HELLBOY™

THE FIRST 20 YEARS

HELLBOY™

THE FIRST 20 YEARS

Art by
MIKE MIGNOLA

Introduction by
PETER DE SÈVE

Editor
SCOTT ALLIE

Associate Editor
DANIEL CHABON

Collection designed by
MIKE MIGNOLA *and* CARY GRAZZINI

Published by
MIKE RICHARDSON

DARK HORSE BOOKS

NEIL HANKERSON ✠ *Executive Vice President*
TOM WEDDLE ✠ *Chief Financial Officer*
RANDY STRADLEY ✠ *Vice President of Publishing*
MICHAEL MARTENS ✠ *Vice President of Book Trade Sales*
ANITA NELSON ✠ *Vice President of Business Affairs*
SCOTT ALLIE ✠ *Editor in Chief*
MATT PARKINSON ✠ *Vice President of Marketing*
DAVID SCROGGY ✠ *Vice President of Product Development*
DALE LaFOUNTAIN ✠ *Vice President of Information Technology*
DARLENE VOGEL ✠ *Senior Director of Print, Design, and Production*
KEN LIZZI ✠ *General Counsel*
DAVEY ESTRADA ✠ *Editorial Director*
CHRIS WARNER ✠ *Senior Books Editor*
DIANA SCHUTZ ✠ *Executive Editor*
CARY GRAZZINI ✠ *Director of Print and Development*
LIA RIBACCHI ✠ *Art Director*
CARA NIECE ✠ *Director of Scheduling*
TIM WIESCH ✠ *Director of International Licensing*
MARK BERNARDI ✠ *Director of Digital Publishing*

Hellboy.com
DarkHorse.com

Published by
Dark Horse Books
A division of Dark Horse Comics, Inc.
10956 SE Main Street
Milwaukie, OR 97222

First edition
March 2014
ISBN 978-1-61655-353-1

1 3 5 7 9 10 8 6 4 2

Printed in China

INTRODUCTION

My artistic puberty took place during a golden time in comics. Although I wasn't a hardcore superhero fan, I read my share of *X-Men*, *Fantastic Four*, and especially *Spider-Man*. In 1973, I was at exactly the perfect age for "The Night Gwen Stacy Died" and must have read it fifty times. "Goblin, you killed the woman I love, and for that, you're going to *DIE!!!*"

But despite these flirtations, my true love was for horror and science fiction comics, and as an early teen I was even convinced that I wanted to draw for them as soon as I was ready to share my genius. Around that time, I discovered the Warren magazines—*Creepy*, *Eerie*, and *Vampirella*—and it was within those pages that I became familiar with some of the greatest comics artists to ever pick up a pencil: Wally Wood, Alex Toth, and Richard Corben, to name just a few.

What set these books apart from all the other comics published during that period was not only their larger, magazine-sized format, but that all the stories were printed in black and white. There was no color to distract from the great draftsmanship and masterful storytelling. Even better, the tales almost always took place in another time period, allowing the artists to explore costumes and landscapes that might not ordinarily be found in a DC or Marvel comic. And of course, there were always monsters. *Lots and lots of monsters.*

I devoured these stories and developed a love of drawing, black humor, and the macabre that remains with me to this day. You might say that much of my youth was spent preparing to become a Mike Mignola fan.

Eventually, I went to art school and found myself drifting away from comics—the desires to both draw and collect them. My tastes had changed and so had comics. To my eye, so much of the artwork had become too burnished and overblown, with every panel competing to be a splash page and every single tendon of every steroid-inflated character rendered to an absurd degree. Of course there were exceptions, but overall, mainstream comics no longer inspired me, so I left them behind.

But not entirely.

Occasionally, I would pop into St. Mark's Comics in the East Village, just to have a peek, just to make sure I wasn't missing something. It was there that I bought my first *Hellboy* comic, *The Corpse*. Rereading it today, I see that it remains the perfect Hellboy tale and could not have been a more ideal introduction to Mignola's work.

The story virtually brims with myth and humor, in equal measure. It is even surprisingly touching. And the drawings. Oh my God, *the drawings*! Such alternately funny and grotesque characters, from the demonic changeling baby to the hideous Jenny Greenteeth and, of course, the titular corpse himself. The story contained everything I had loved about comics and everything I missed about them. From that point on, I became a Mignola fan and collector. And I thought I was a pretty avid one, too.

That was until Scott Allie, the editor of this volume and most everything *Hellboy*, invited me to write this introduction and, in preparation, sent me a veritable refrigerator box full of *Hellboy* books. Inside were six thick hardcover volumes containing tons of work I had never seen before. He followed this up with a download of scans so large it gagged my computer for an hour. How could Mignola have created so much artwork? And how could it all be so damned good?

Mignola himself wouldn't be quite so generous in his estimation of the work. Like most good artists, he's his own toughest critic. He'll tell you that he can hardly bear to look at his early *Hellboy* work, which is more detailed than his more distilled work of recent years. When he talks about his first *Hellboy* story, *Seed of Destruction*, he can be pretty harsh on what he sees as his overreliance on detail. He'd tell you he's learned a lot since then and has spent the last twenty years resisting the impulse to draw every follicle on every hairy arm. Where once he would draw fifty parallel lines along a muscled limb, these days four or five dashes do quite nicely to suggest that a creature is shaggy. It's the kind of confidence that comes with age and experience—knowing exactly what to throw out, and daring to do it.

Among Mignola's early influences were artists like Frank Frazetta and Bernie Wrightson, two of my early favorites as well, and both virtuosos in the use of heavy, inky shadows. Not coincidentally, both were also masters of shape and composition, having a huge effect on Mignola's style. But it was Jack Kirby who just may have been the guy to really cause something pivotal to click inside Mignola's head. Kirby's work taught him much about the sanctity of shapes, and gave Mignola permission to forgo the nuisance of drawing realistic anatomy in place of what simply looks *cool*.

There's an increasingly sculptural quality to Mike's work as the years go by. The more detail Mignola casts aside, the more his drawings take on a craggy volume, as if all the elements, including Hellboy's pitted face, are carved in stone. In fact, most Hellboy drawings practically beg to be brought into the third dimension. They are composed like solid hunks of granite that fit

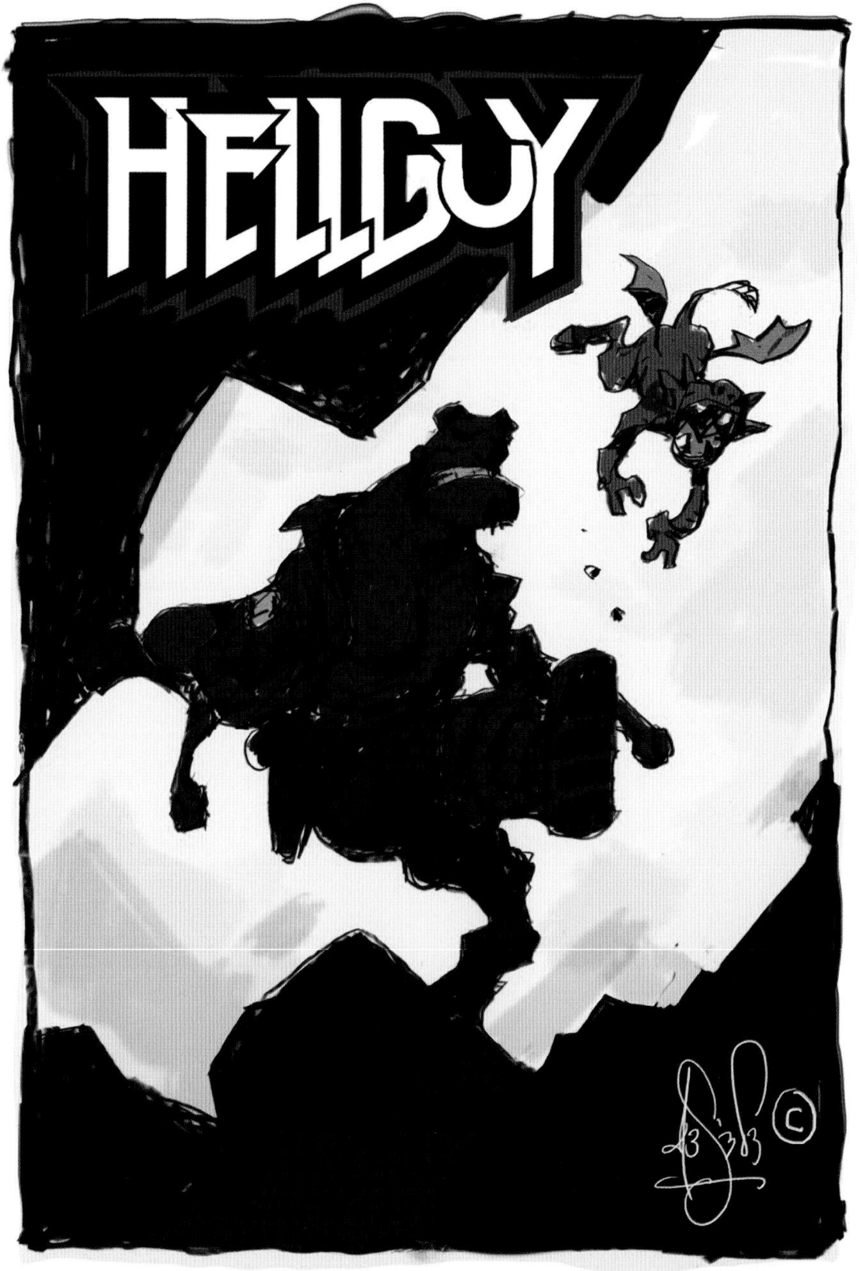
HELLBOY

together in such a chunky, pleasing way that they make you want to turn the forms around and admire them from every angle.

One of the things I love most about the *Hellboy* artwork is the design of Hellboy himself. Mignola has no interest in the perfect muscle-bound physique that is the hallmark of almost every single superhero out there. To the contrary, Hellboy's shoulders slope, he wears a baggy trench coat, and he has the wrists of a schoolgirl (well, one of them, anyway). Perhaps that's because Mignola never quite saw him as a superhero in the first place, but more as a character from a pulp story. Mostly, though, it's because that's the way Mignola *likes* to draw him, and if you don't like it, tough darts.

That's the secret behind *Hellboy*'s success, of course. Mignola left mainstream comics and its restrictions behind to create his own character, who exists in his own universe. And that universe exists because Mike likes to draw it. Working in the trenches of Marvel and DC for the first chunk of his career, he lived in mortal fear of having to draw cars and skyscrapers, and did everything he could to avoid the living death of drawing the boring stuff that makes up our own dull world. What he *does* like to draw are rocks and ruins and crags and moors. And those are the places you'll find Hellboy. That's also where you will find some of the most wonderful character designs ever committed to a piece of paper.

As a character designer myself, I envy the sheer variety and invention Mignola brings to the creatures that haunt Hellboy's world. From his sinister leprechauns (those "rough little men") to his ancient leviathans and his invented iconography of randomly appearing frogs, flies, and floating crowns, each one suggests mythologies we will never fully know, but should be nervous about just the same. Mignola loves our traditional monsters, but even the most familiar of them—vampires, ghosts, and zombies—are rendered completely fresh and new. Have you ever seen a Frankenstein monster quite as DIY as on the cover of *House of the Living Dead . . .* ? And then there are those creatures we've never heard of: the underwater god, the Bog Roosh; the mud dragon, Ogdru Jahad; and the boar-headed demon, Gruagach— all plucked from forgotten folklore from every corner of the world.

Mignola has an exquisite sense of design and pattern and applies it to the most incongruous subjects. Look at the gnarled tentacles that form the backdrop to the poster Mike did for the 2008 H. P. Lovecraft Film Festival (see page 73); or the vast ribbon of coral and teeth looming above Abe Sapien on the cover of *The Devil Does Not Jest* (page 107); or the spiral runes carved on a boulder, their pattern reversing to white as they flow into shadow, on page 15 of *The Corpse*. Mignola consistently manages to depict even the most grotesque monstrosity and make it somehow beautiful.

Recently, Mike and I found ourselves invited to speak at the Illustration Master Class, a weeklong seminar in Massachusetts for illustrators interested in developing traditional drawing and painting skills. Knowing Mike would be in the audience, I began my talk by stressing that originality is, above all else, absolutely crucial in designing a character. I then showed my first slide, an example of my own work, to demonstrate my point. "I call him Hellguy," I said. "He's got a giant stone boot and uses it to kick demon ass."

I share this story not because it was funny but because, in attempting to mimic Mike's style, I had to put myself in his head to somehow figure out how he does what he does.

I still have absolutely no idea.

Peter de Sève

Peter de Sève's illustrations and character designs are known throughout the world. His work spans three decades and various media, including magazines, books, print, and television advertising, animated feature films, and magazines. He is perhaps best recognized for his many covers for the New Yorker *magazine and his character designs for the blockbuster* Ice Age *franchise (Scrat is a veritable international celebrity). De Sève has also contributed to such films as* Mulan, A Bug's Life, Arthur Christmas, *and* Finding Nemo. *Most recently, de Sève was the lead character designer on a French animated feature based on the beloved classic* The Little Prince, *due for release in 2015.*

His many distinctions include the prestigious Hamilton King Award from the Society of Illustrators, a Clio Award for a Nike television commercial, and a Daytime Emmy Award for best character design in a daytime television show.

FOREWORD

ABOUT THIS BOOK—
This is not *The Art of Hellboy* Volume 2. We (long-suffering editor Scott Allie, designer Cary Grazzini, and I) put that first *Art of* book together back in 2003. Since then we've talked about doing a Volume 2, and really would love to one of these days— but this isn't it. What this *is* is a celebration of Hellboy and (maybe more importantly) his world hitting the twenty-year mark. The idea here is to show the evolution of the whole Hellboy thing, from a single drawing of a big, shaggy monster to a whole bunch of different books about a whole bunch of different characters, all functioning in one world, one history, and telling (sort of) one big story. When I started *Hellboy* I had no plan other than to do the kind of book that I would enjoy reading if it were done by someone else. Guess it worked out well for me that no one else was doing it, because creating this world and watching it grow has been the greatest joy of my career. I couldn't have done it alone and I certainly didn't (more about that in a bit), but editor Scott Allie and I decided that since I started this thing, we'd keep the focus here on my work—so in addition to the evolution of the Hellboy world, you'll hopefully notice an evolution in my artwork. *I* look at it as evolution. If you're one of those people who miss all the little lines that used to be there, you might call it *de*-evolution, but there you go. It is what it is.

I've tried to select my favorite pieces from the last twenty years. I probably went a little light on art from the first ten years—not just because I like the newer stuff better (though there was some of that), but because the earlier stuff is well covered in that *Art of Hellboy* book. I did, however, want to include enough of that early work to give a clear picture of what this Hellboy thing was way back when, and how it grew into what it is now.

About page 27—

I have a real love-hate relationship with painting. Every time I do one, I swear I'll never do another one, and then six months later I'm chomping at the bit to do it again. There are a few examples of finished paintings scattered through this book, but the one on page 27 is only about half-finished. It does give a look into my painting technique (or lack thereof)—I start with an ink wash drawing to establish my darks and lights, then build up layers of watercolor over that. The Hellboy in the middle of this one is still in the early ink wash stage, while some of those little angel guys look pretty close to finished. No idea now why I gave up on this one—might have just been having one of those days.

And now to thank some people—

First, my lovely wife Christine. She's the one who gently suggested I try making up my own character and, after the first miniseries, when I was thinking of sliding back to DC Comics (to draw another Batman comic or something), she gently suggested that I maybe do another Hellboy comic instead. Without her nothing (other than maybe that shaggy-looking guy on page 9) in this book would exist.

Second, John Byrne. John scripted the first Hellboy series, and without his help I might never have had the confidence to try doing my own character. I certainly would not have attempted it back in 1994. I shudder to think where I would be now if he hadn't been with me back then.

I have to thank Mike Richardson for saying yes to a not terribly commercial artist who said he wanted to do a comic called *Hellboy*. Mike said yes without seeing any art, and I don't even remember him asking what the book was about. I'm pretty sure there's no other publisher out there who would have done that.

Thank you, Barbara Kesel, first *Hellboy* editor, and Scott Allie, editor of everything since. Scott's been sounding board, cowriter, and reluctant therapist. He's been organizing the larger part of my life for the past nineteen years, and I just do not have the words to thank him for all he's done, so I won't try—instead I dedicate this book to him, and promise to get moving on the next twenty years.

Thank you to all the colorists who have had to put up with me over the years—mostly and especially the great Dave Stewart, in so many ways the glue that holds the whole Hellboy/B.P.R.D. world together.

And, finally, thanks to all the other artists, writers, designers, and letterers who have contributed to building this world over the years. A special thank-you to John Arcudi, who's been doing most of the heavy lifting for a long time now; Guy Davis, who, with John, deserves so much credit for building the B.P.R.D. into what it is now; and Duncan Fegredo and Richard Corben, who did so much to keep Hellboy alive till it was time for him to not be.

And, of course, the fans—
Thanks—

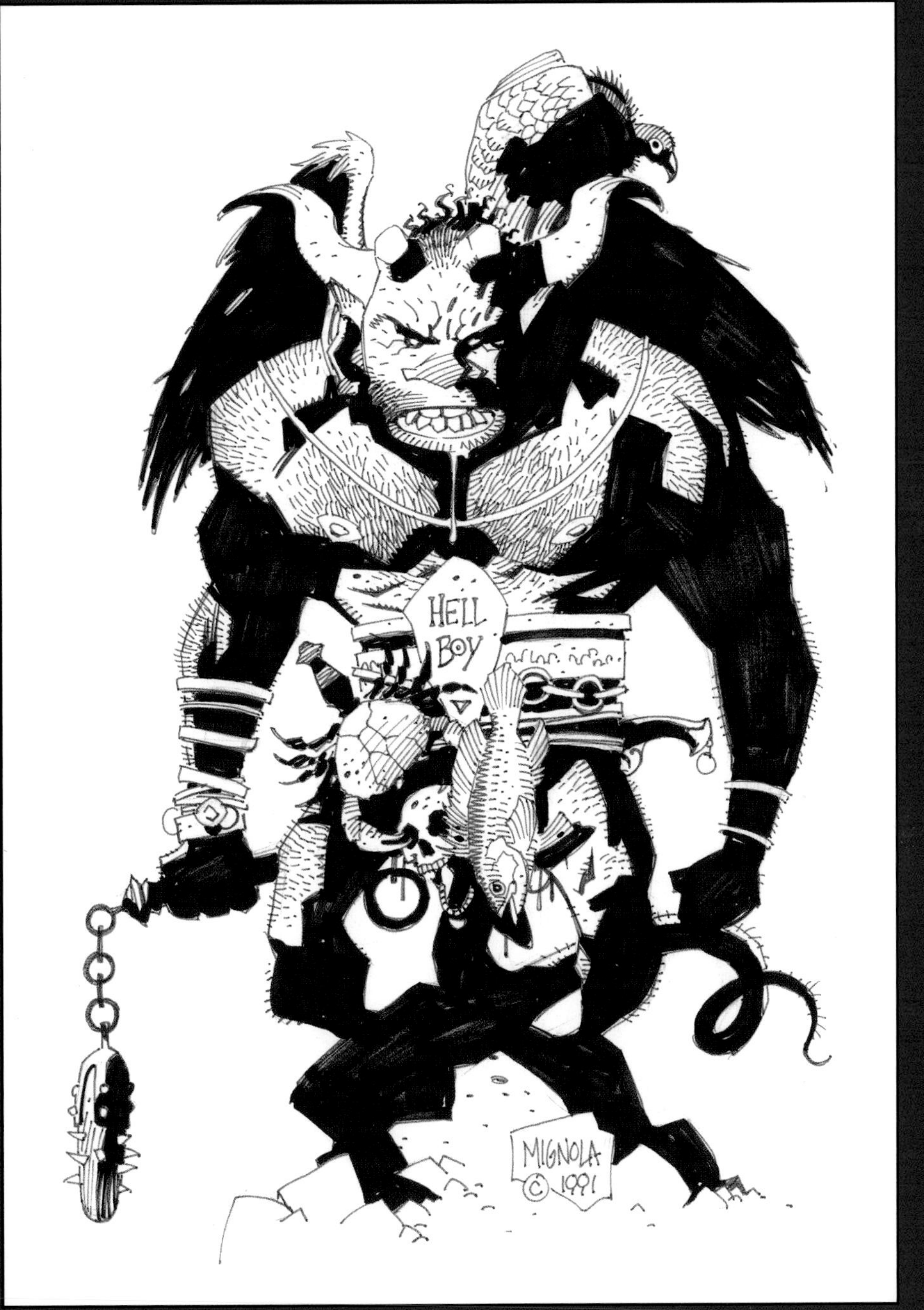
HELL BOY
MIGNOLA © 1991

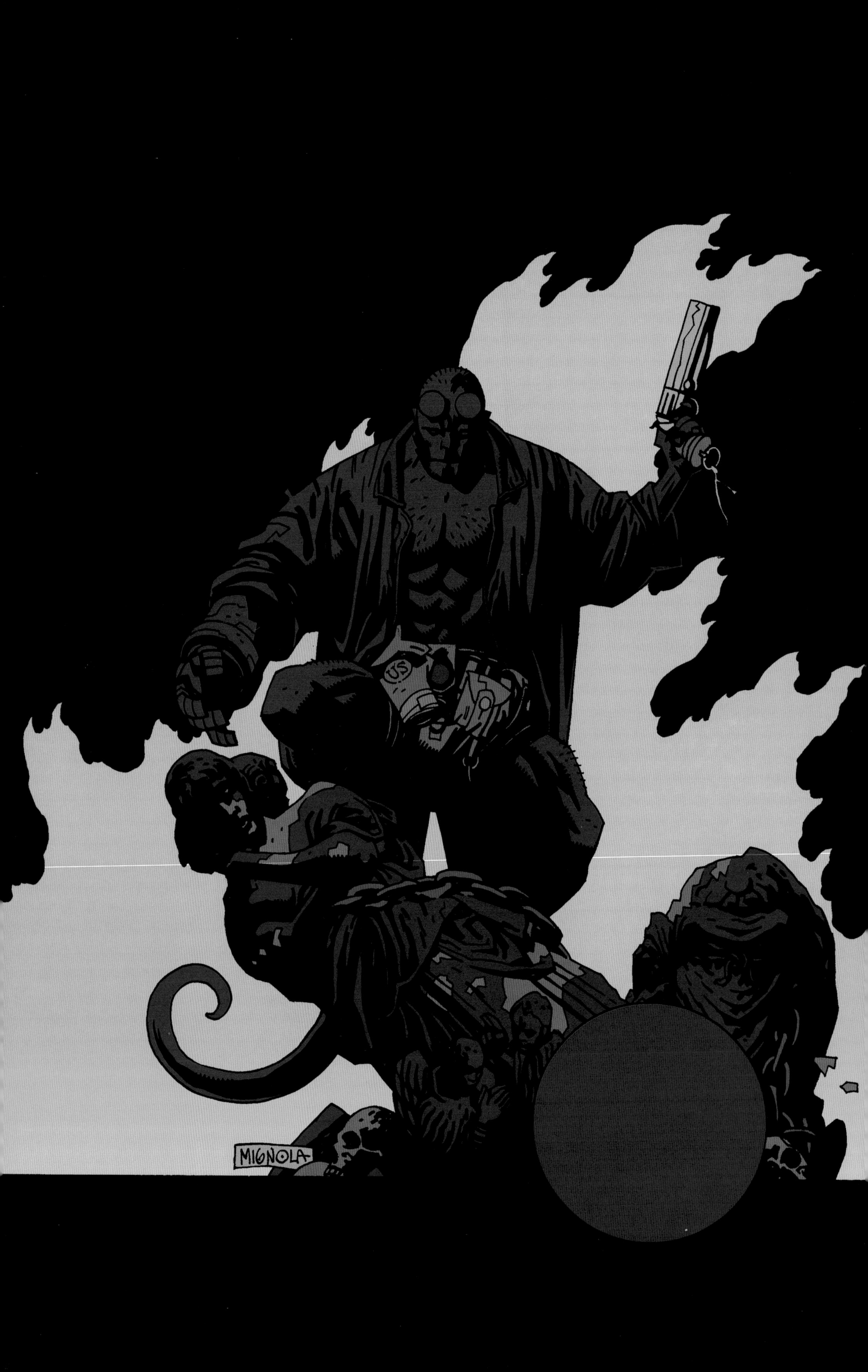
MIGNOLA

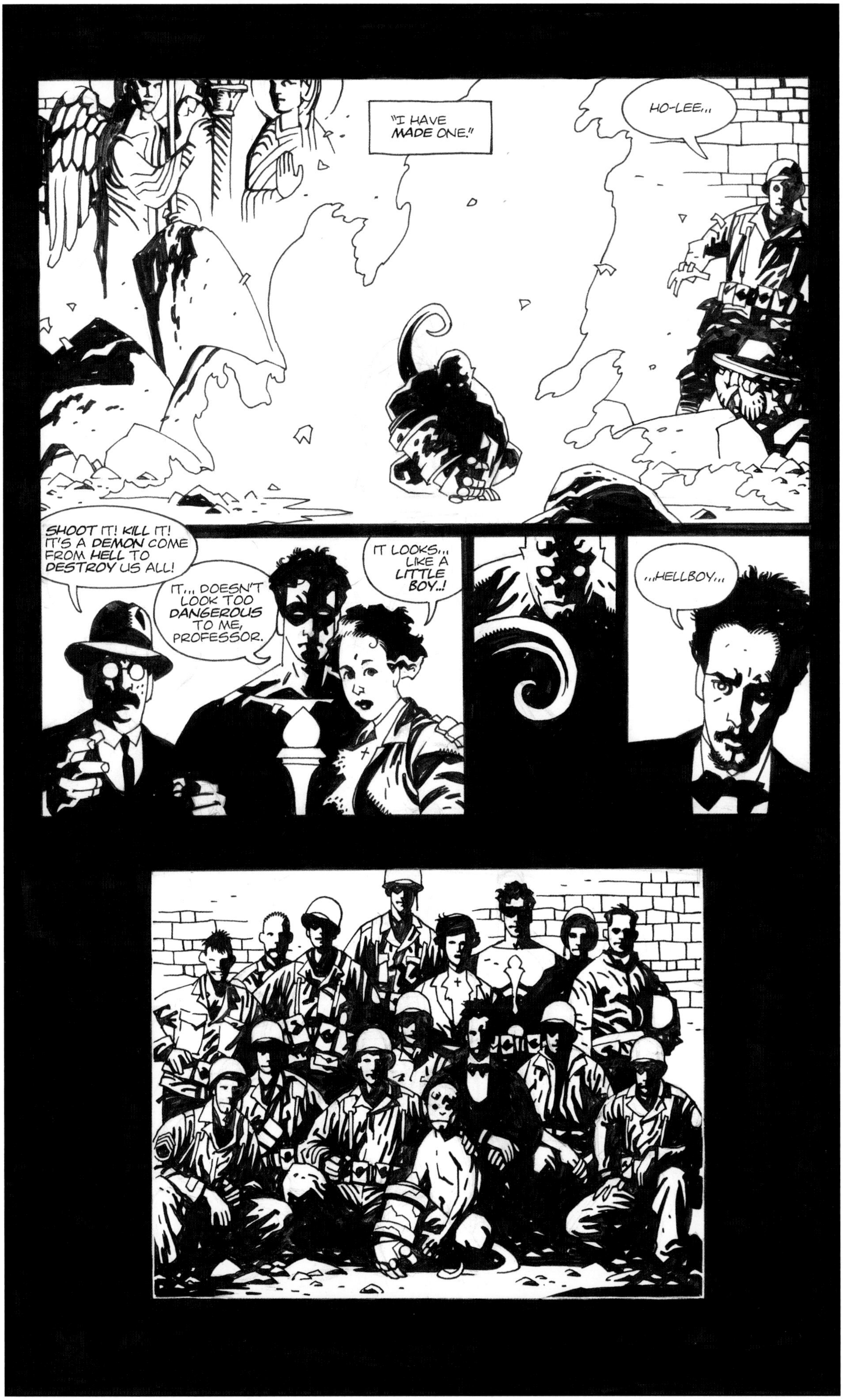
"I HAVE MADE ONE."
HO-LEE...
SHOOT IT! KILL IT! IT'S A DEMON COME FROM HELL TO DESTROY US ALL!
IT... DOESN'T LOOK TOO DANGEROUS TO ME, PROFESSOR.
IT LOOKS... LIKE A LITTLE BOY..!
...HELLBOY...

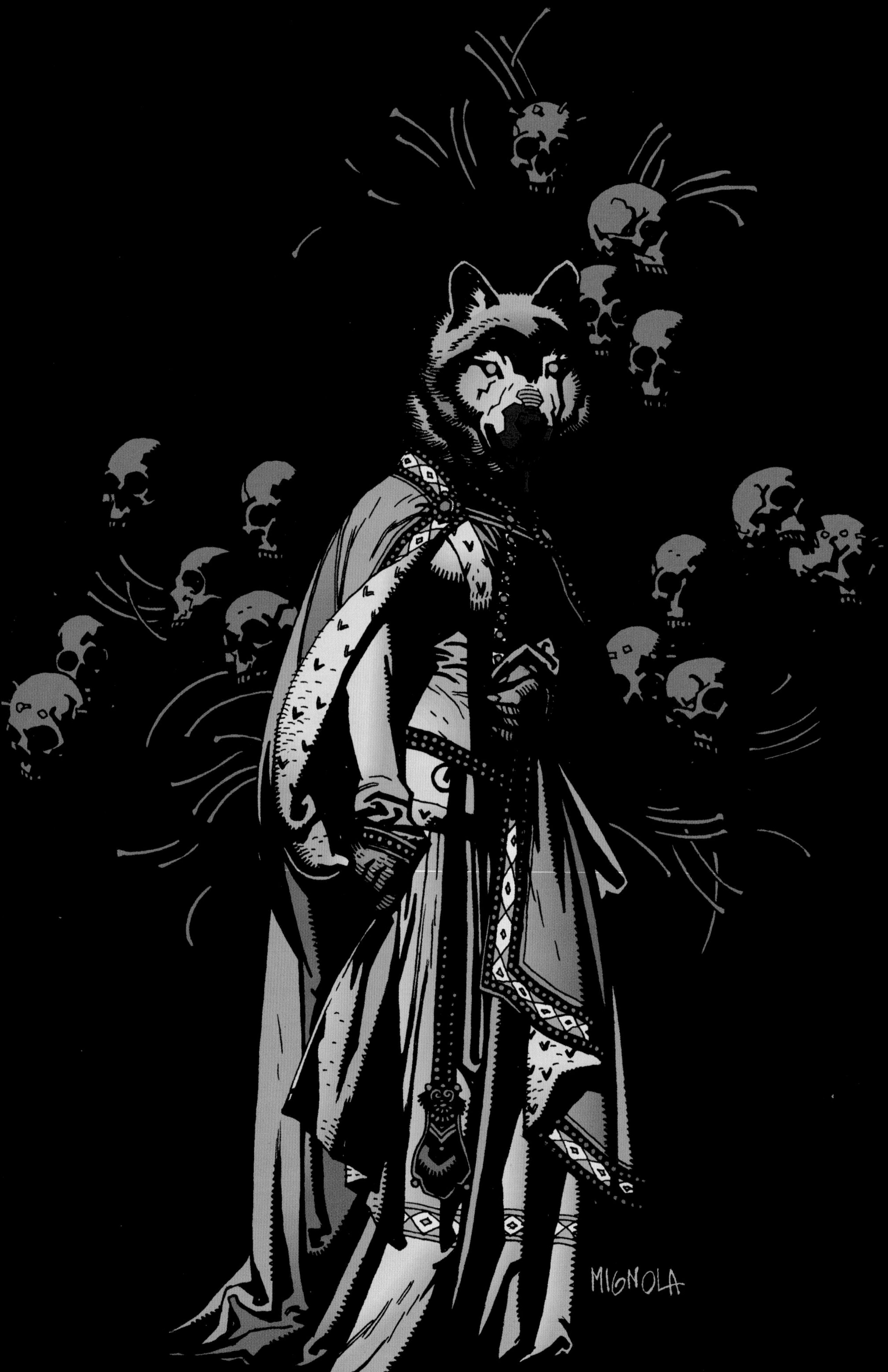
MIGNOLA

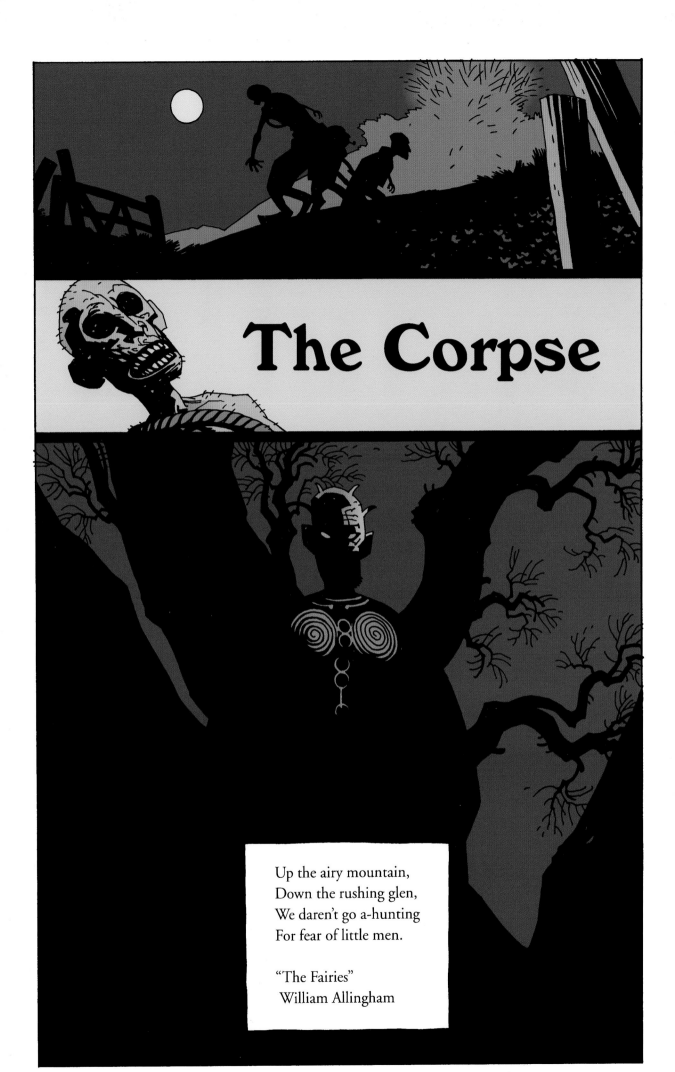

The Corpse

Up the airy mountain,
Down the rushing glen,
We daren't go a-hunting
For fear of little men.

"The Fairies"
William Allingham

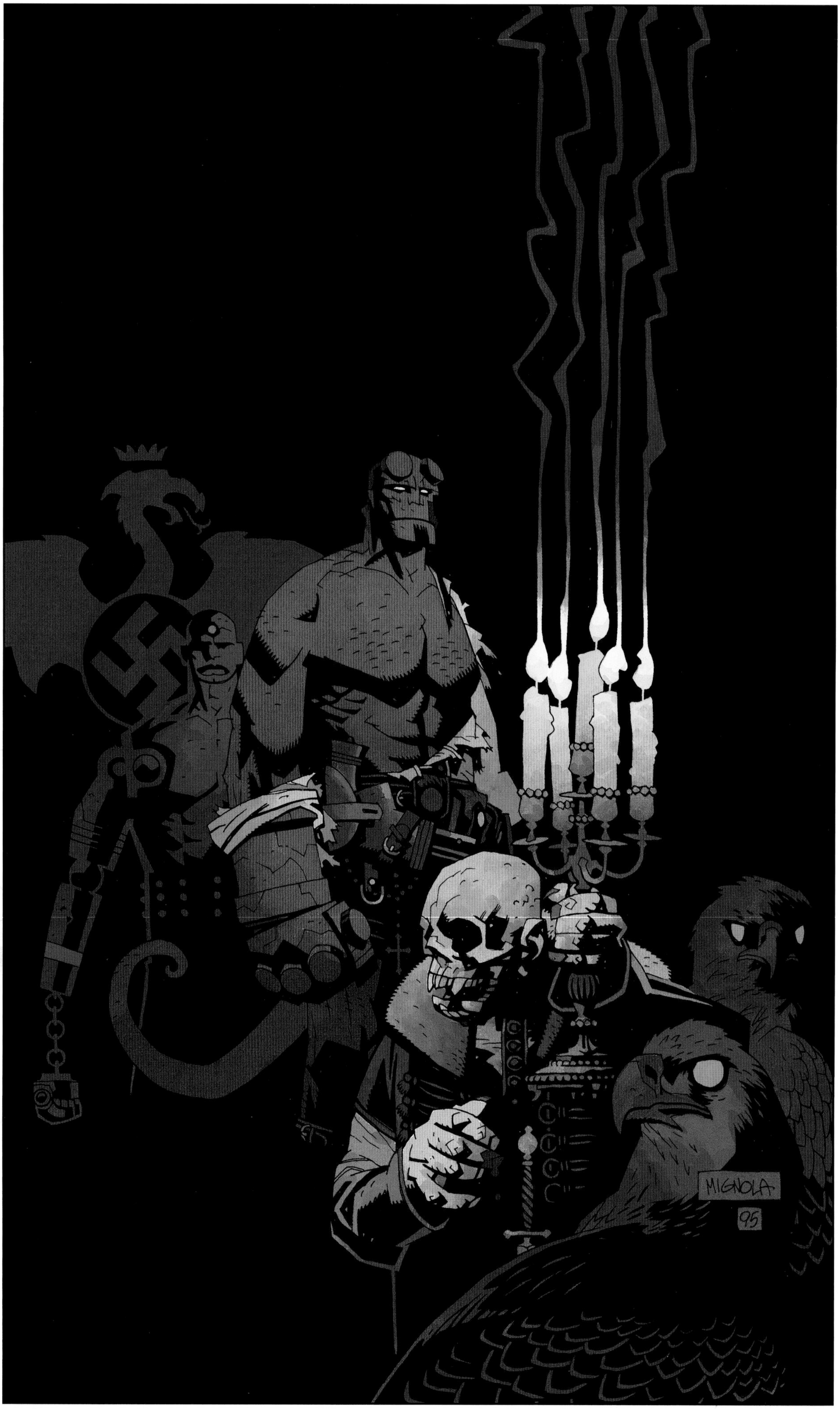
MIGNOLA
95

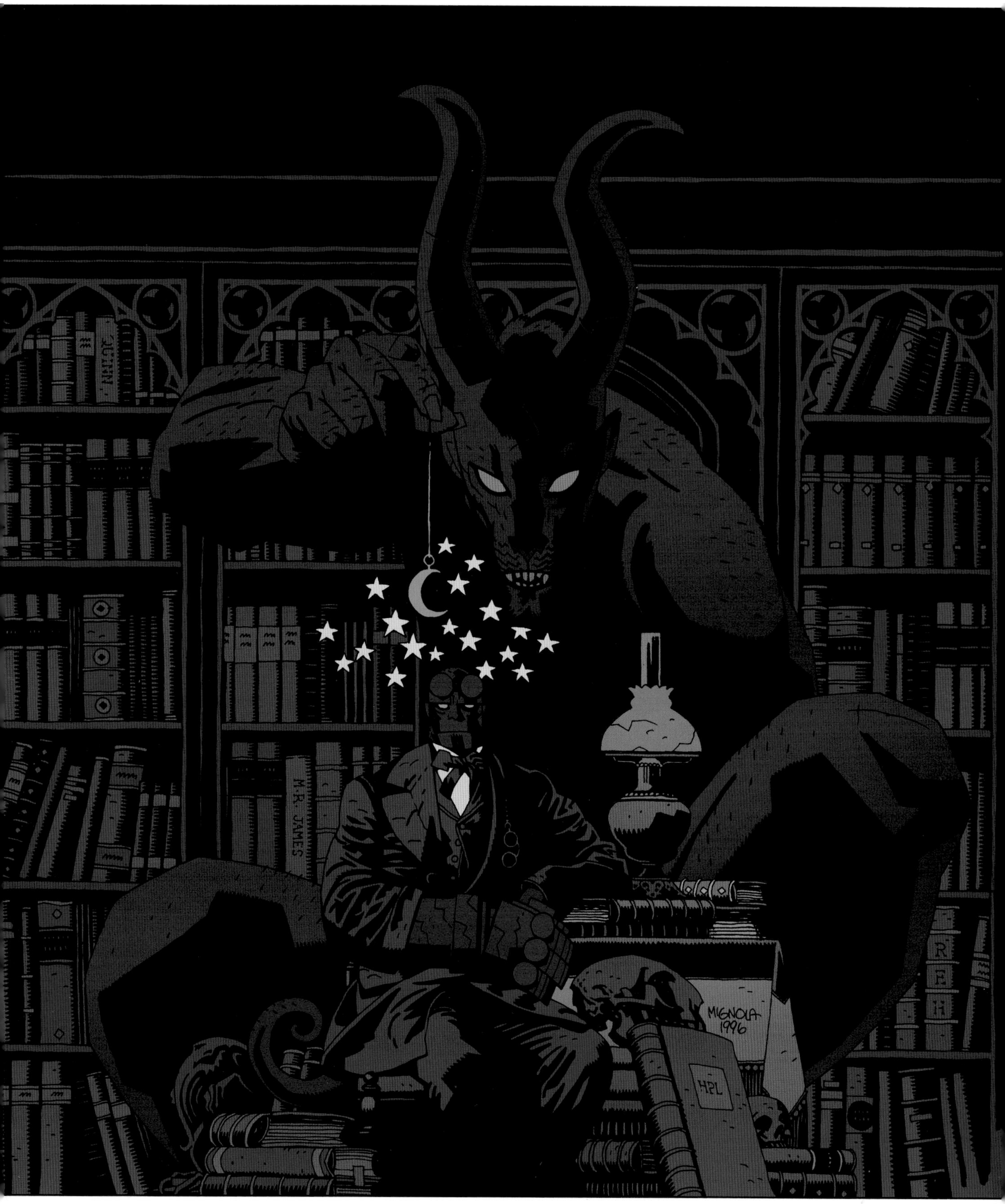
M.R. JAMES
MIGNOLA 1996
HPL
R E H

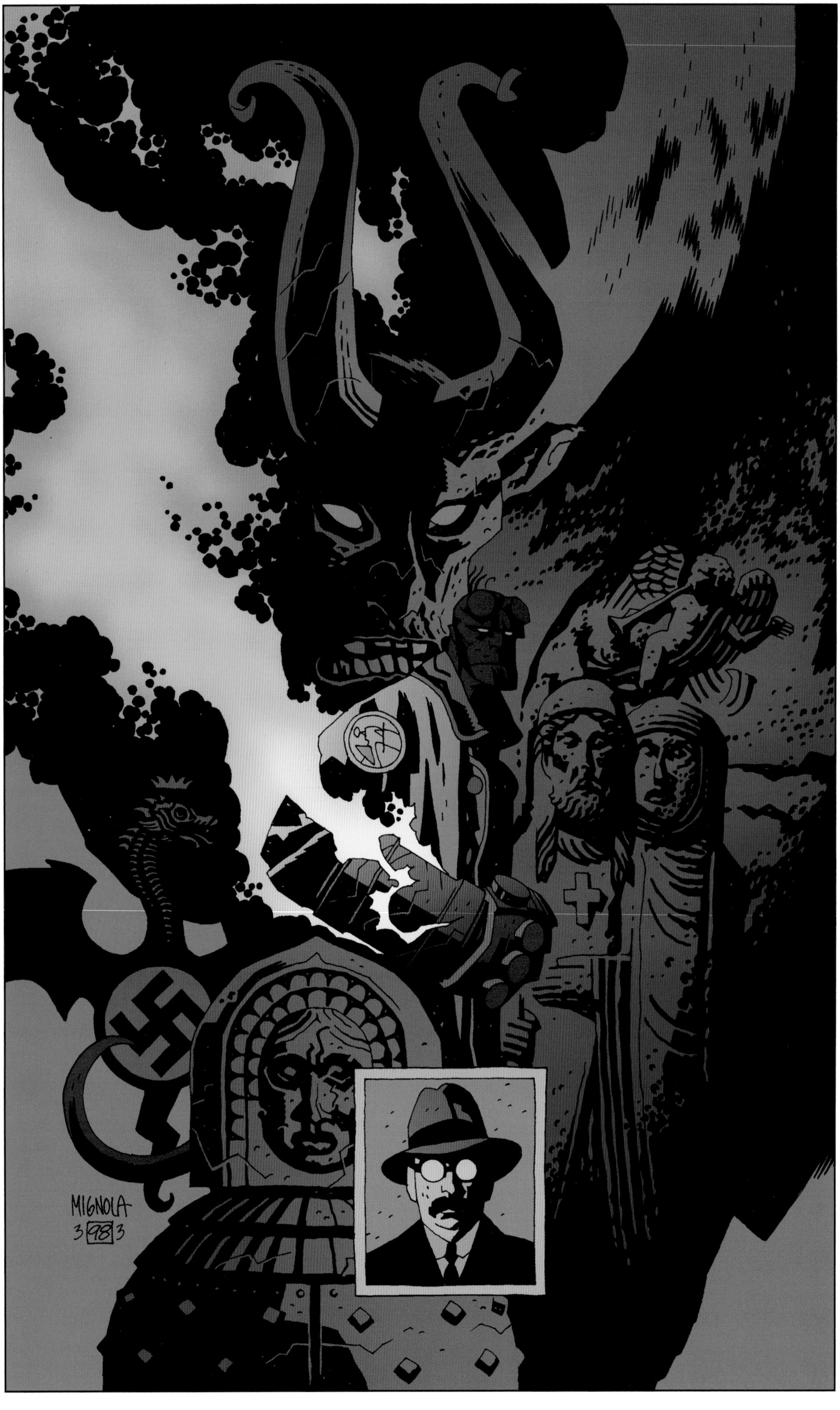
MIGNOLA
3 98 3

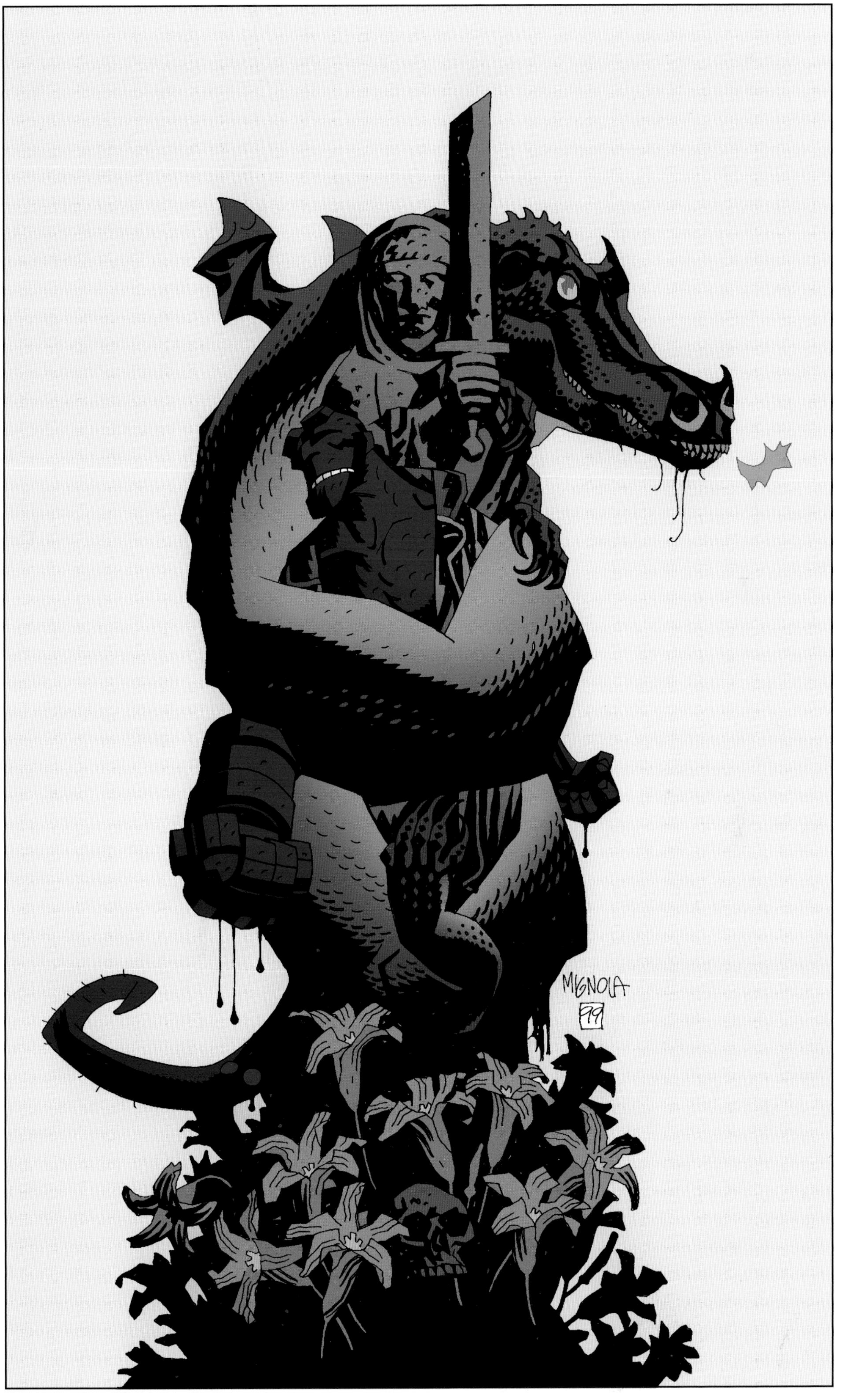
MIGNOLA
99

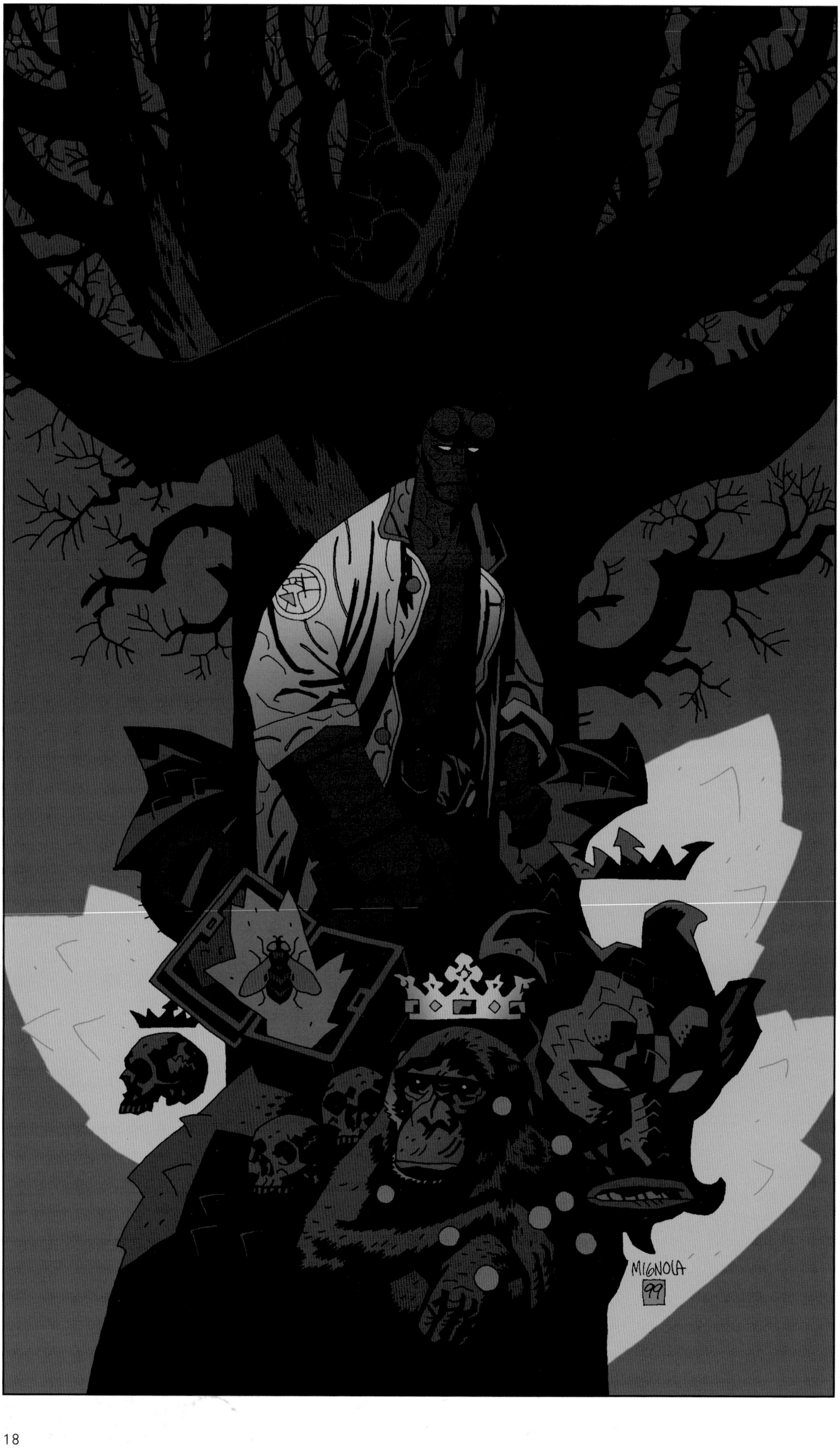
MIGNOLA
99

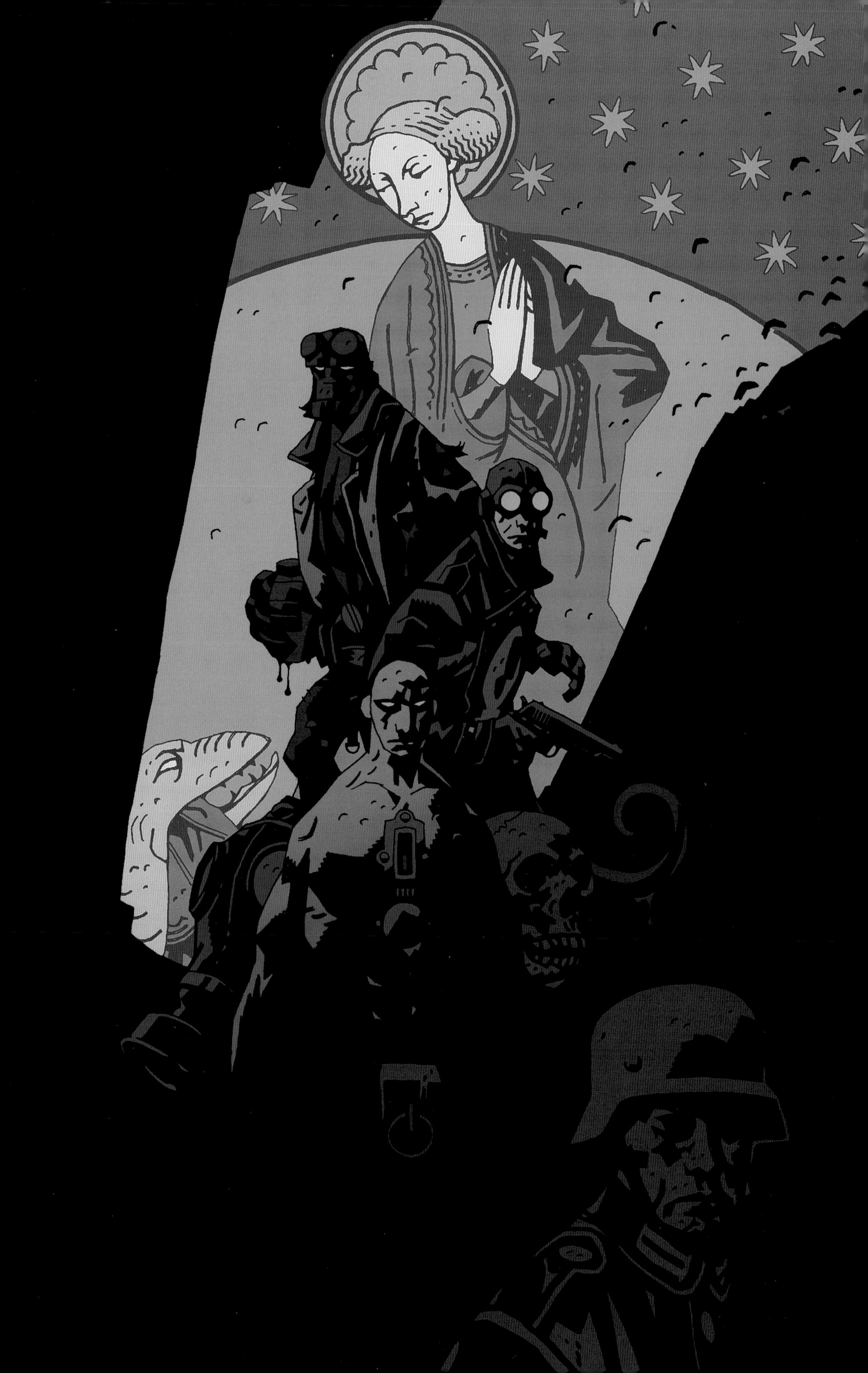

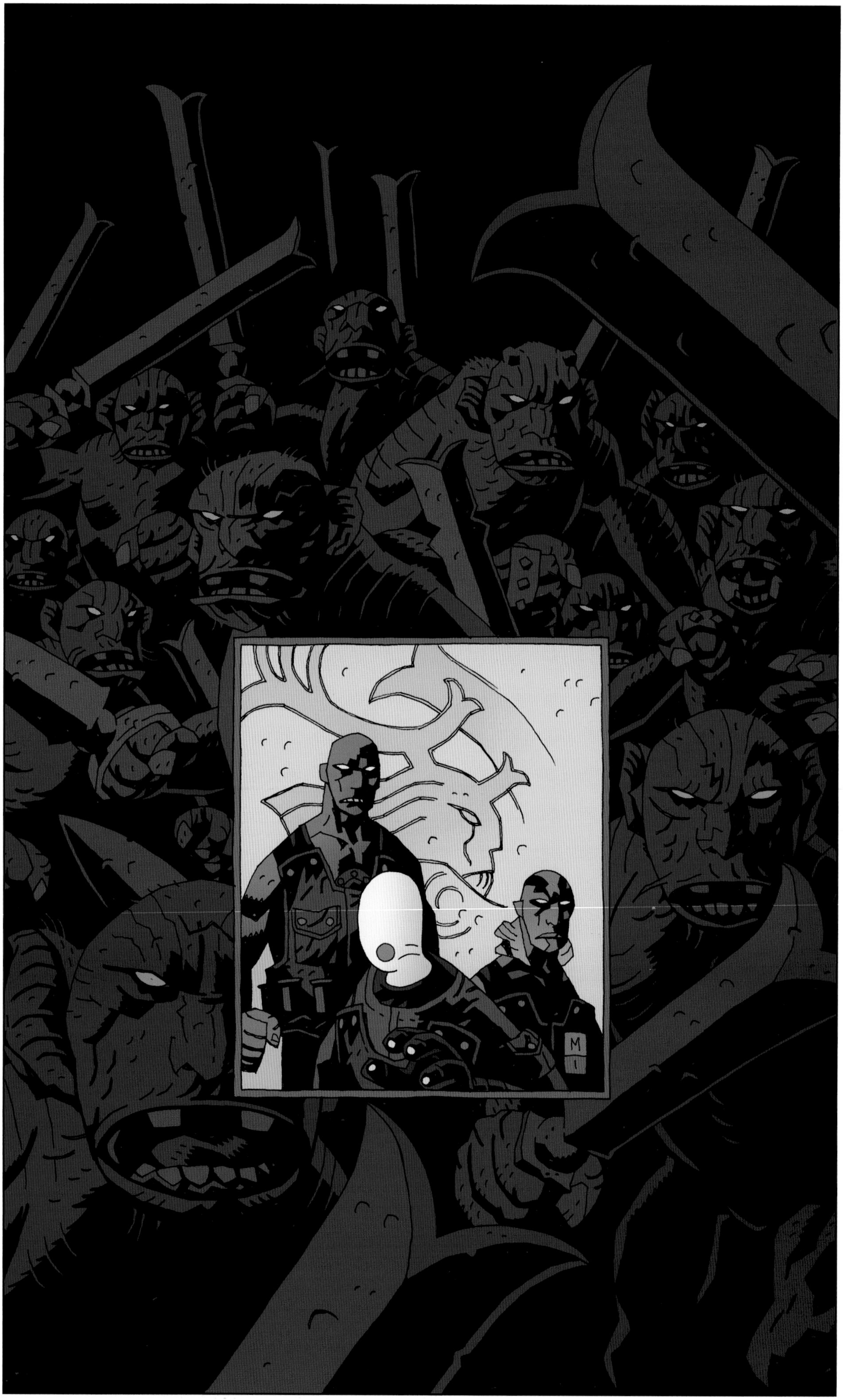

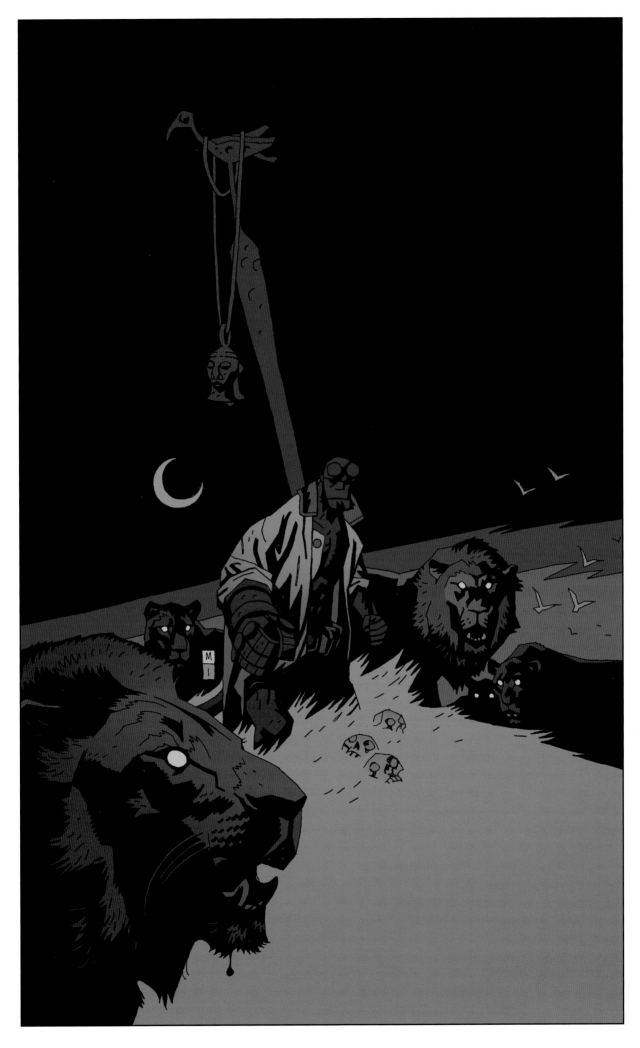

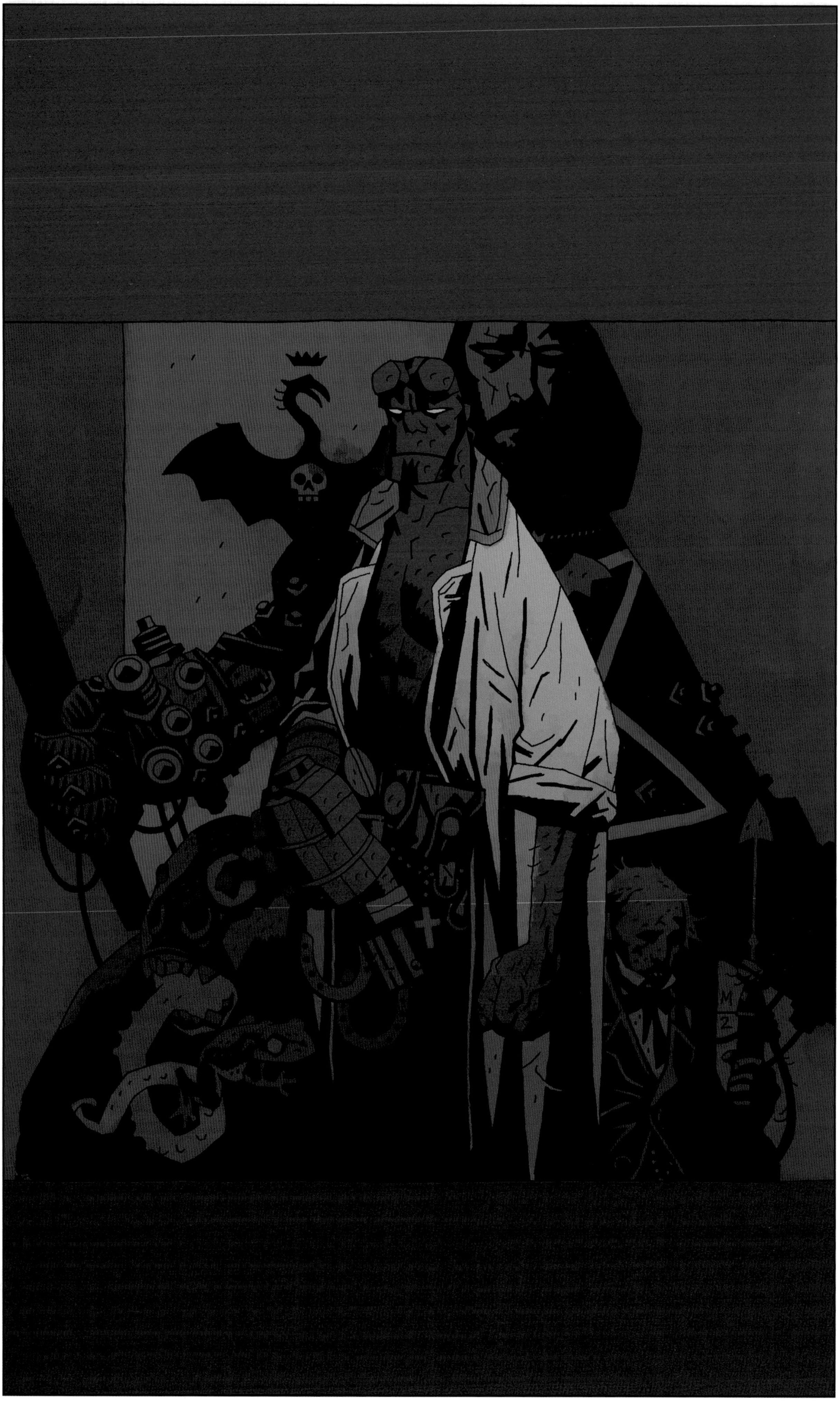

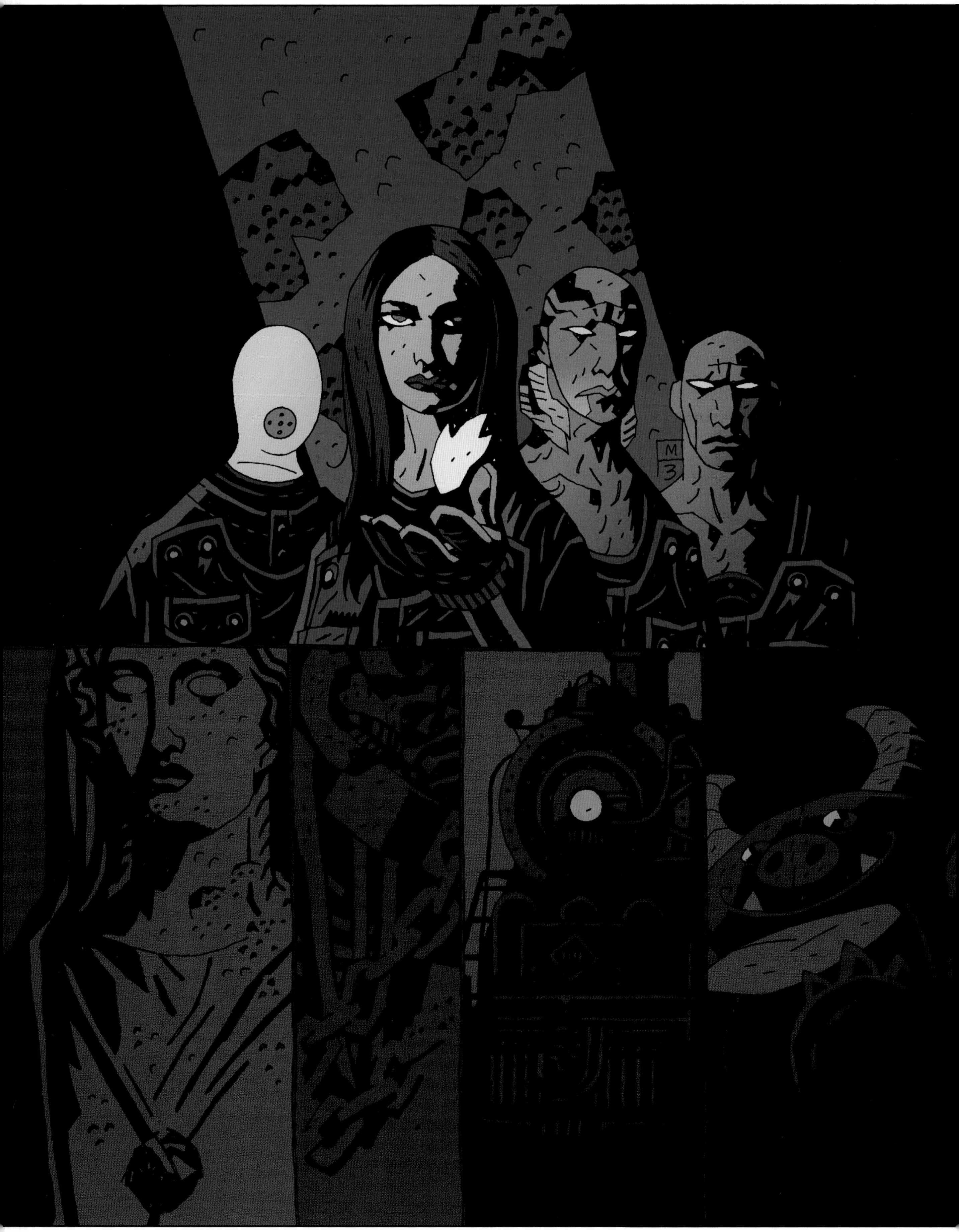

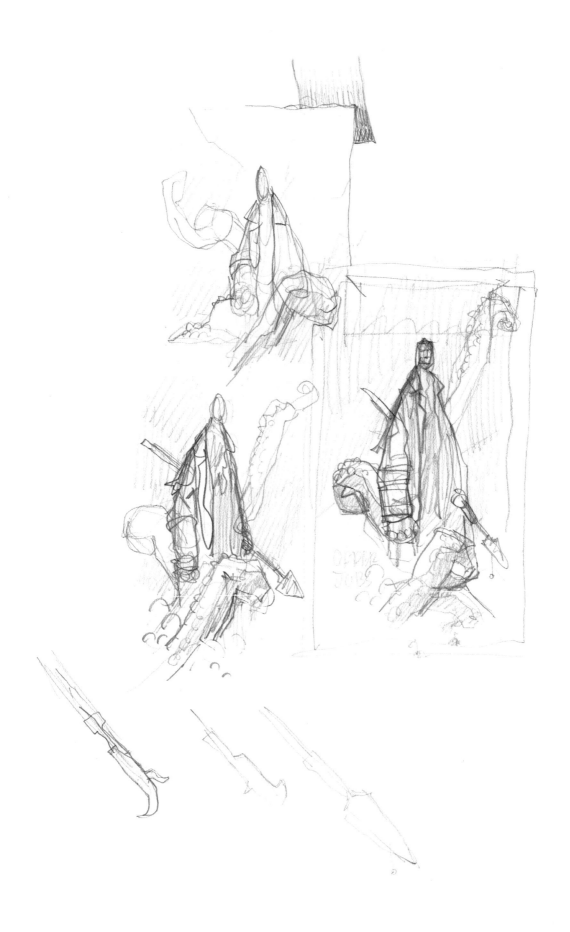

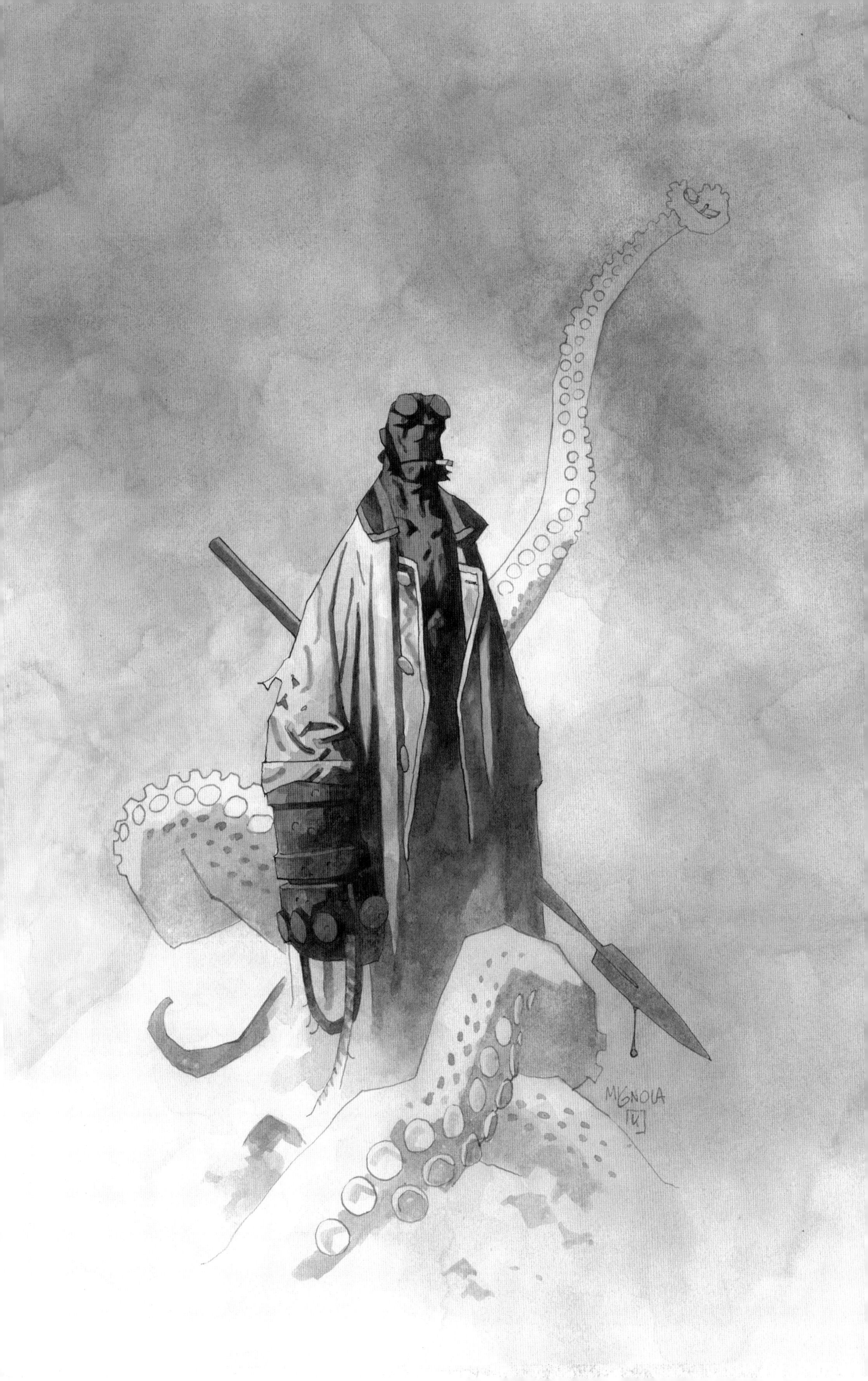
MIGNOLA

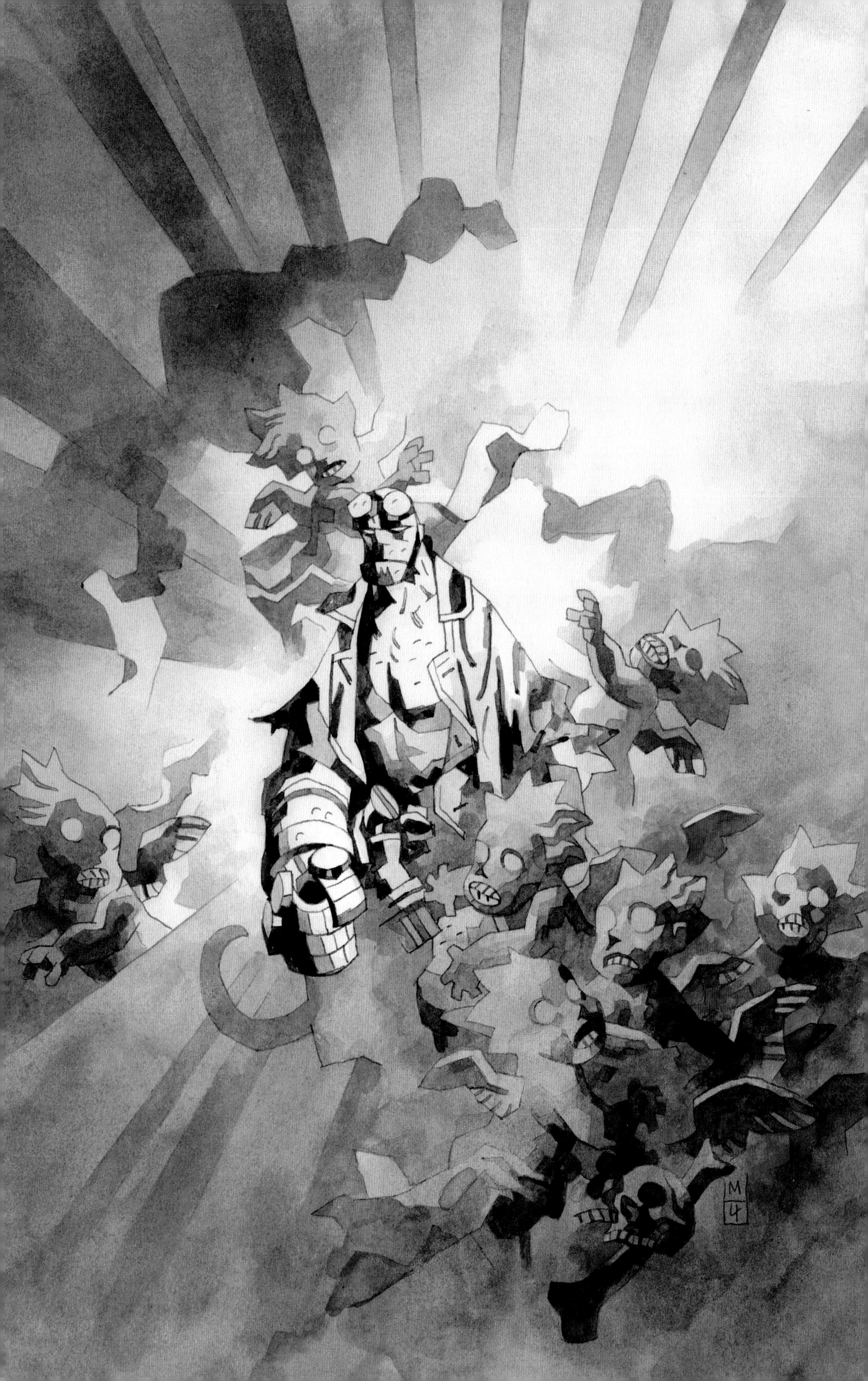

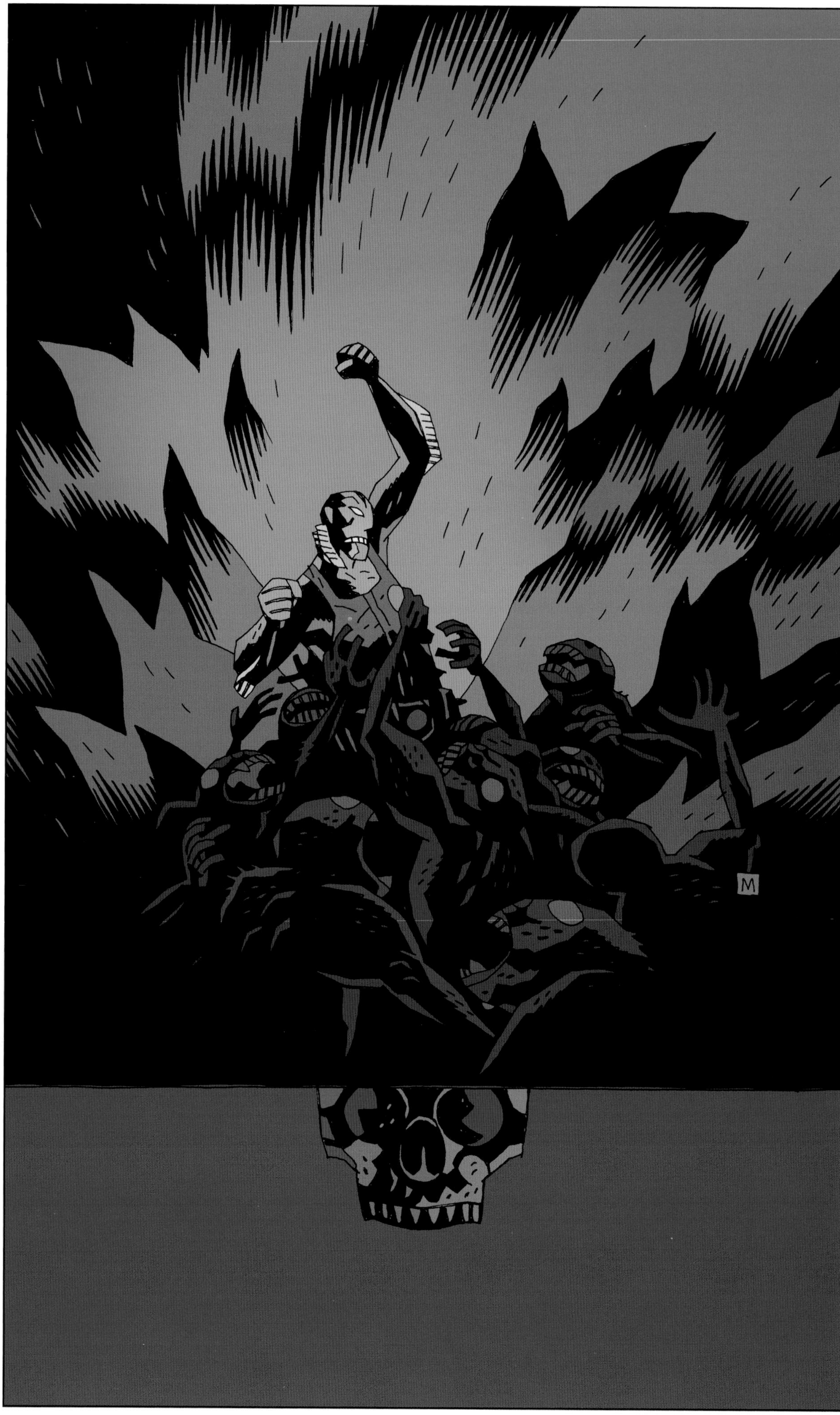
M

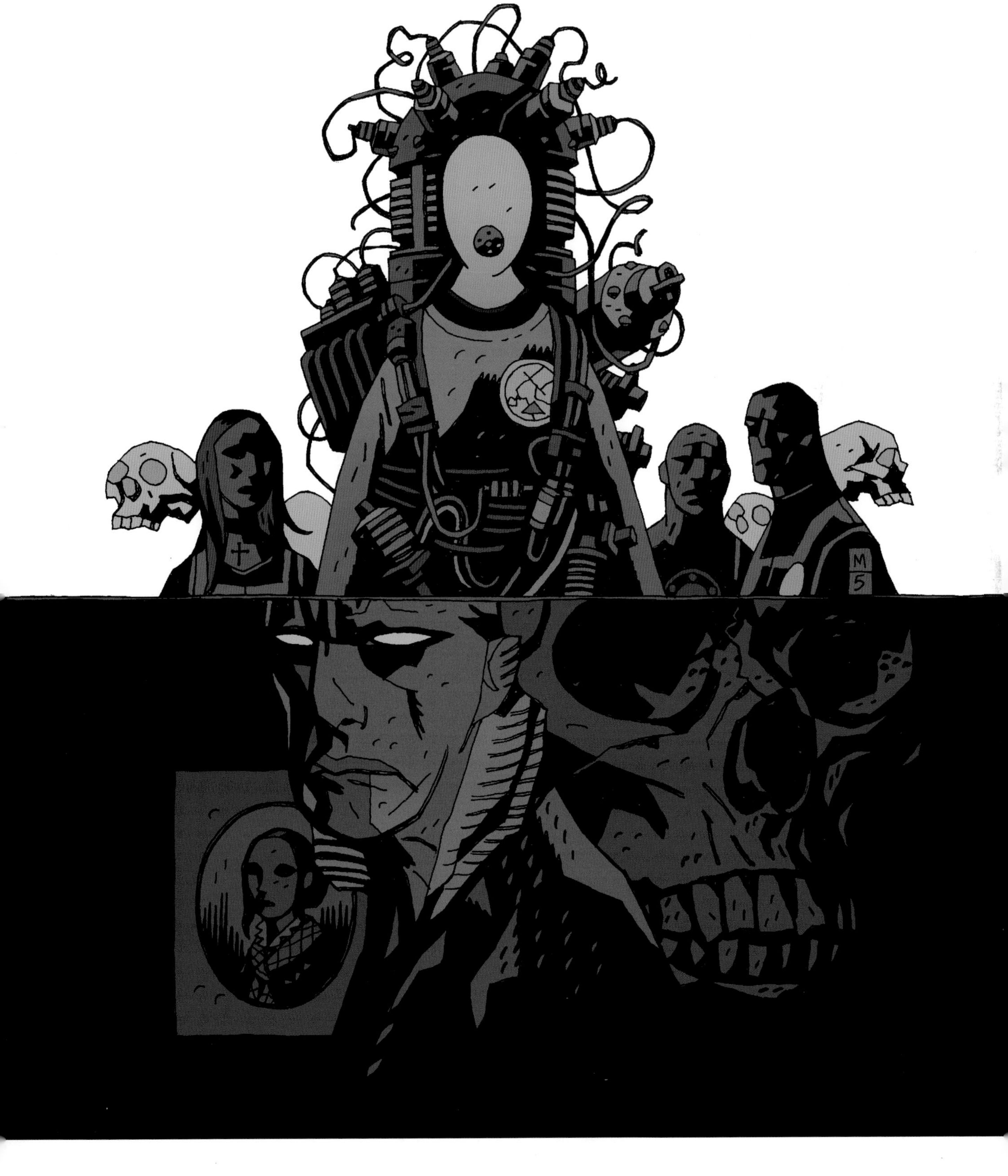

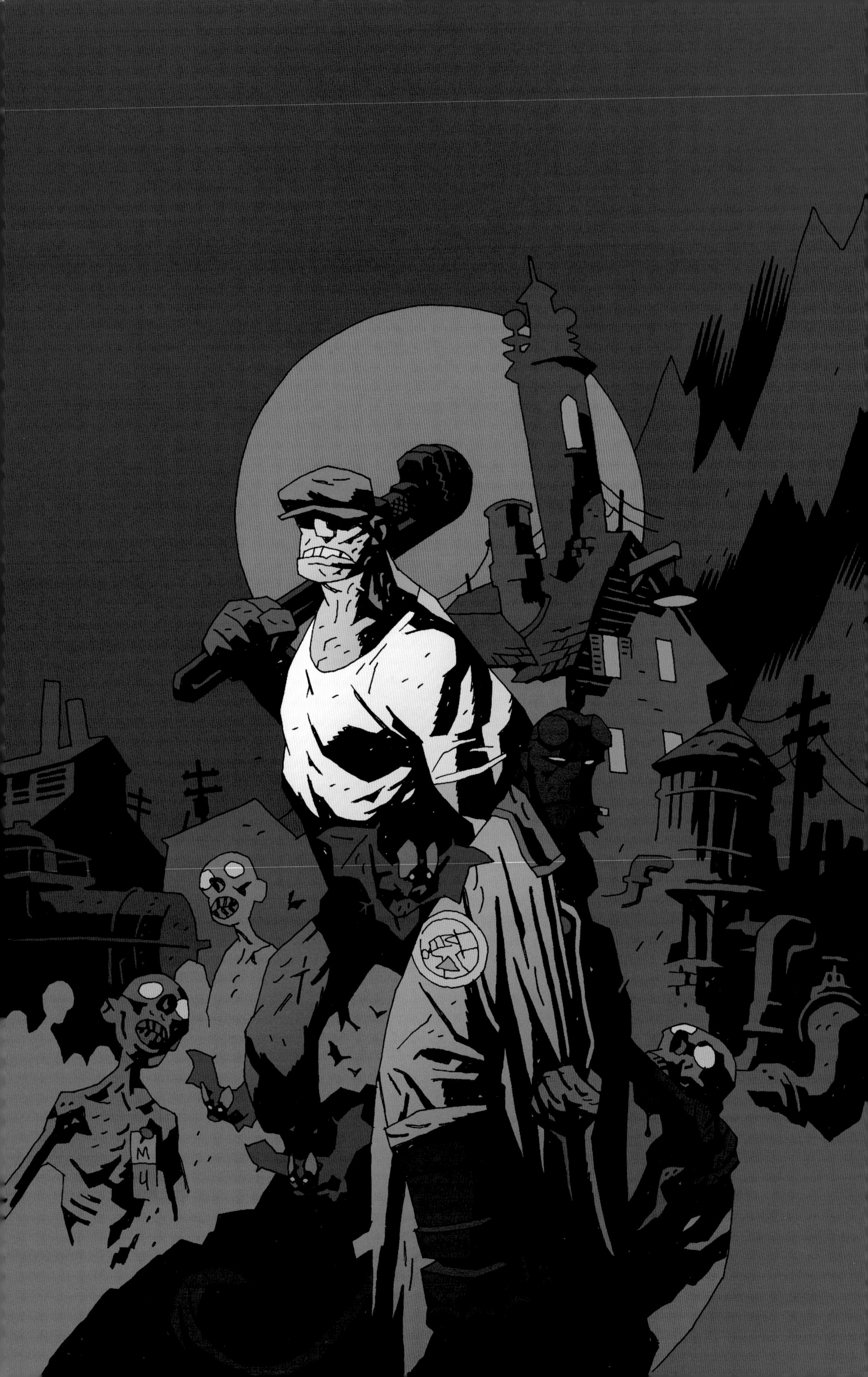

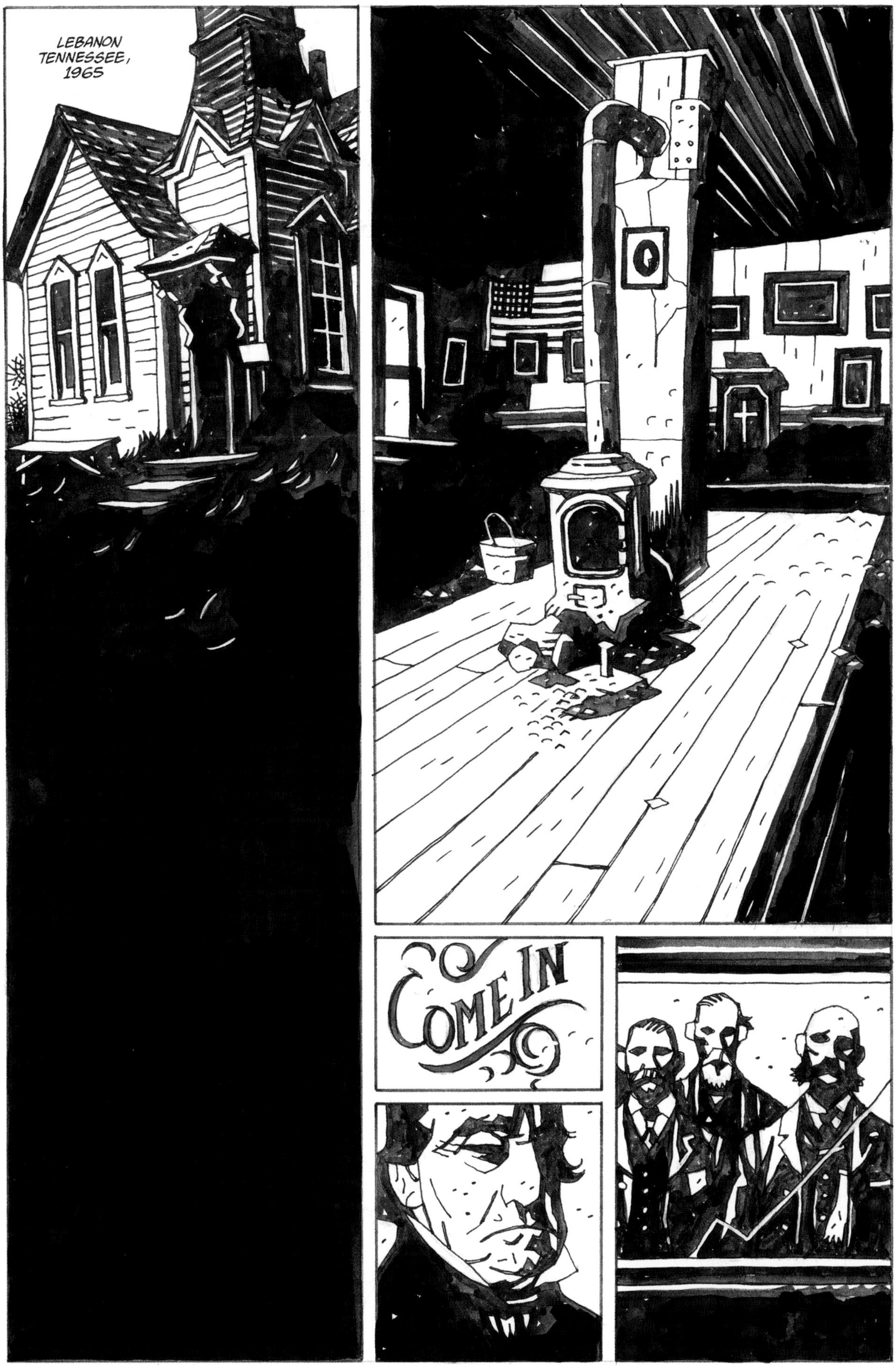
LEBANON TENNESSEE, 1965
COME IN

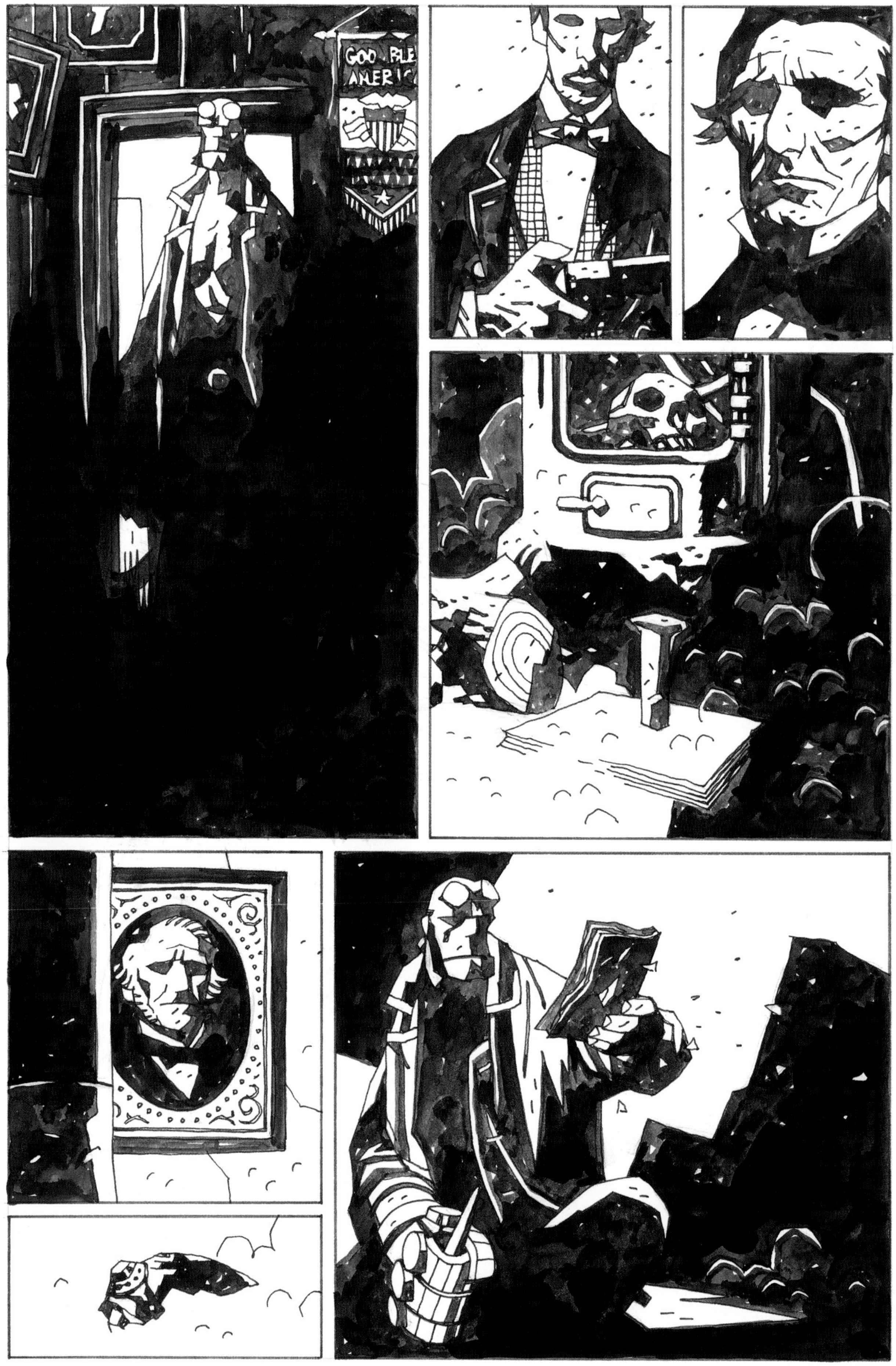

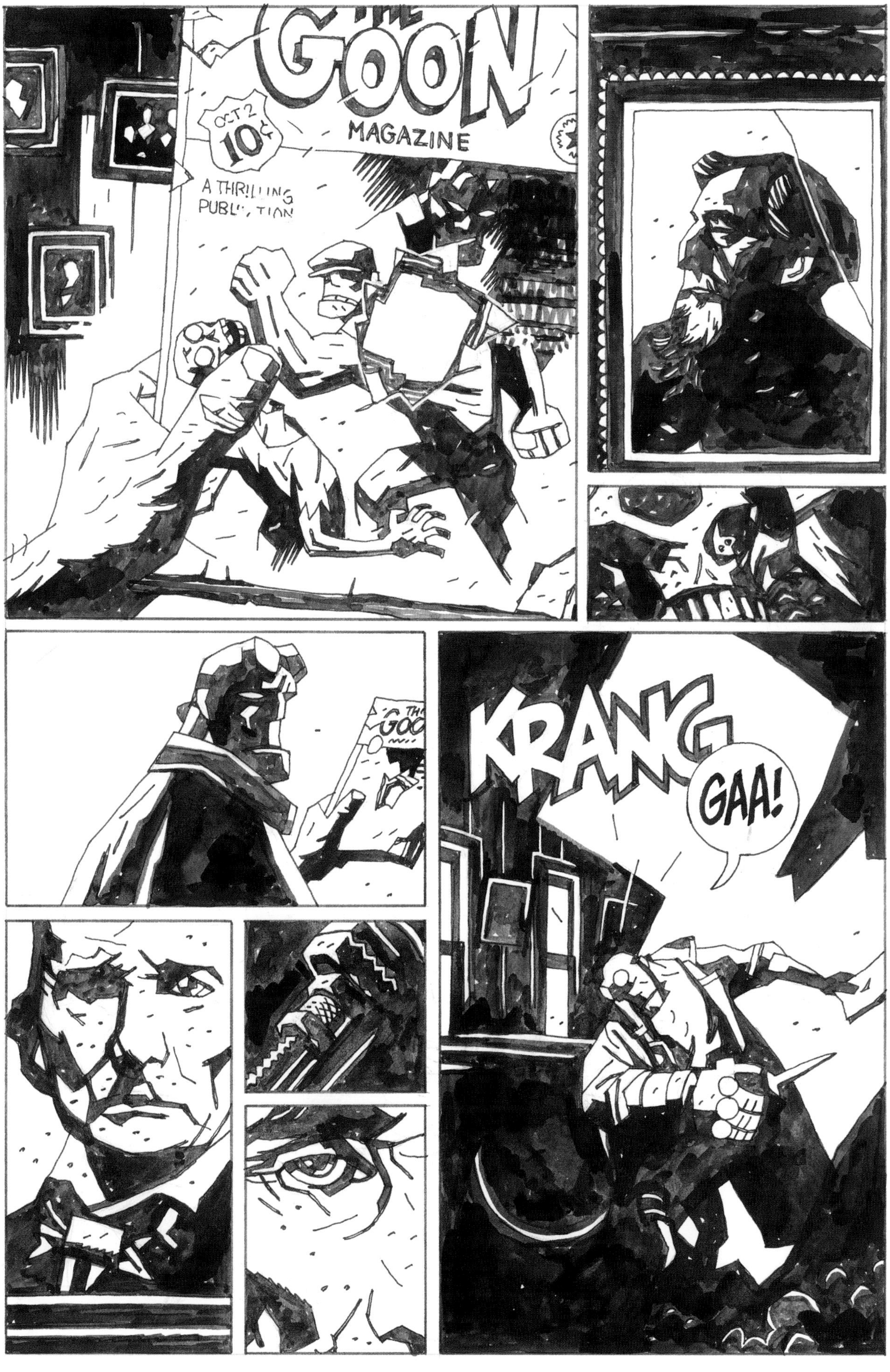
THE GOON
MAGAZINE
OCT 2
10¢
A THRILLING PUBLICATION
KRANG
GAA!

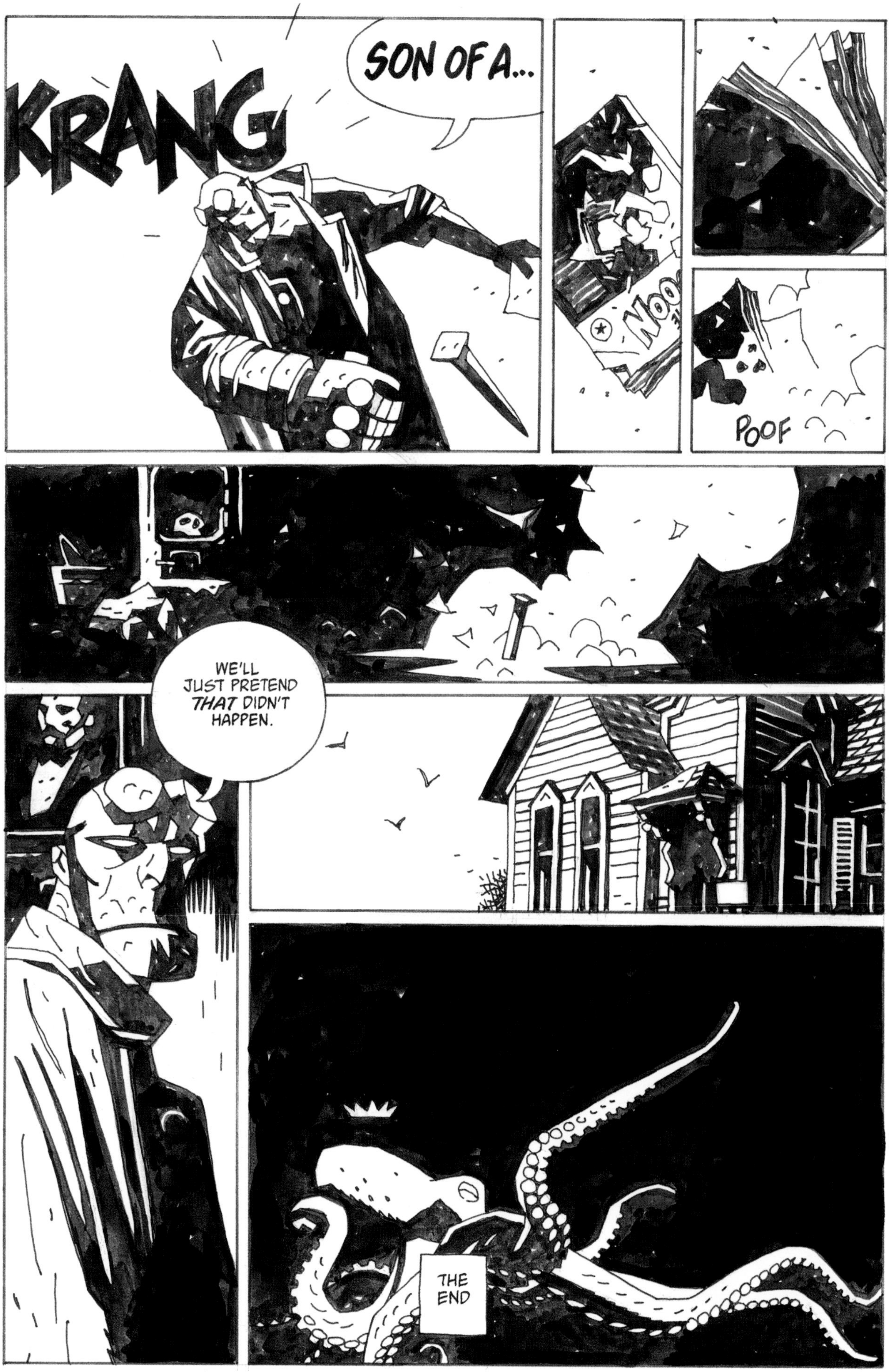
KRANG
SON OF A...
POOF
WE'LL JUST PRETEND THAT DIDN'T HAPPEN.
THE END

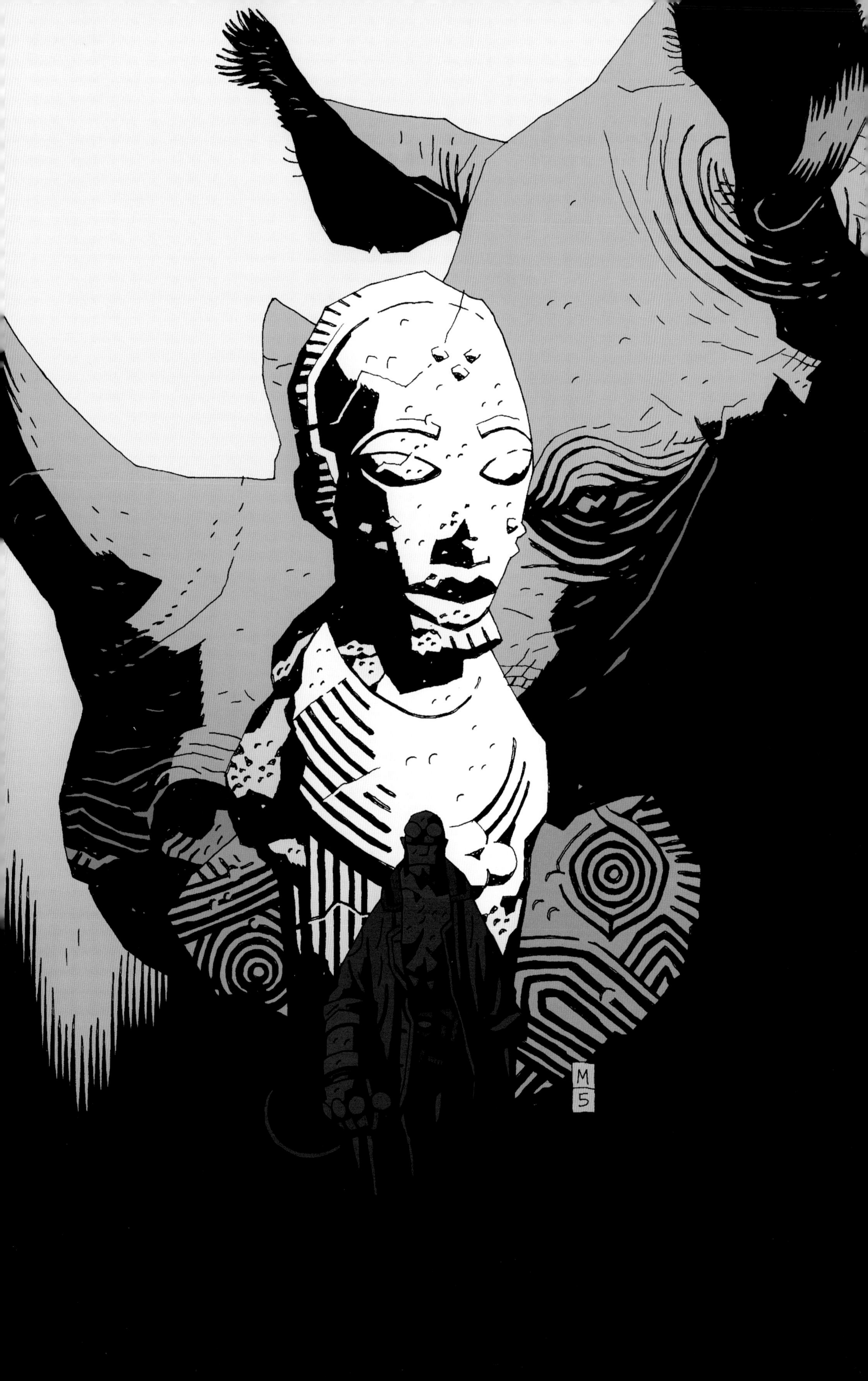

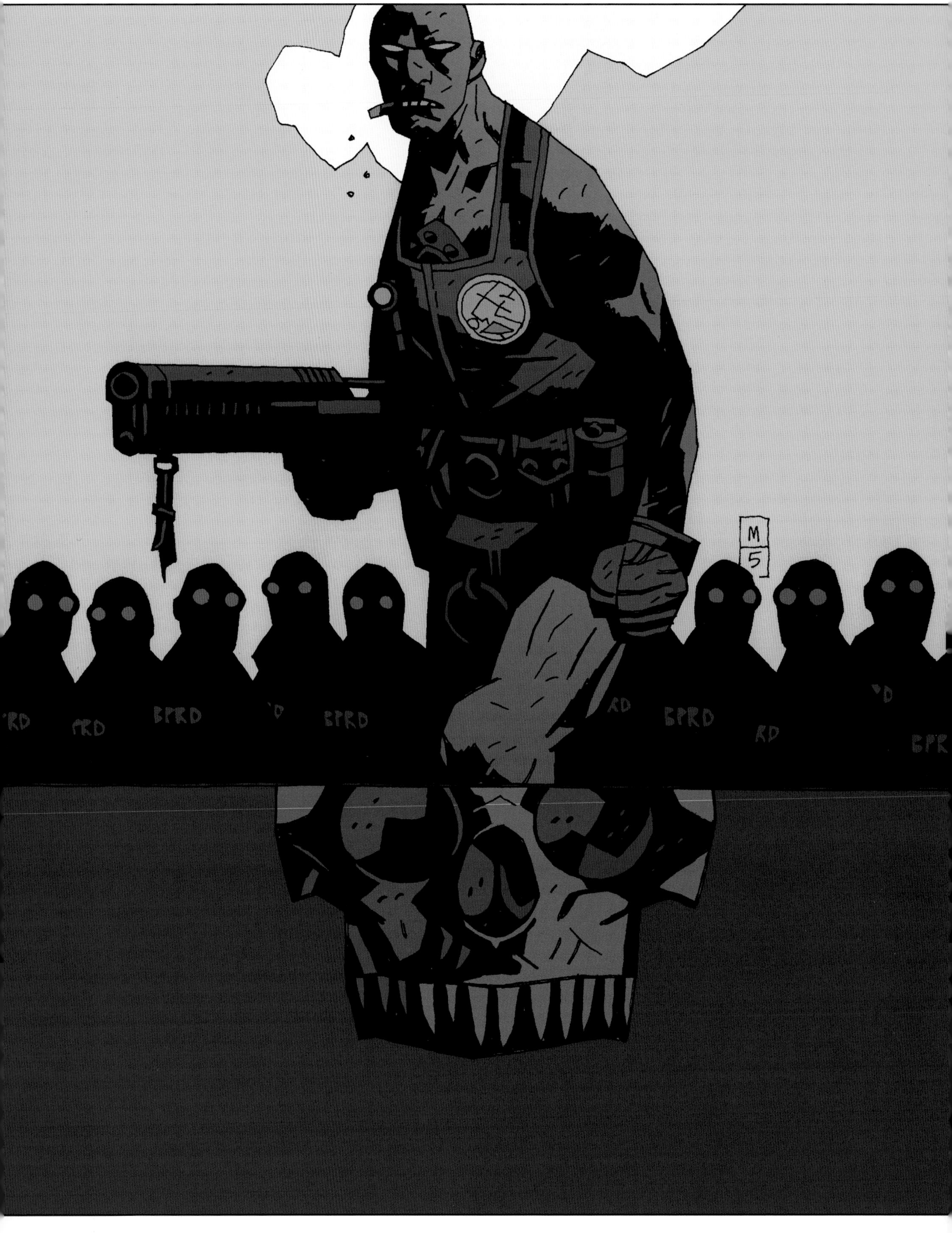
BPRD

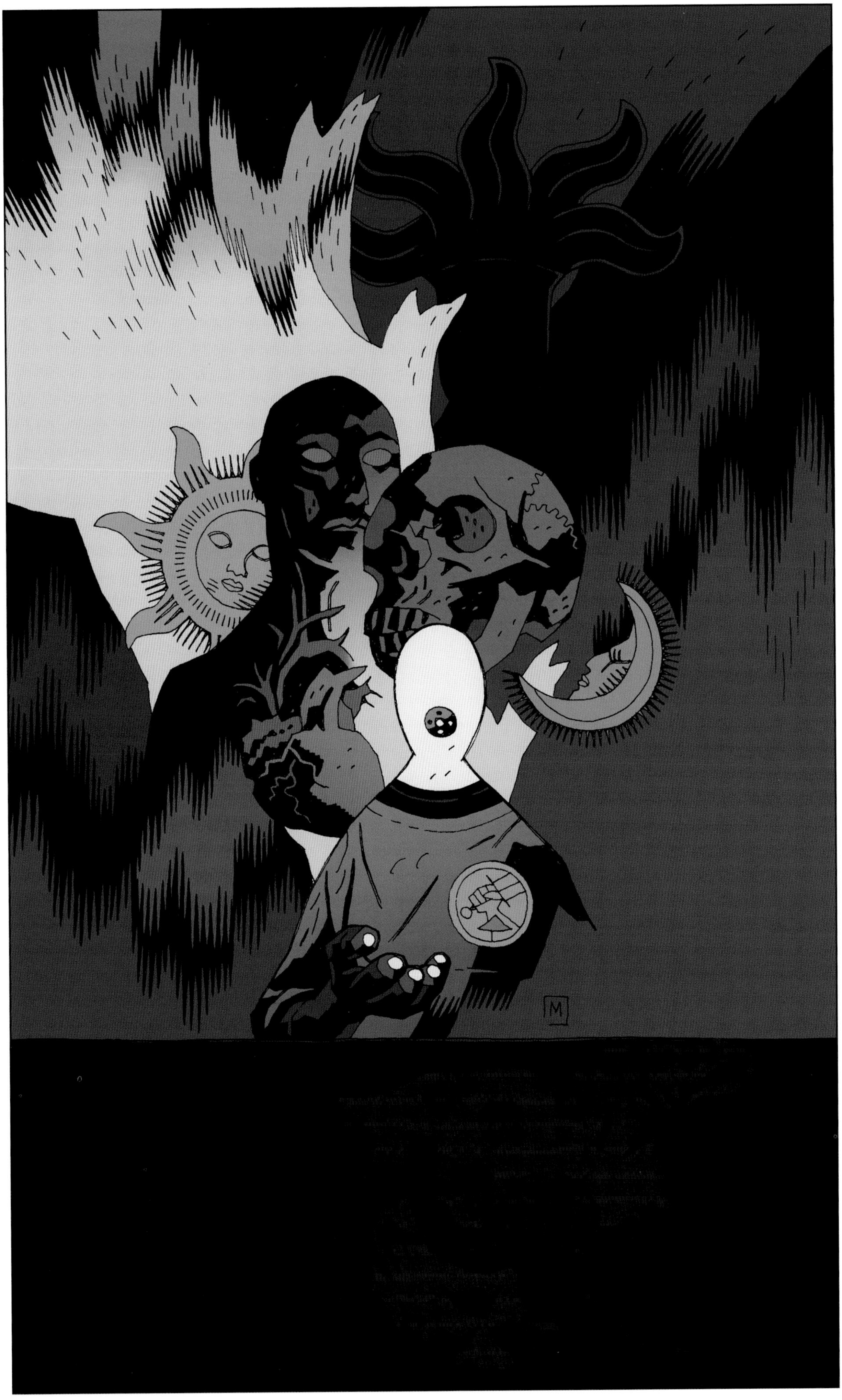

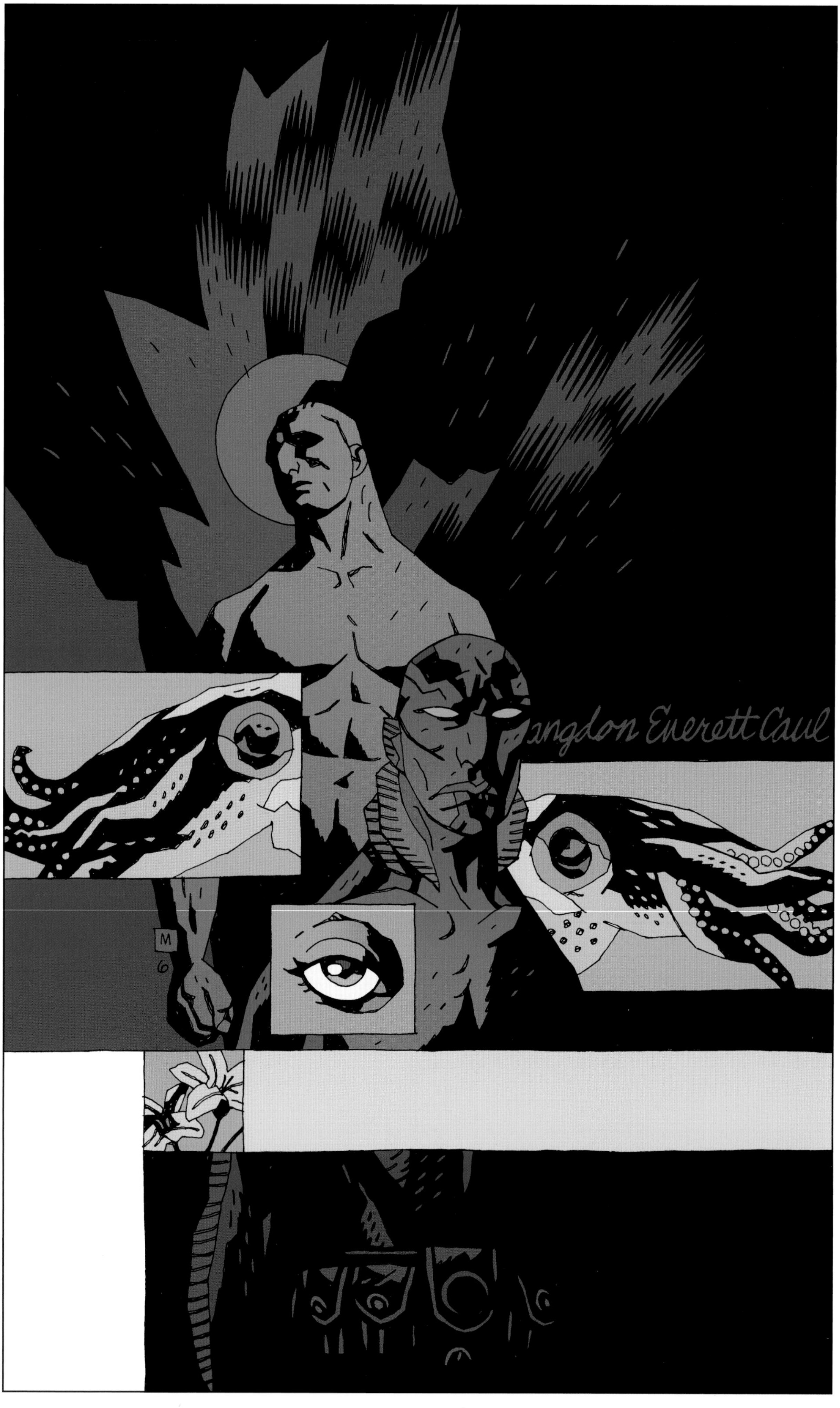
angdon Everett Caul

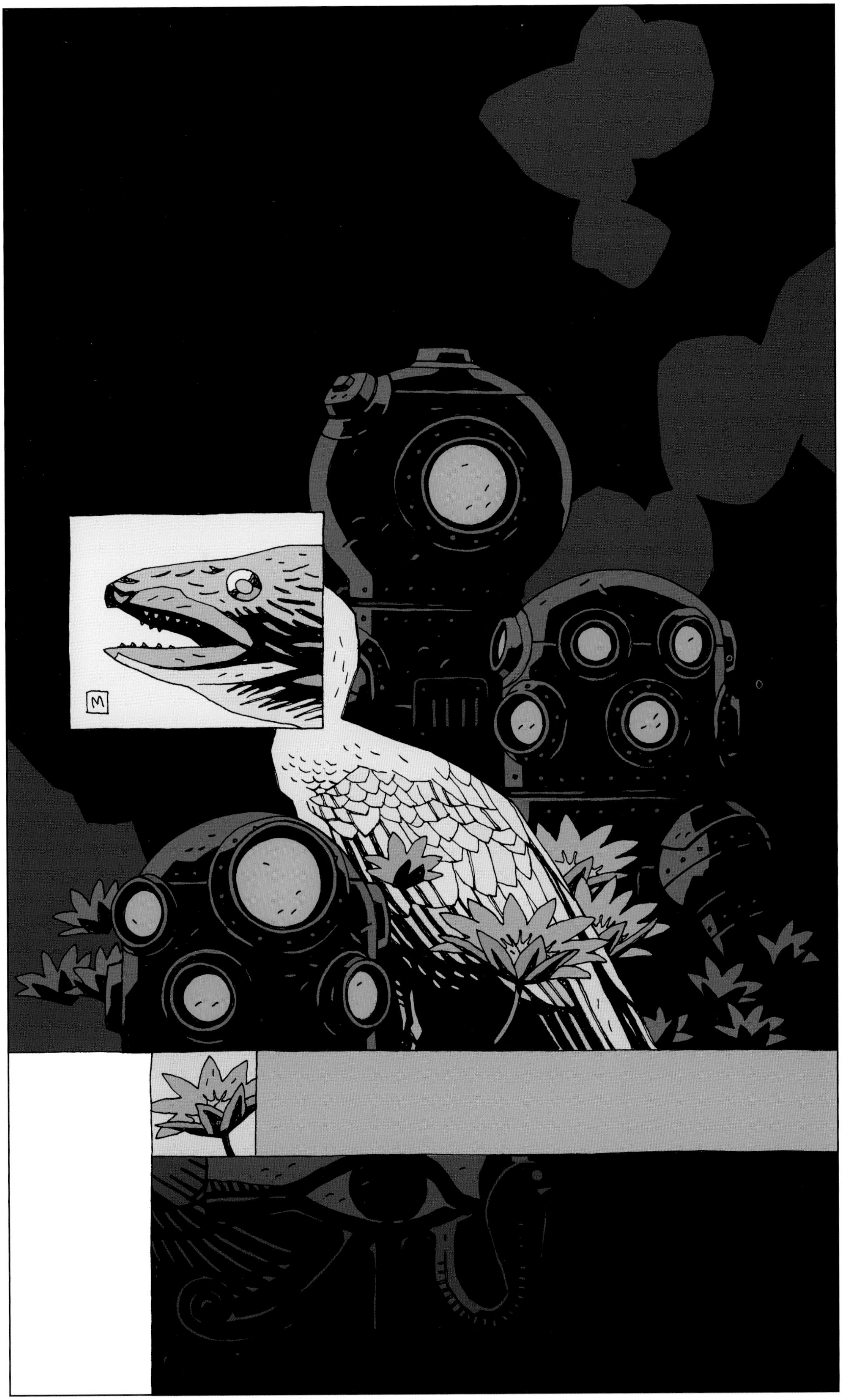

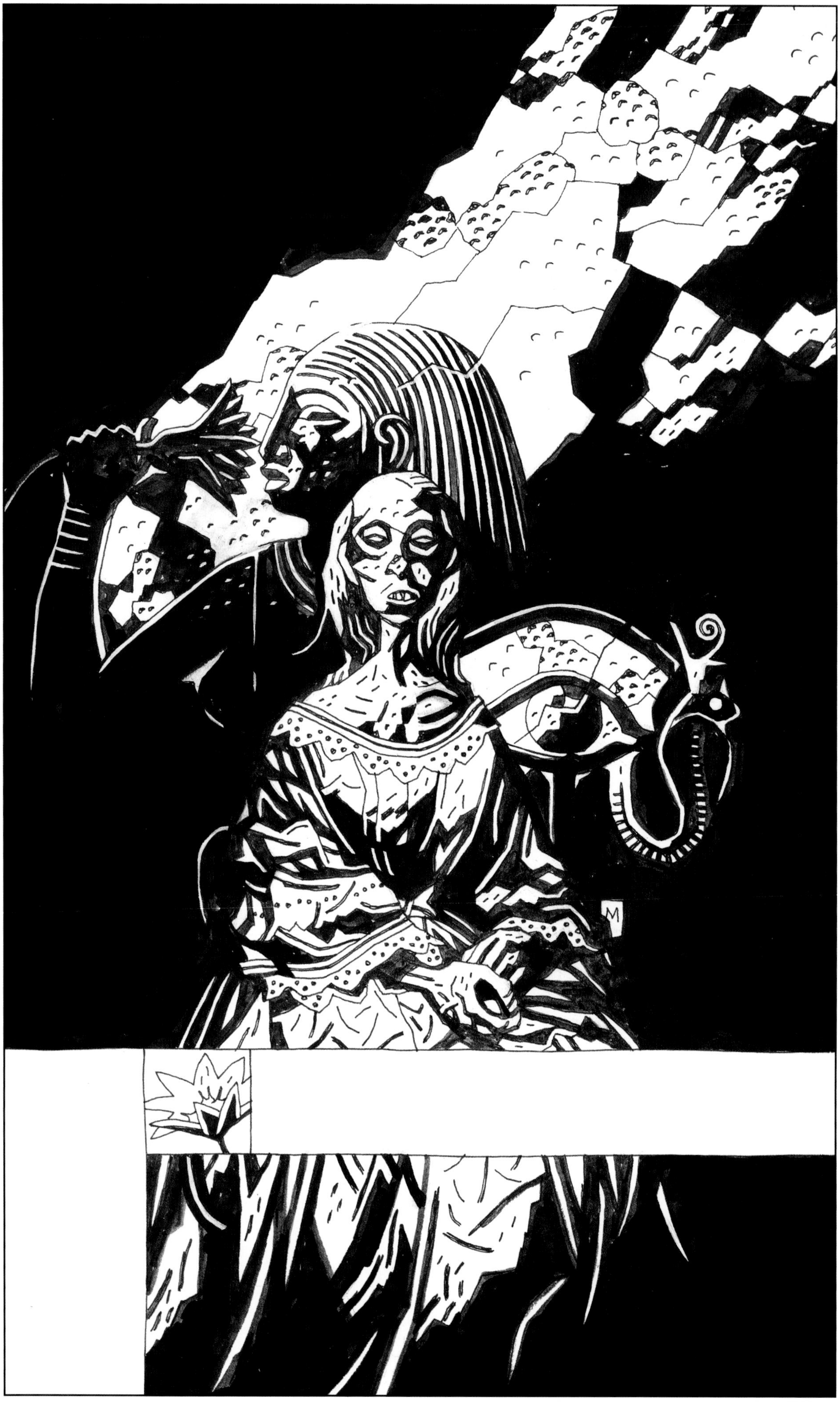

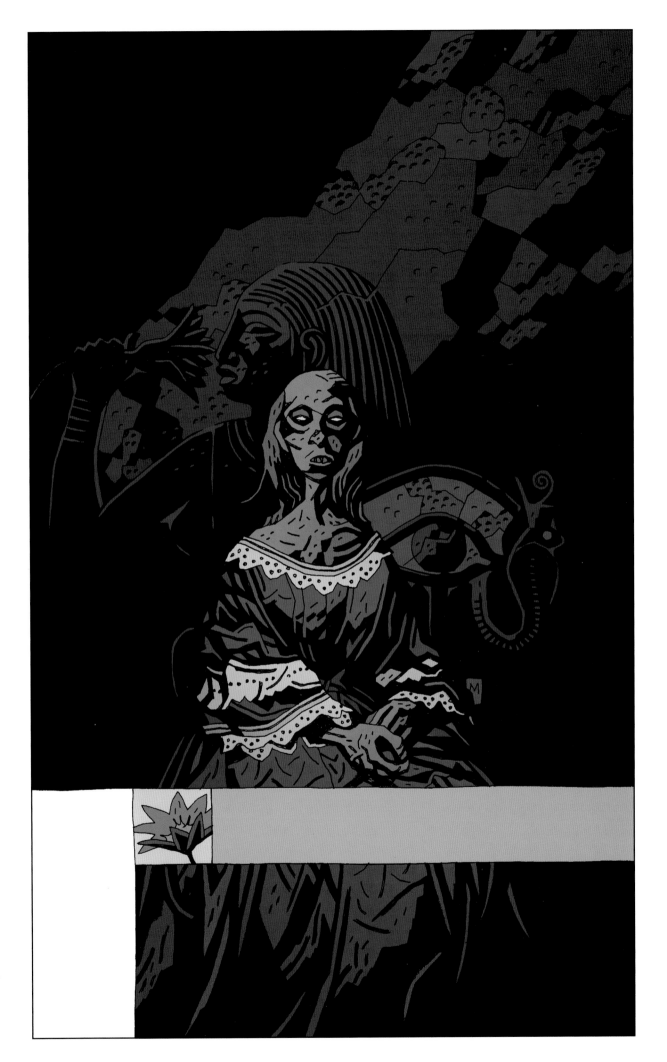

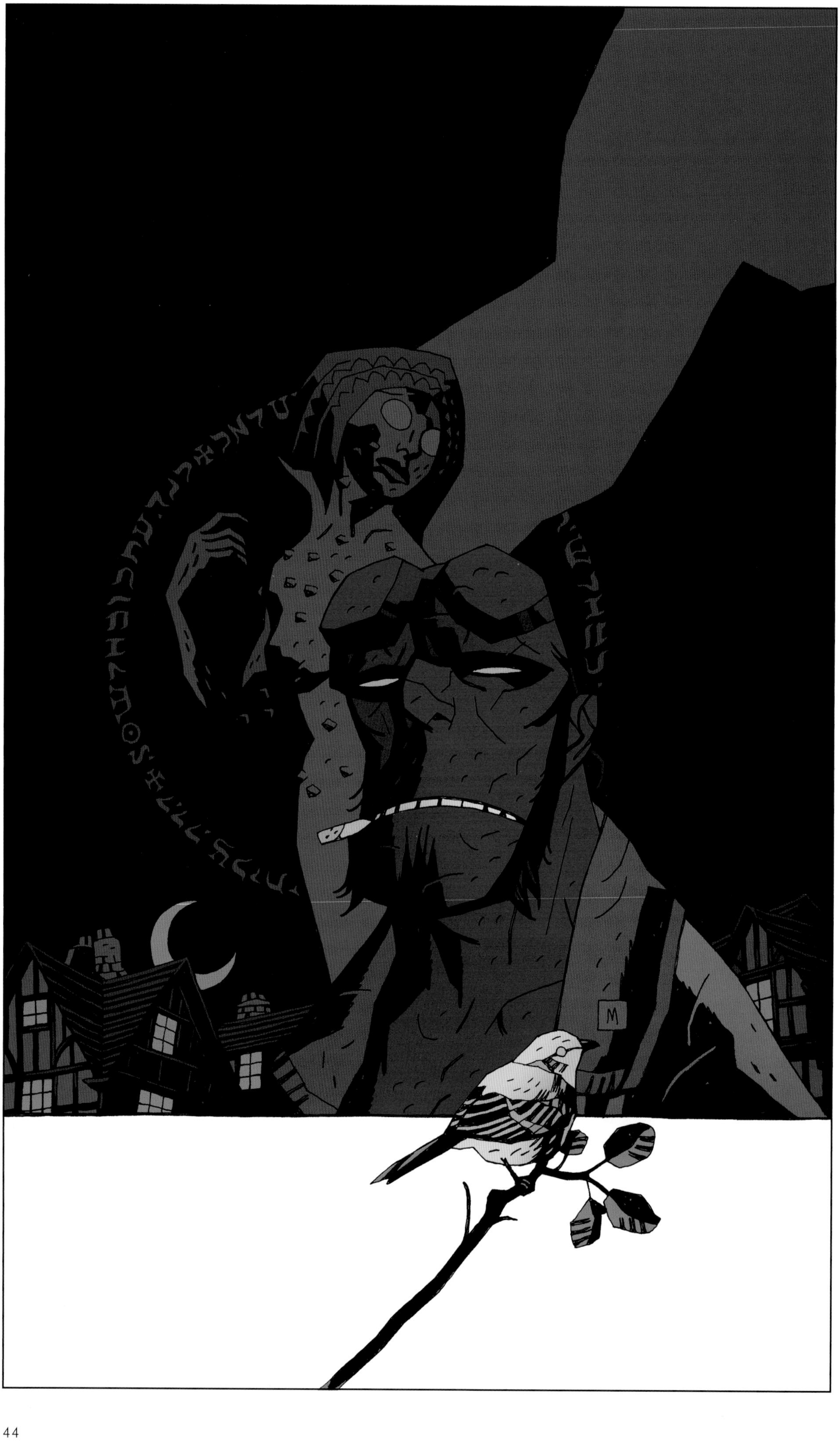

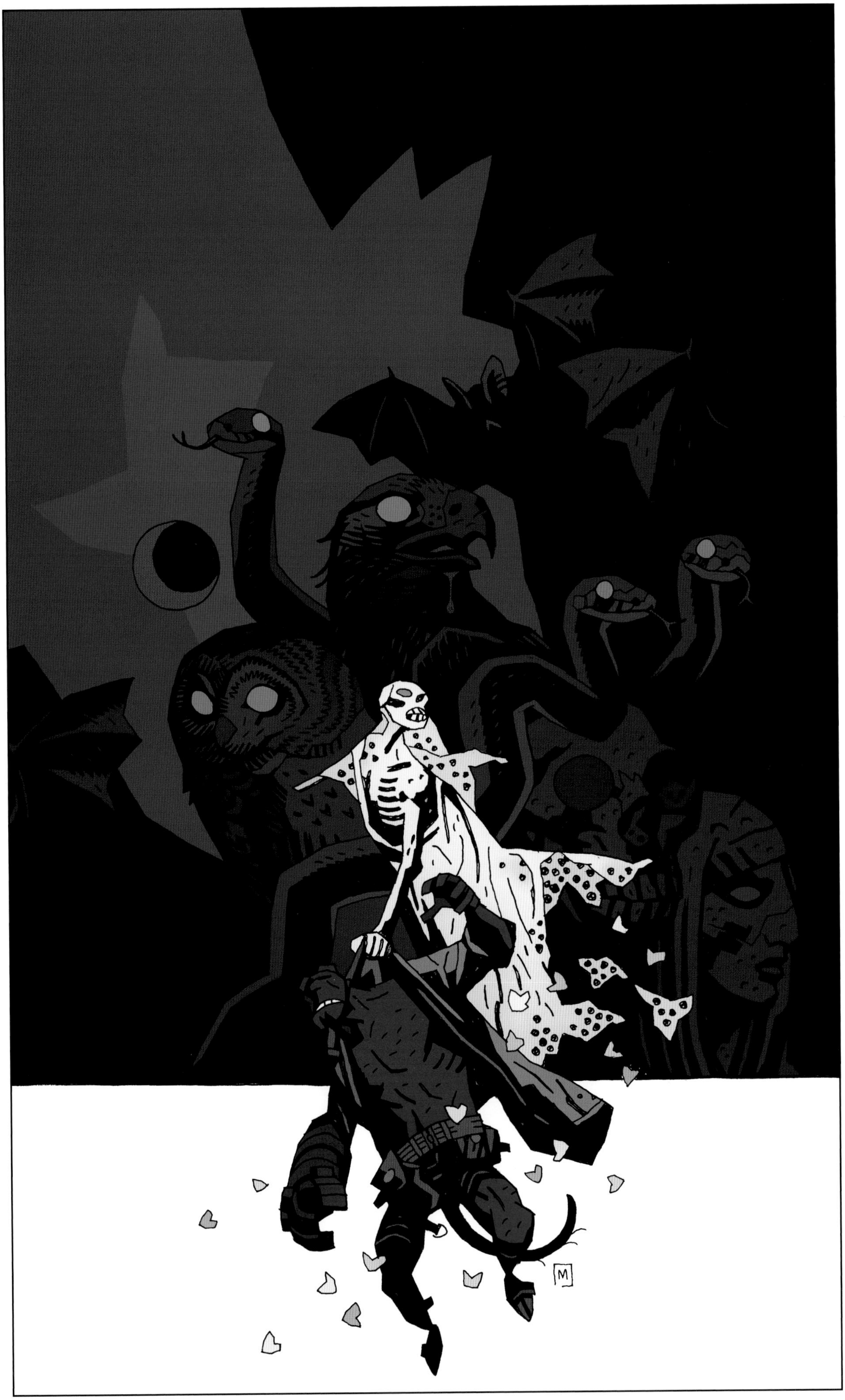

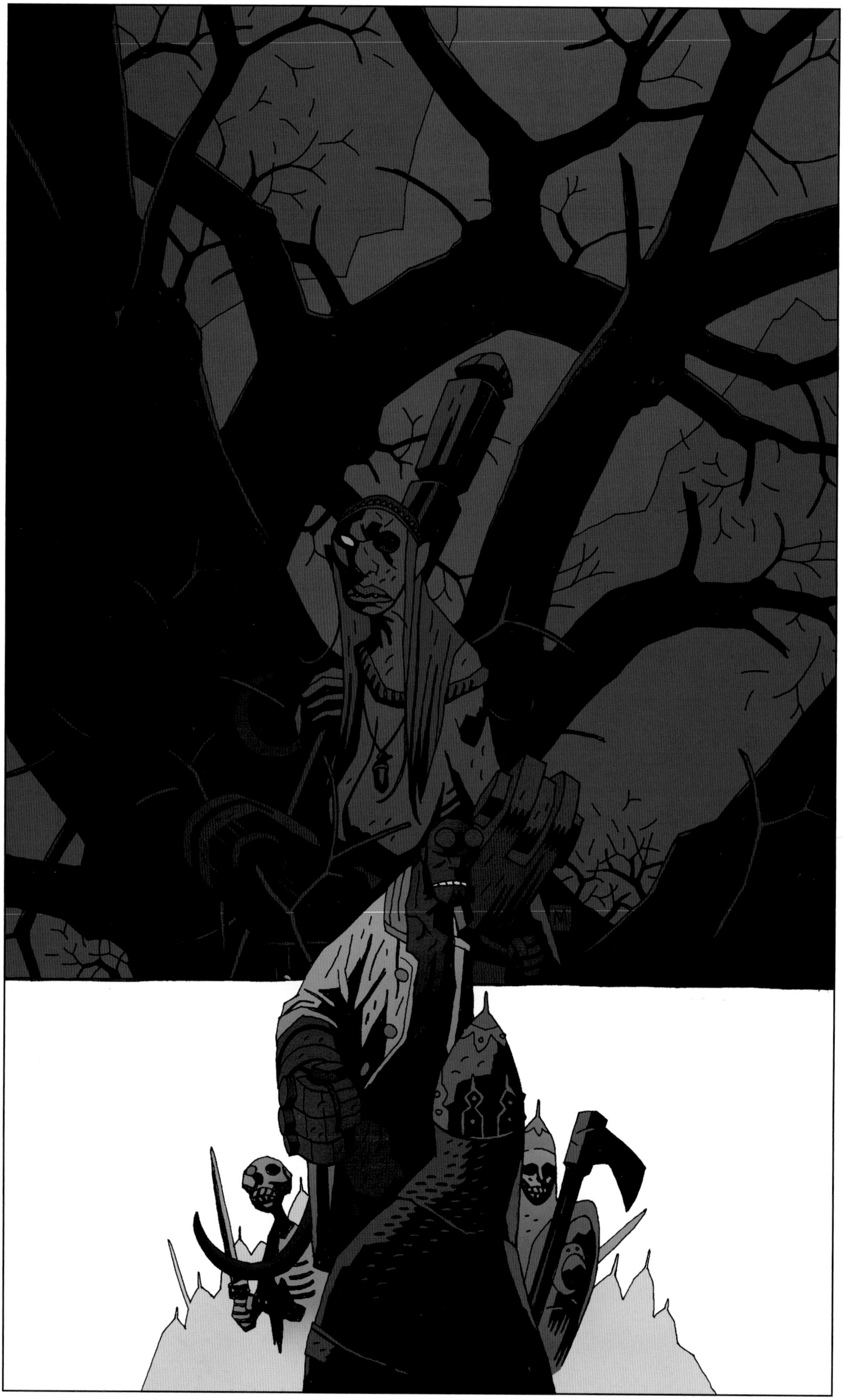

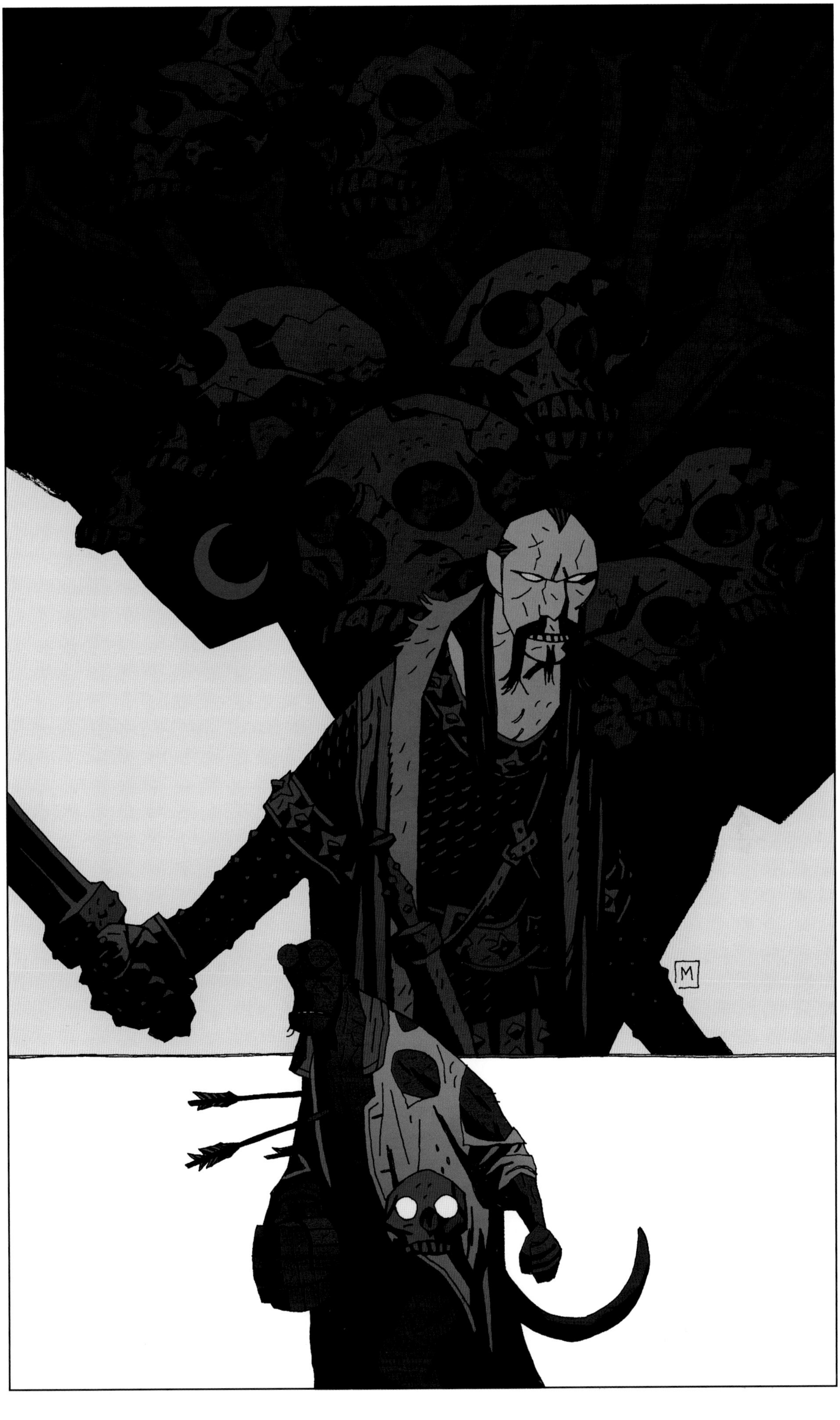

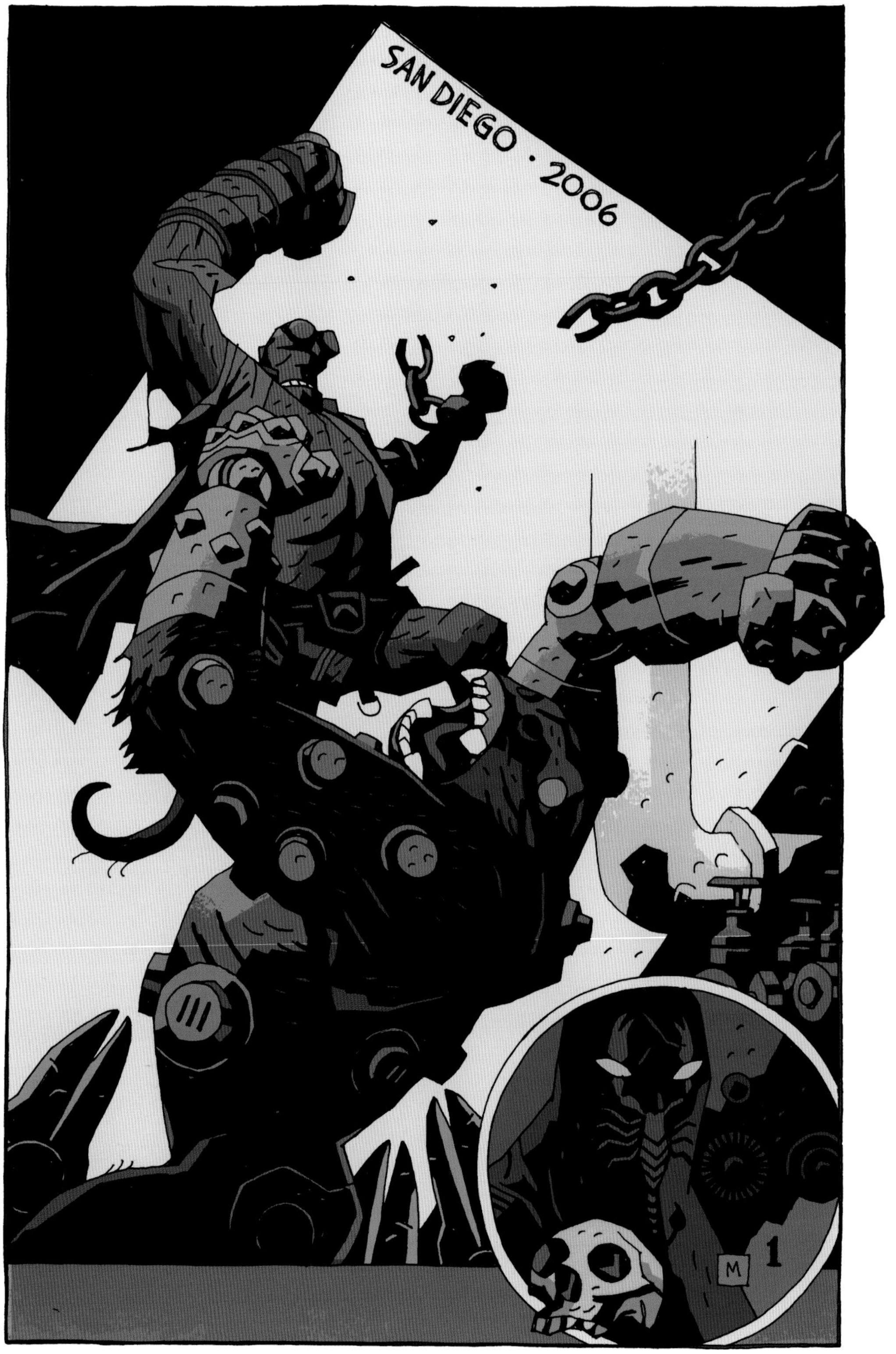
SAN DIEGO · 2006
M 1

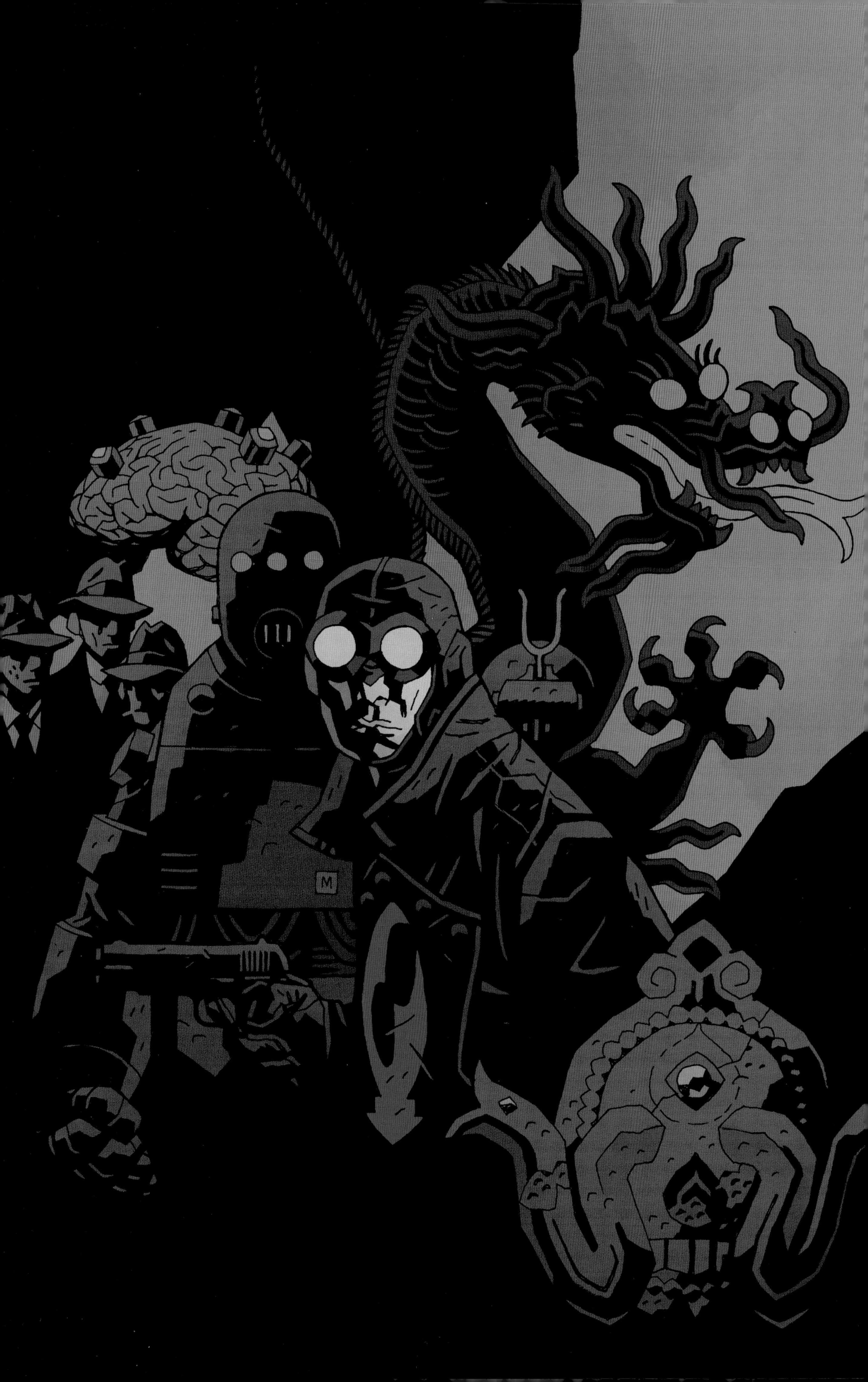

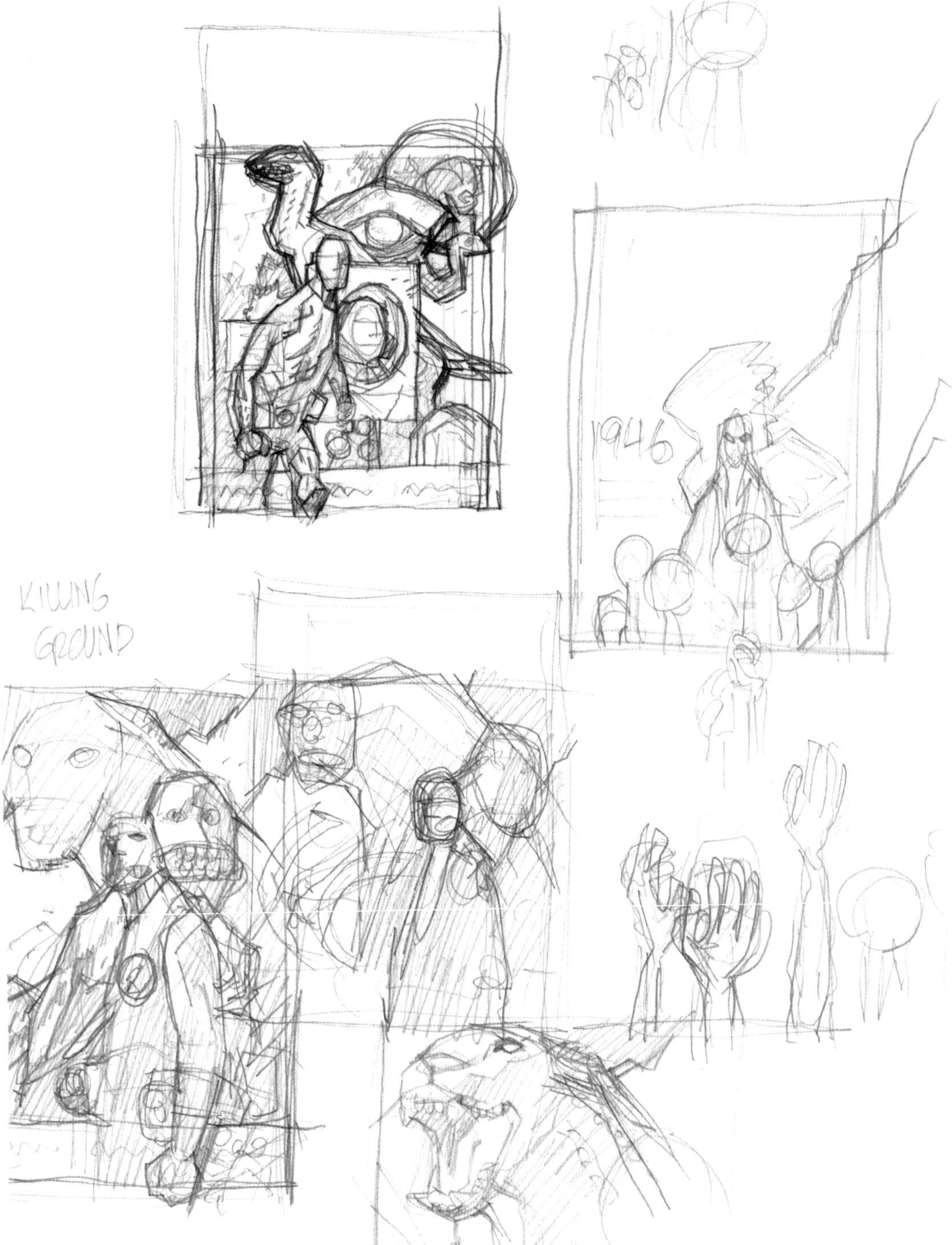
KILLING GROUND
1946

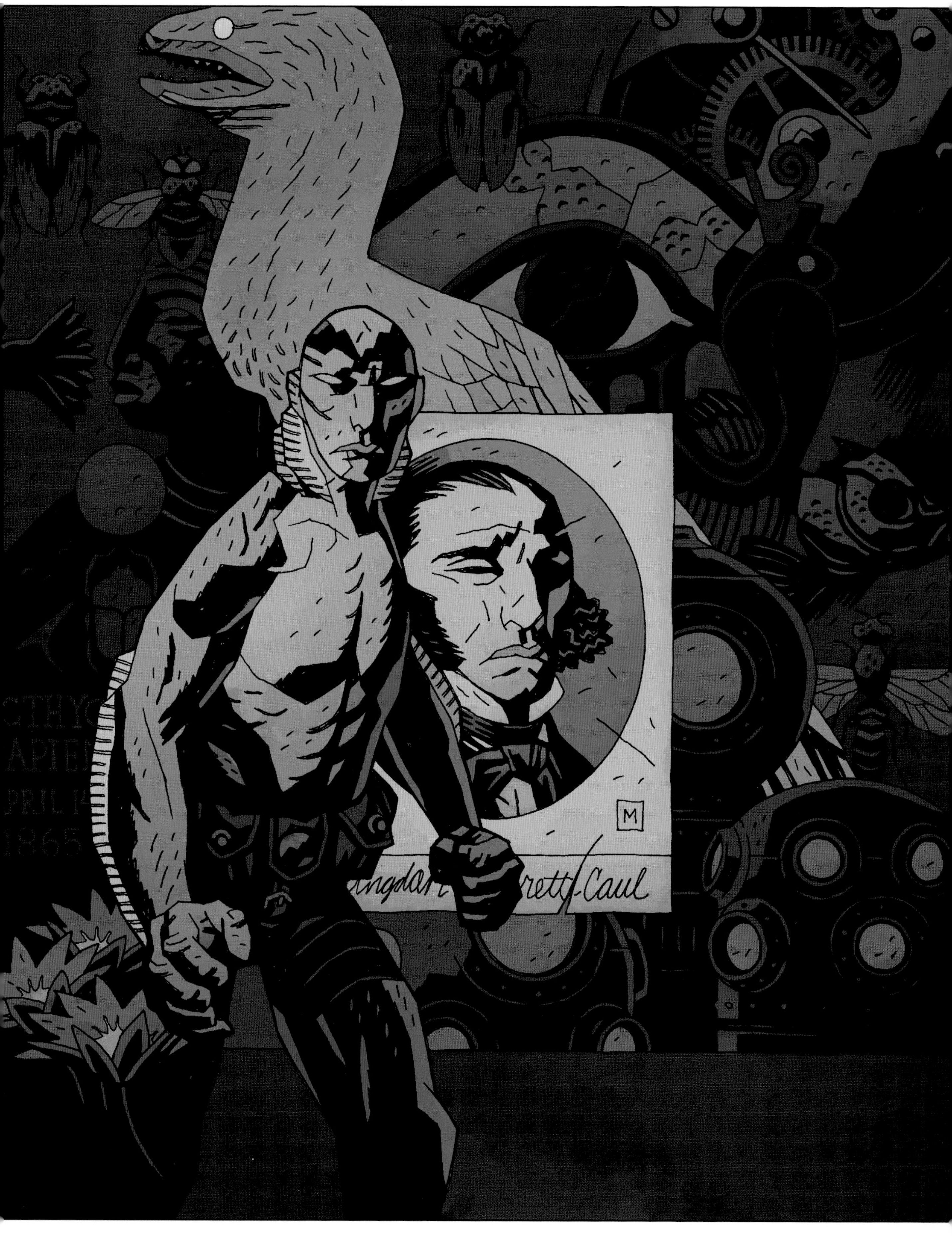
1865

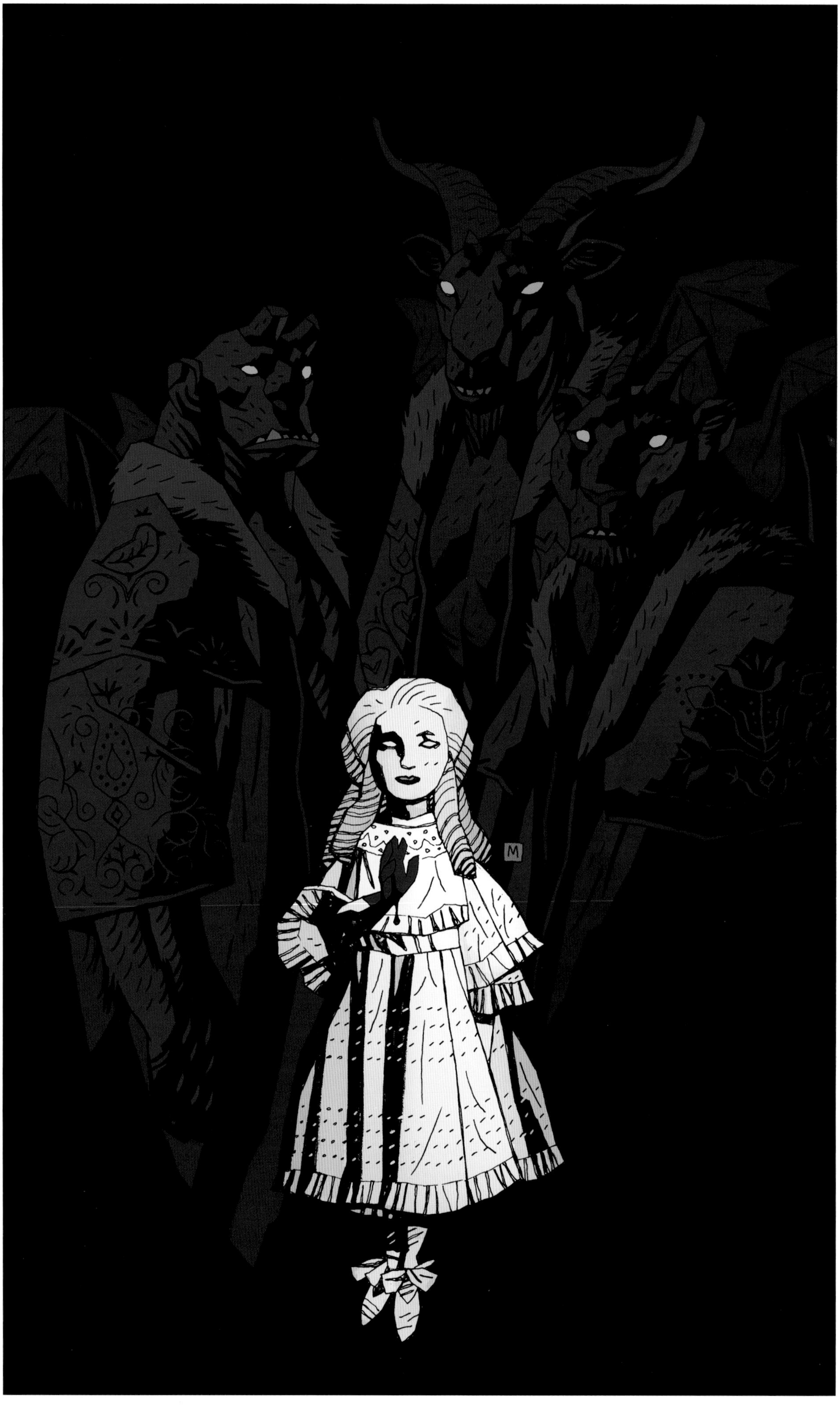

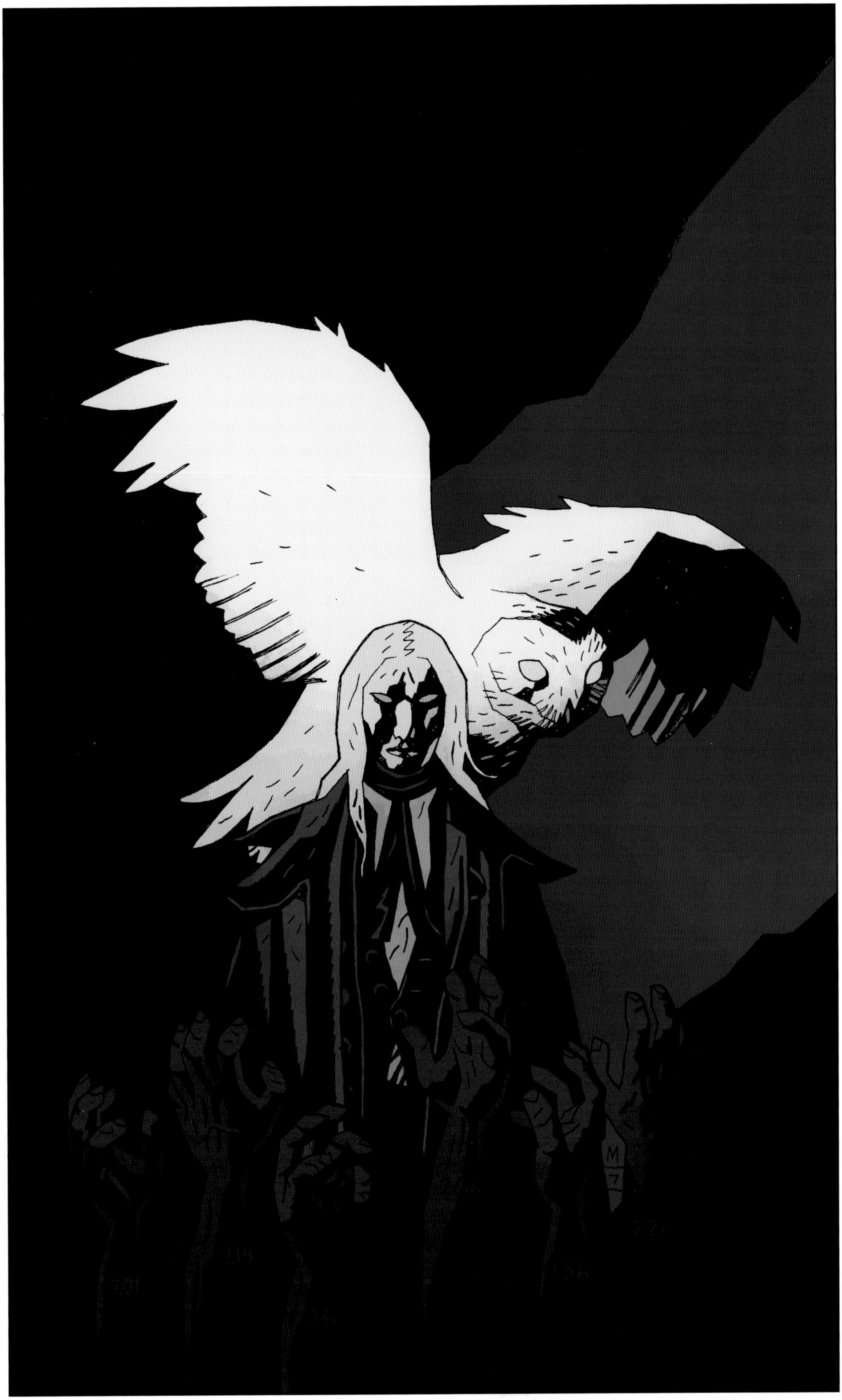

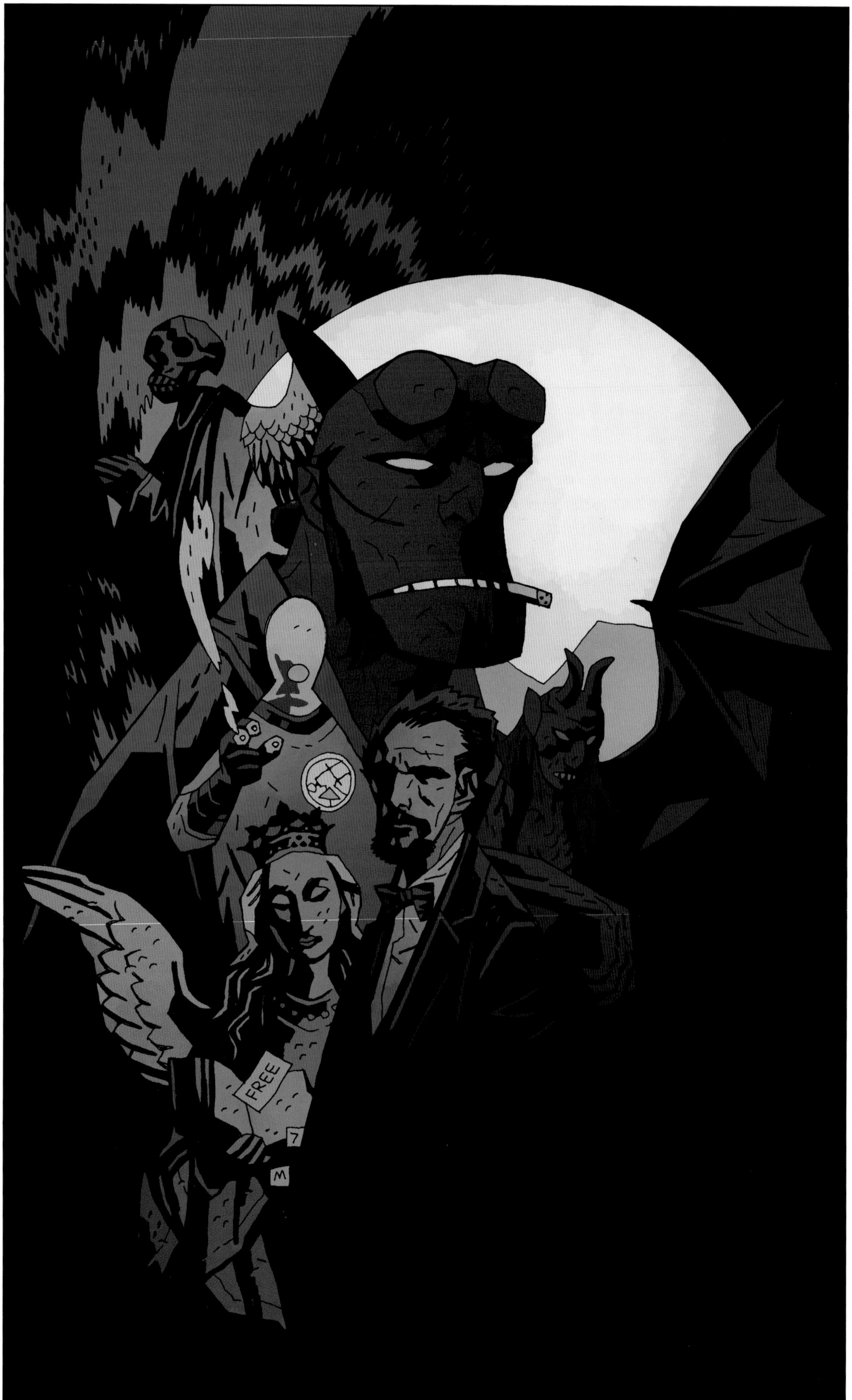
FREE

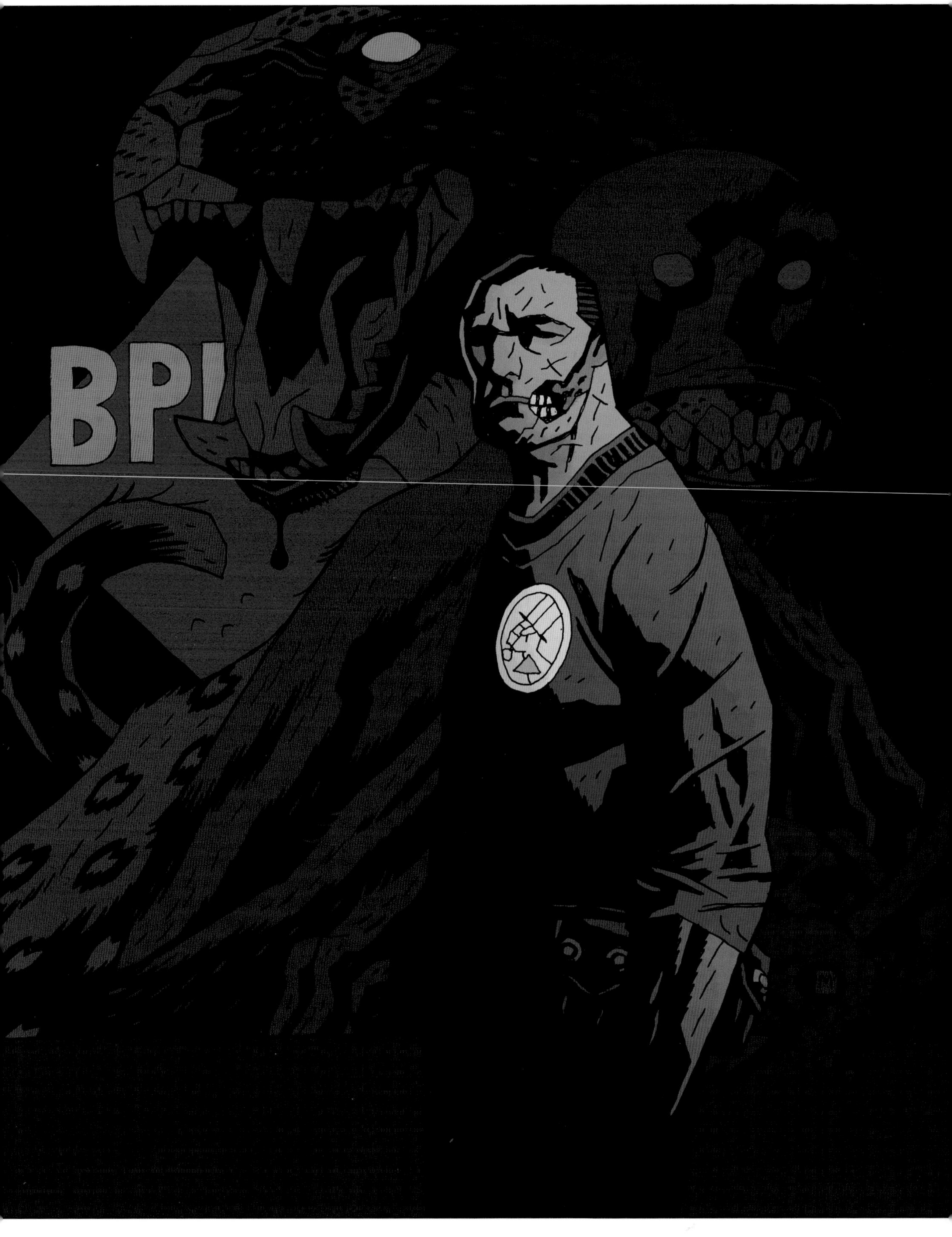

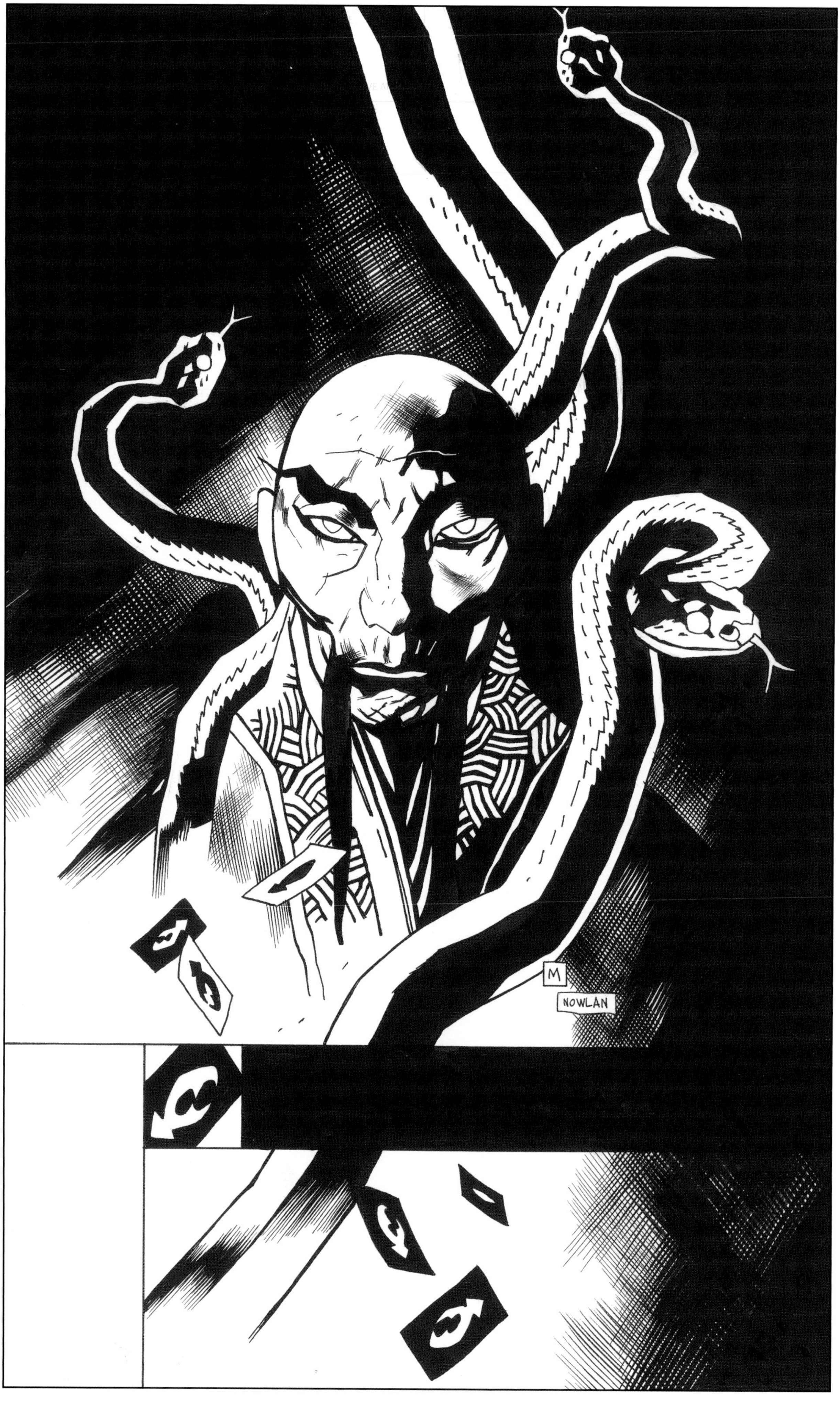
M
NOWLAN

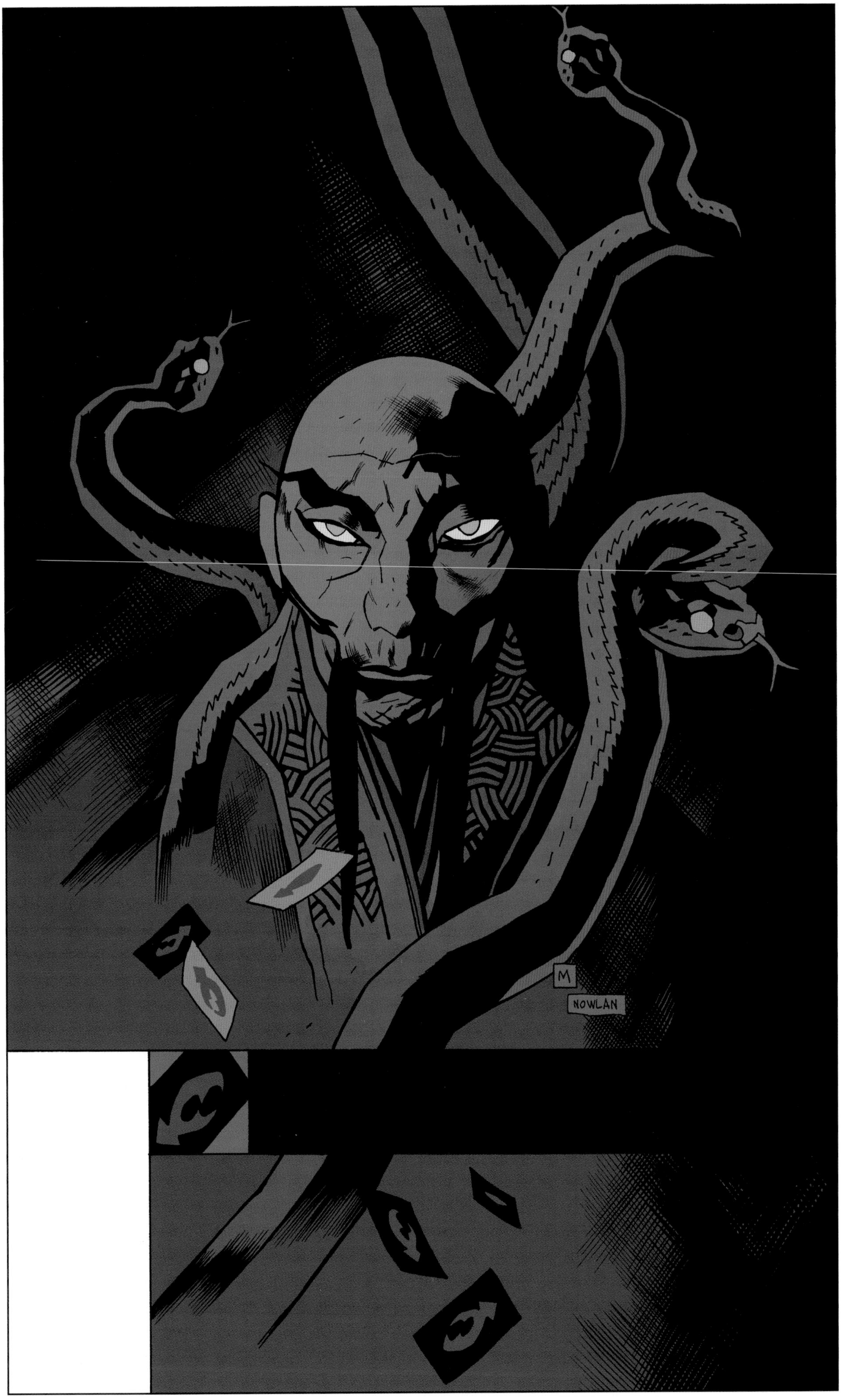
M
NOWLAN

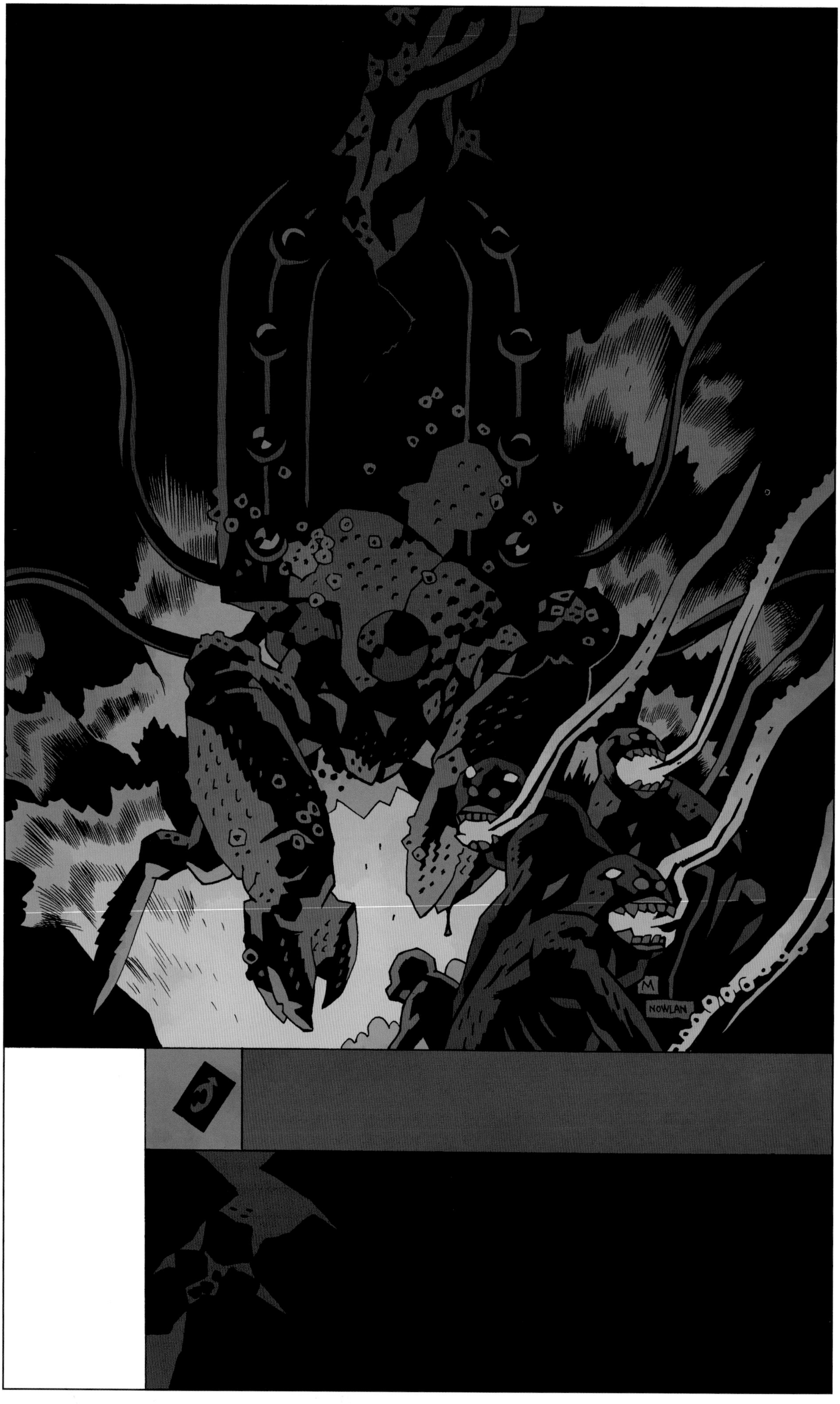
NOWLAN

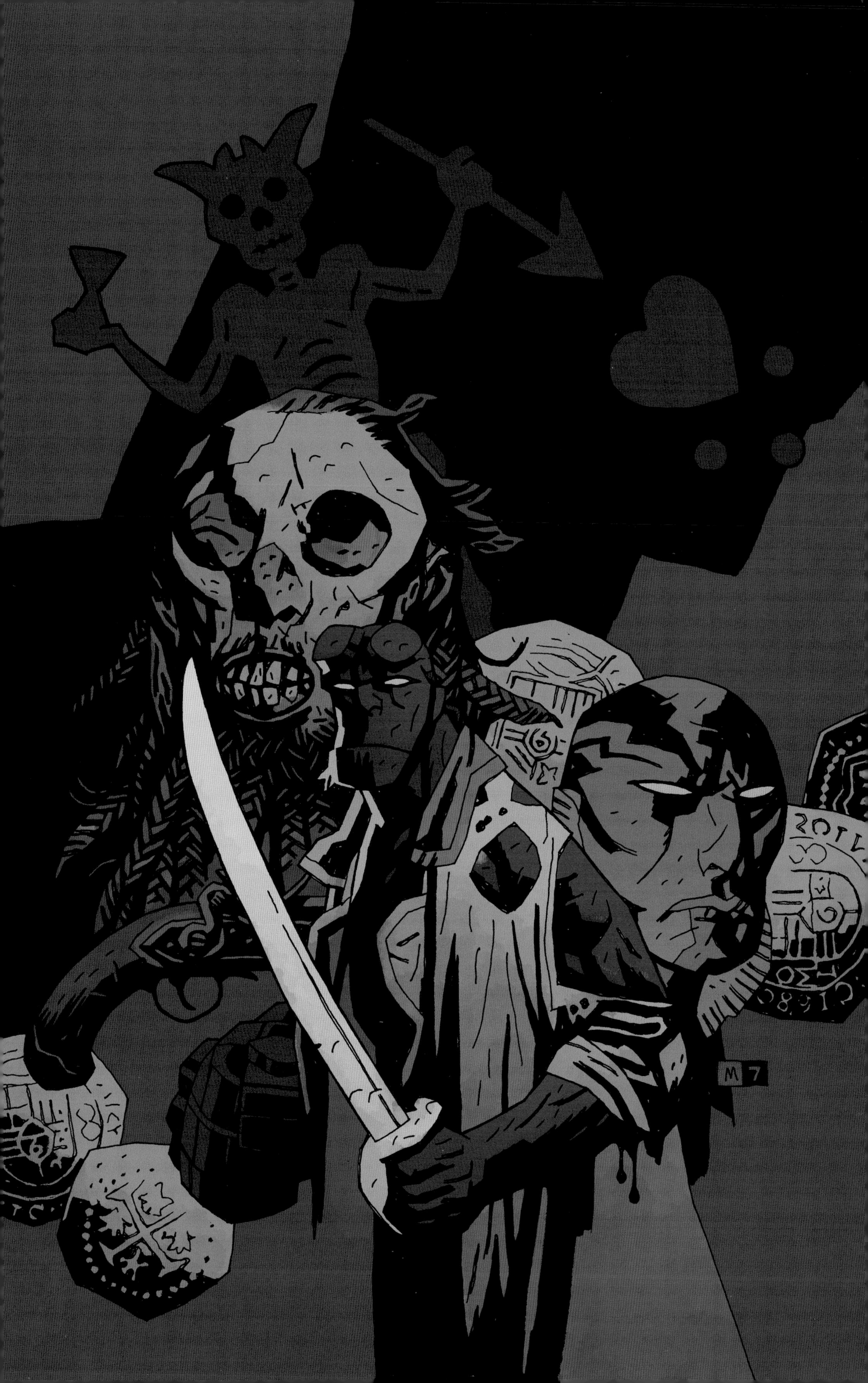

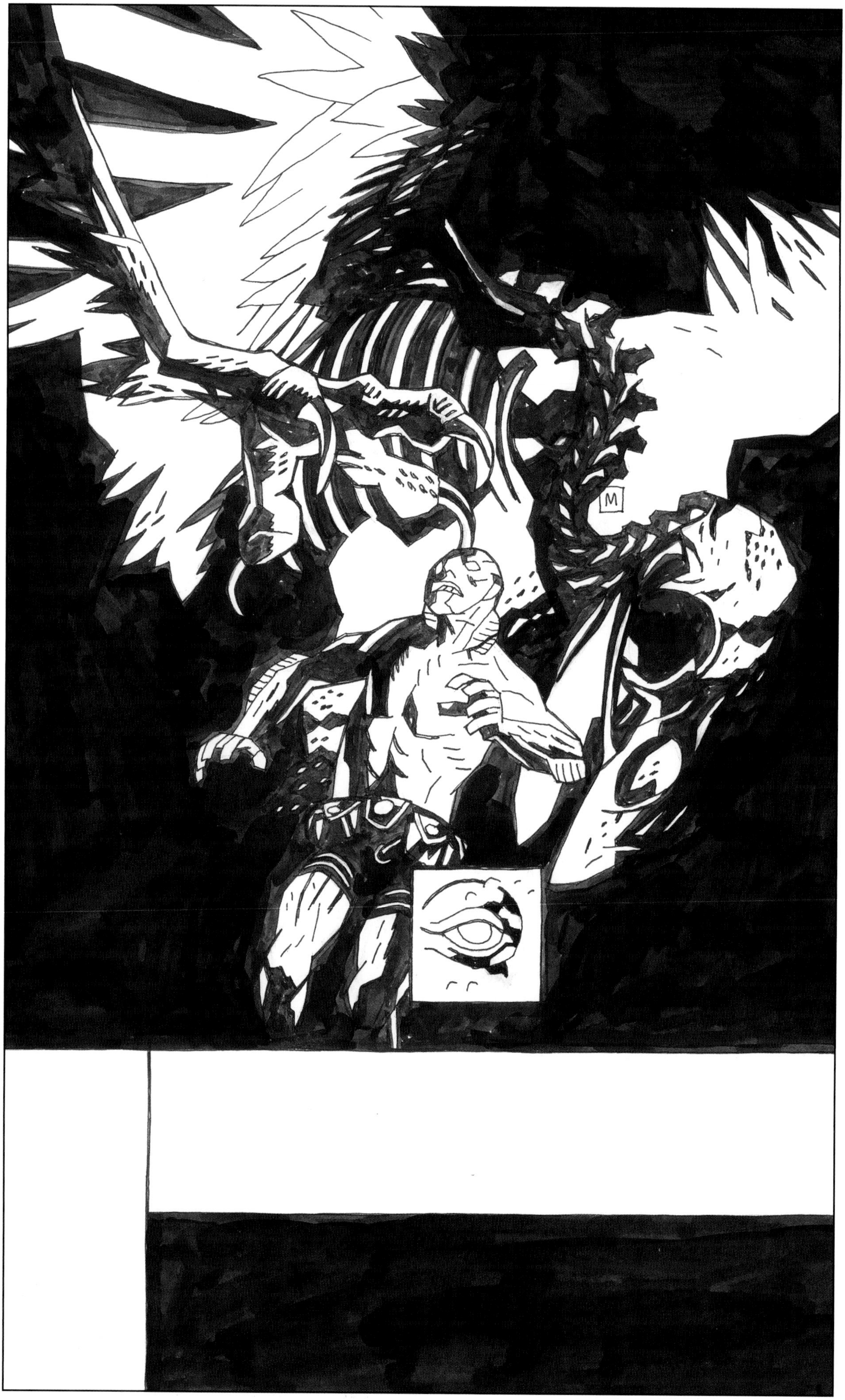

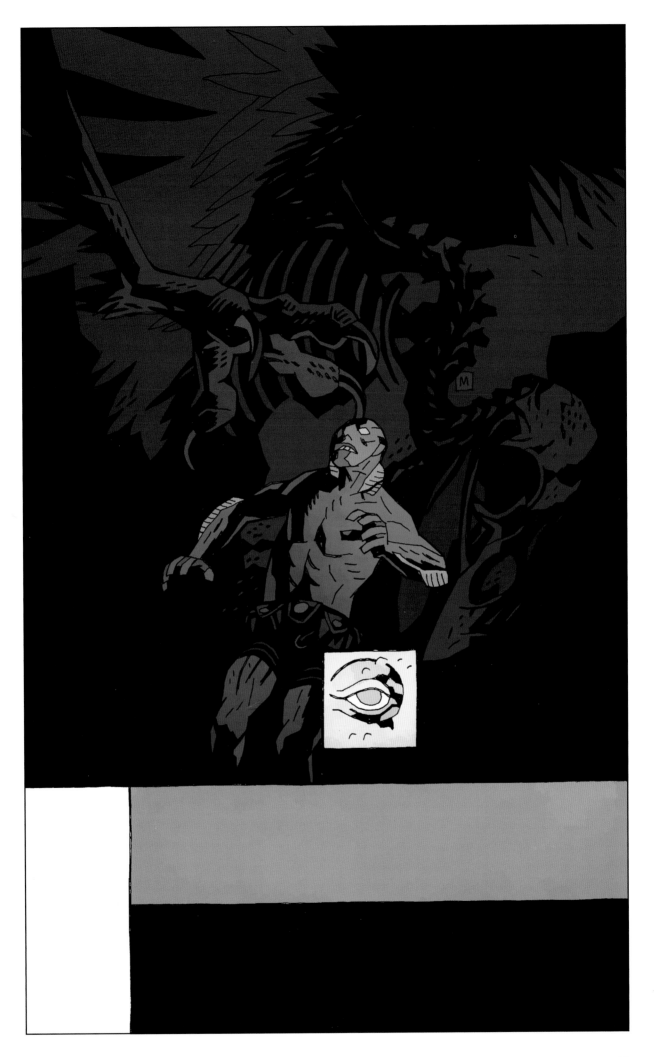

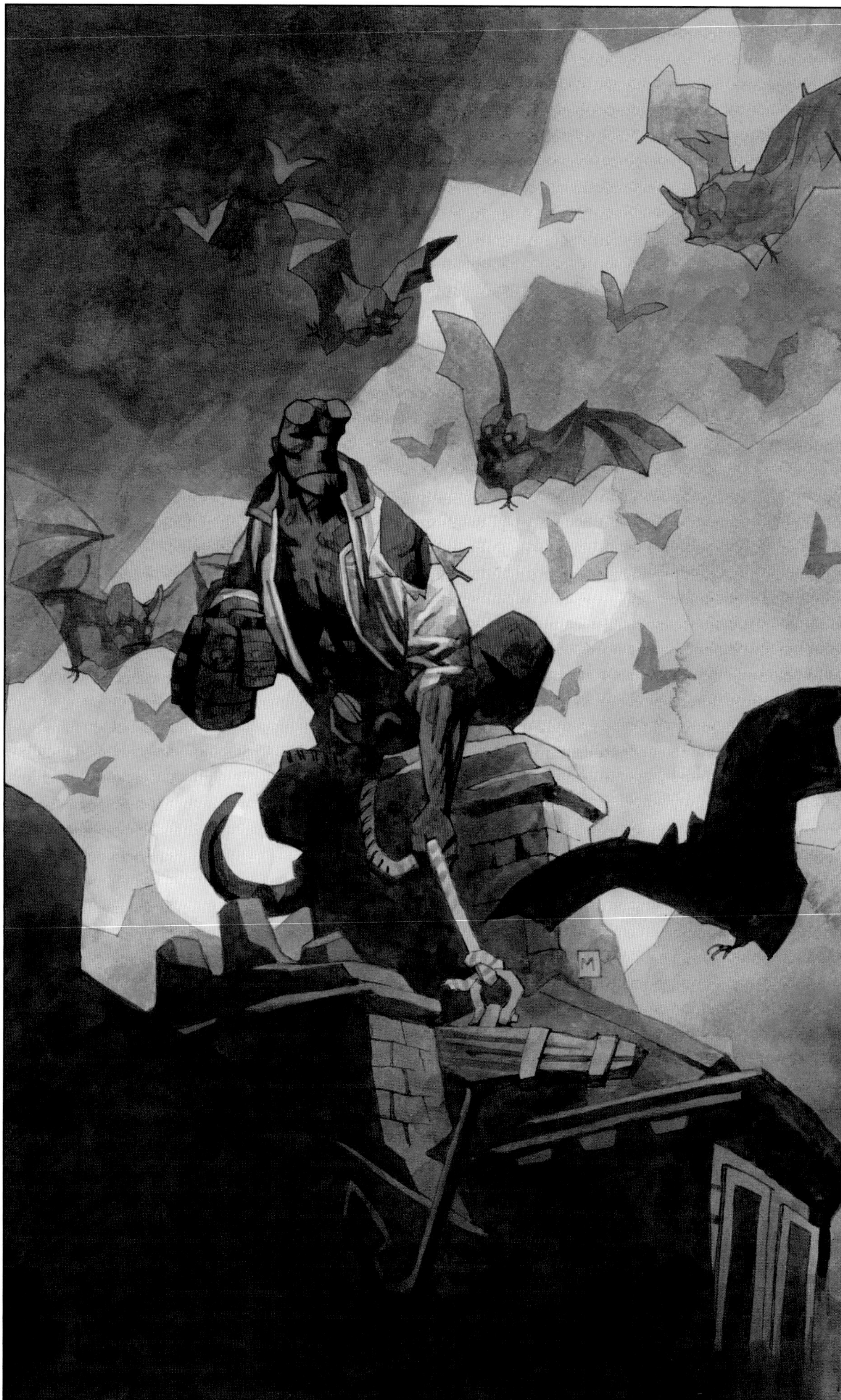

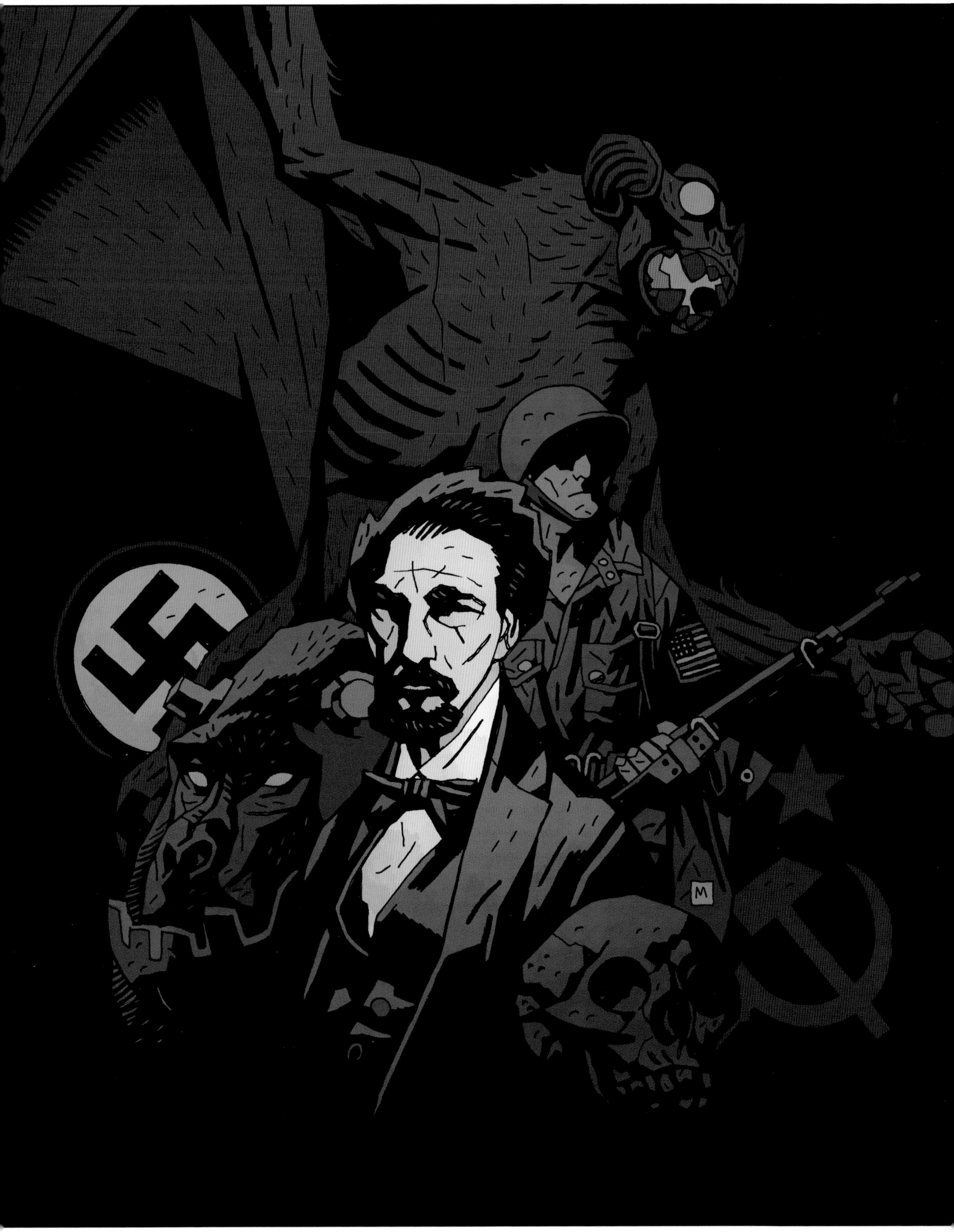

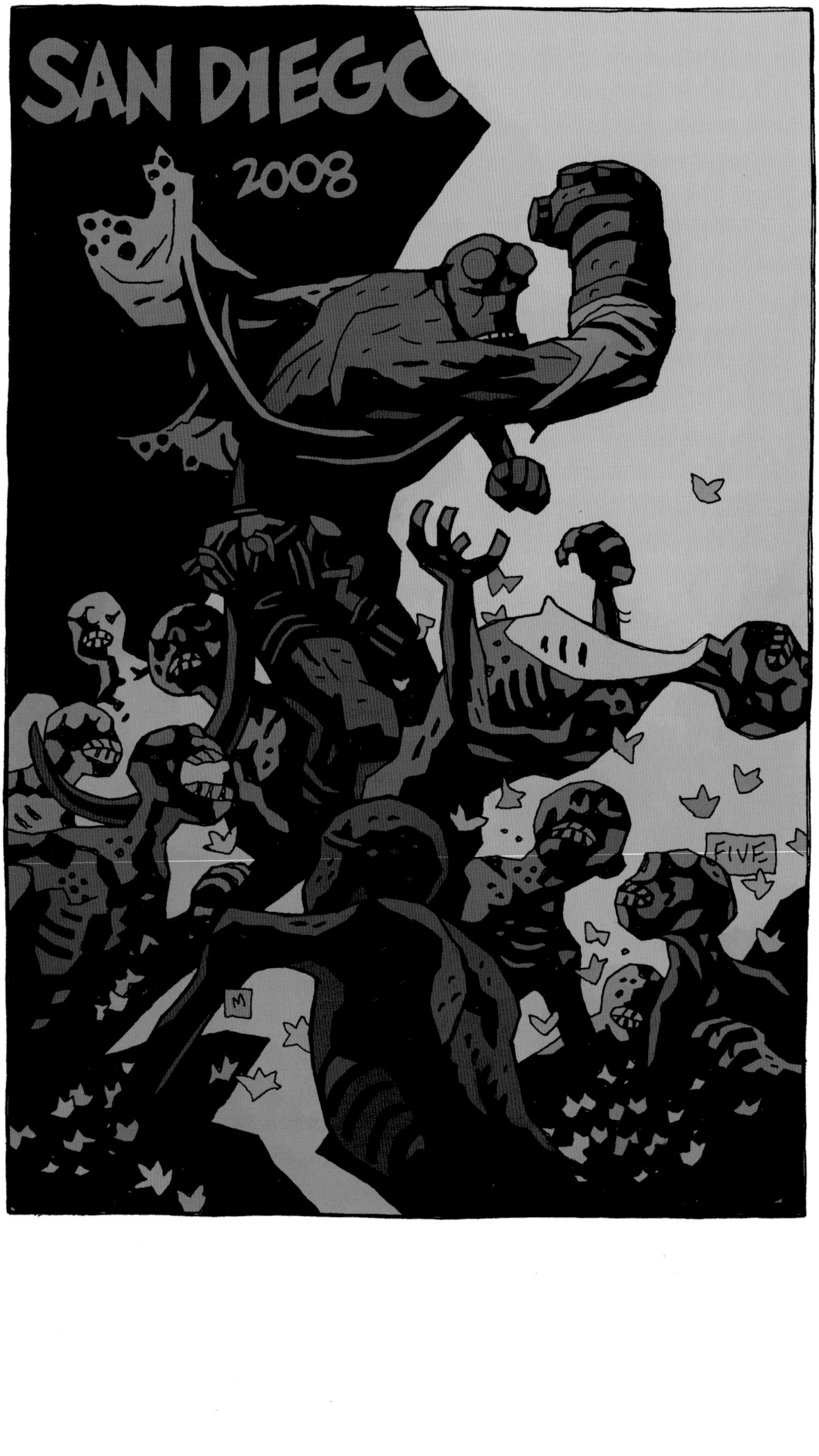
SAN DIEGO
2008
FIVE

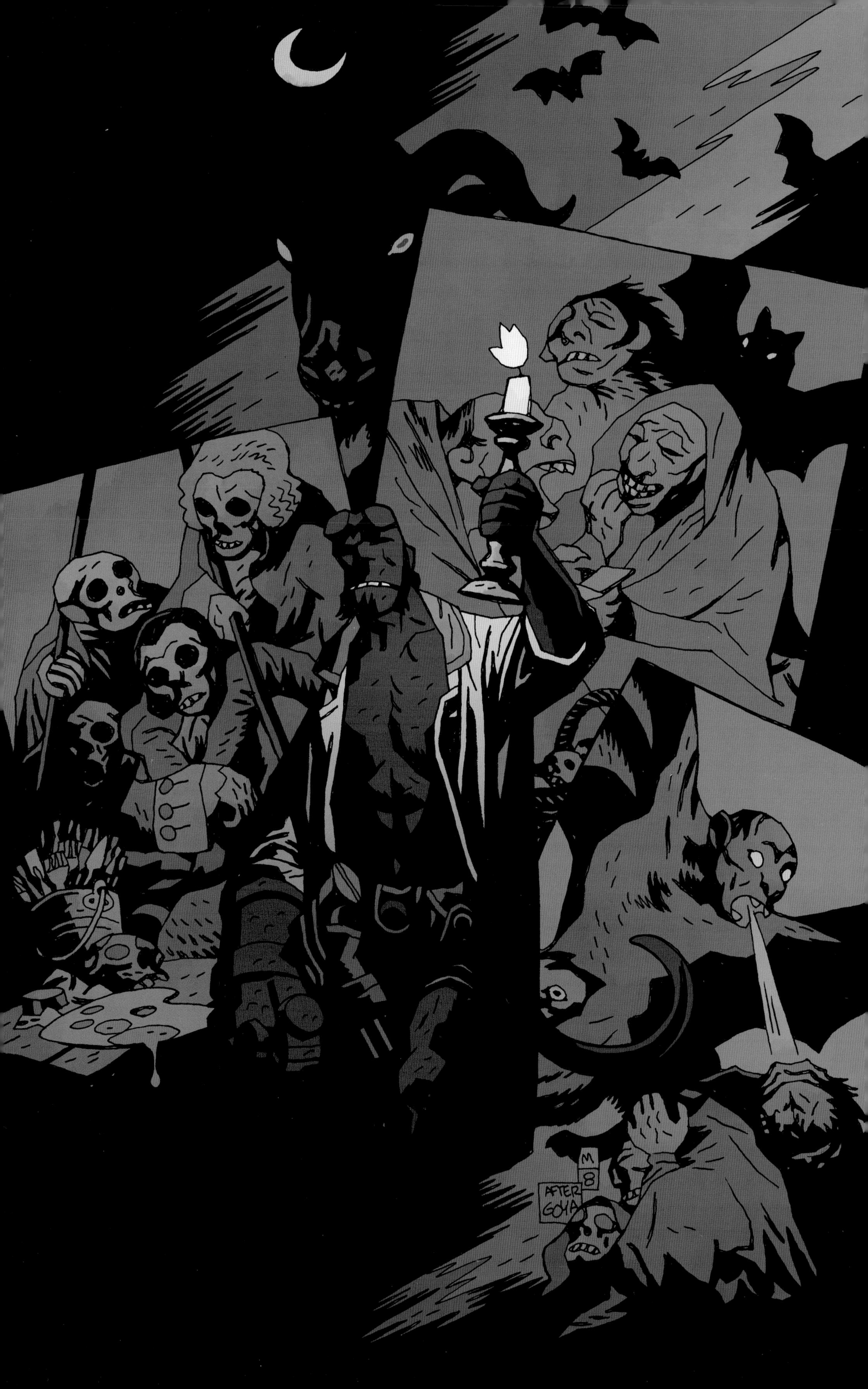
M 8
AFTER GOYA

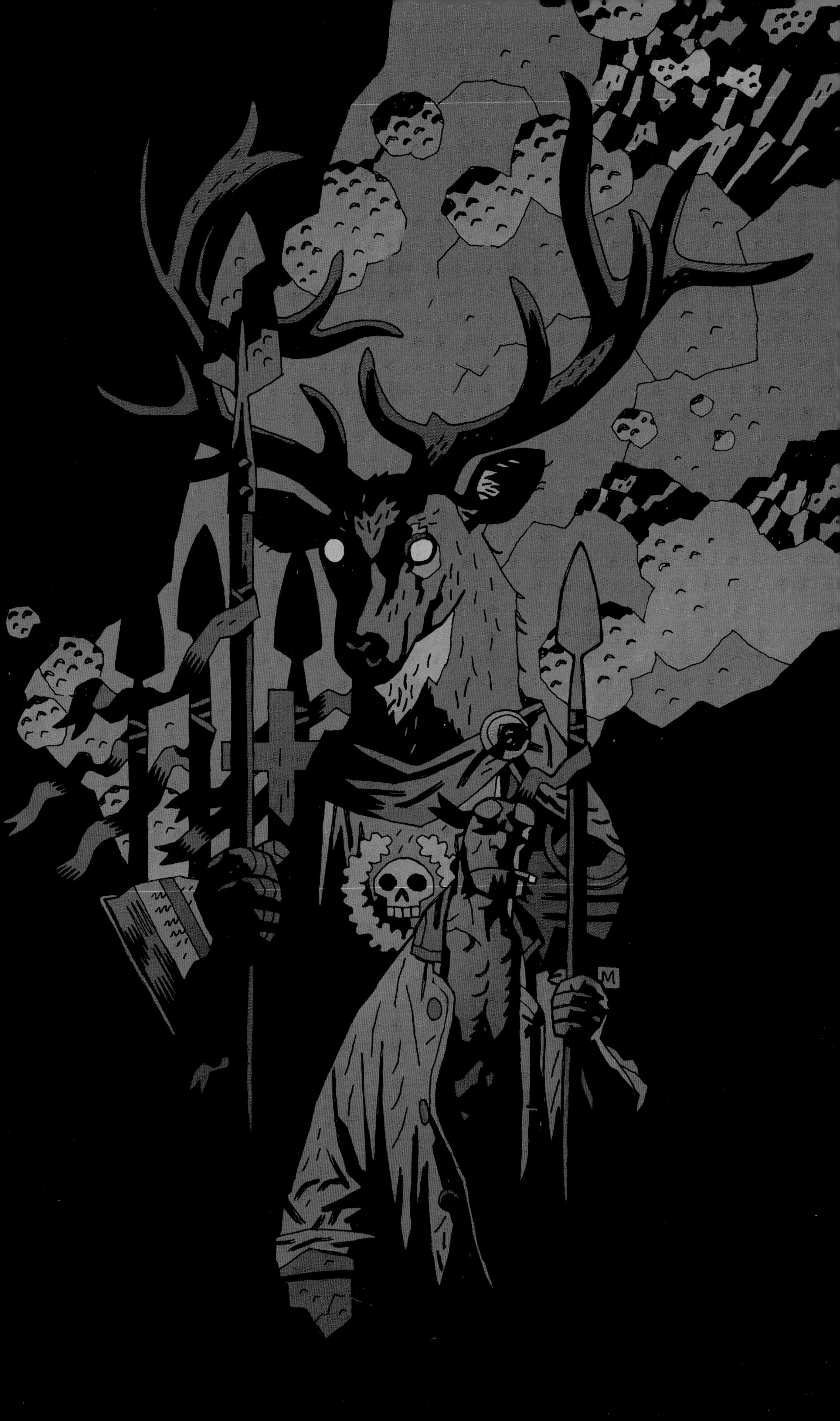

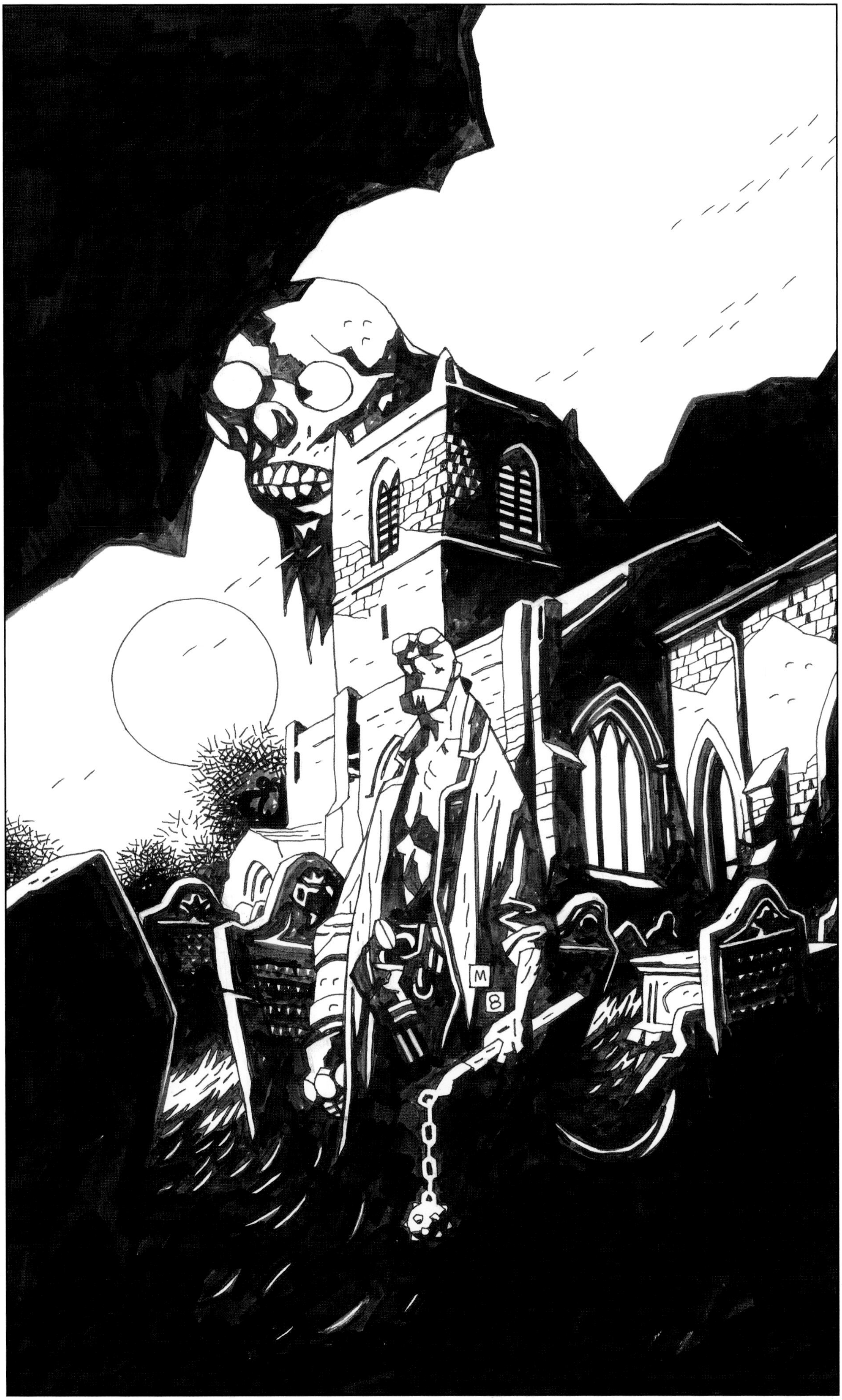

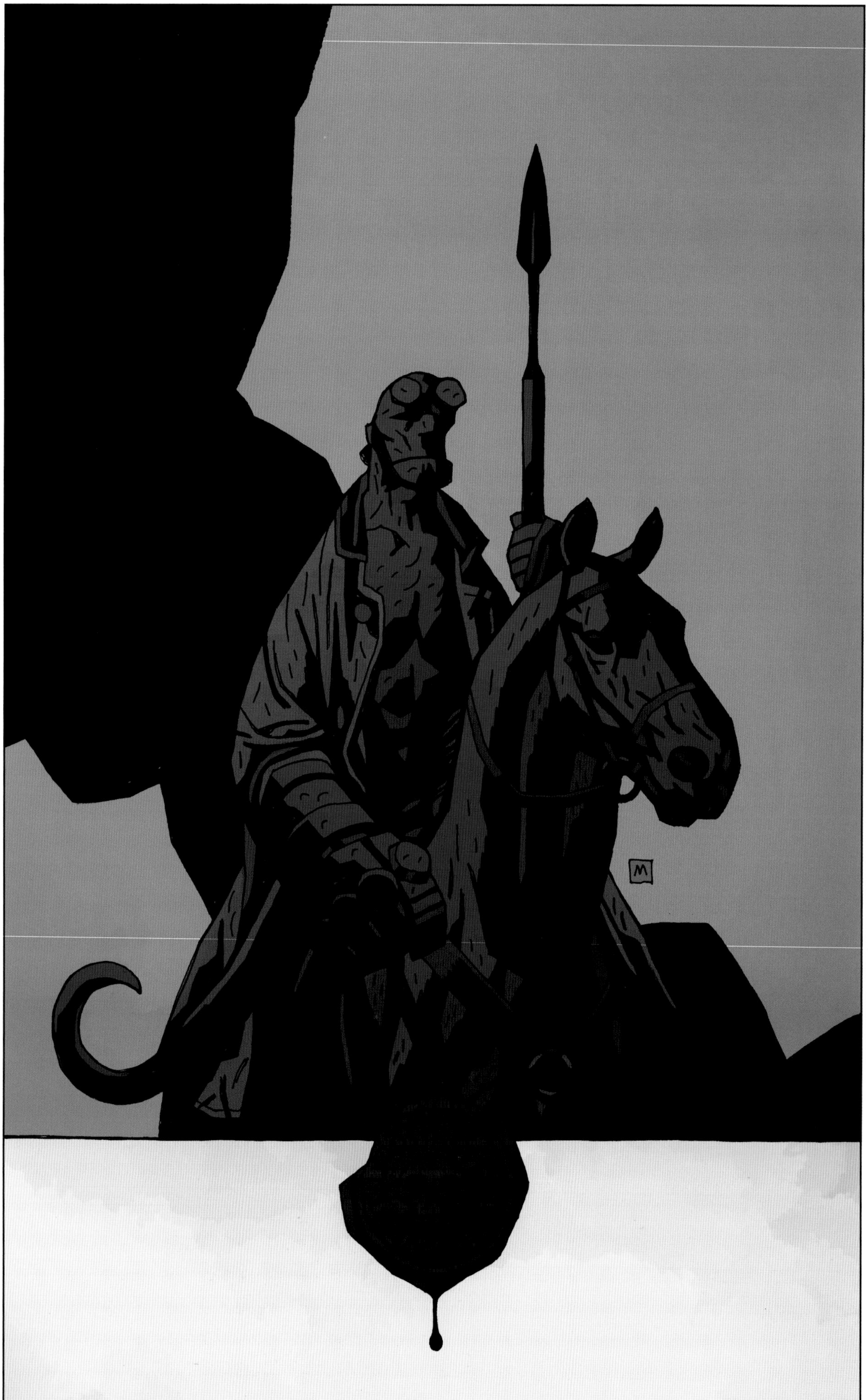

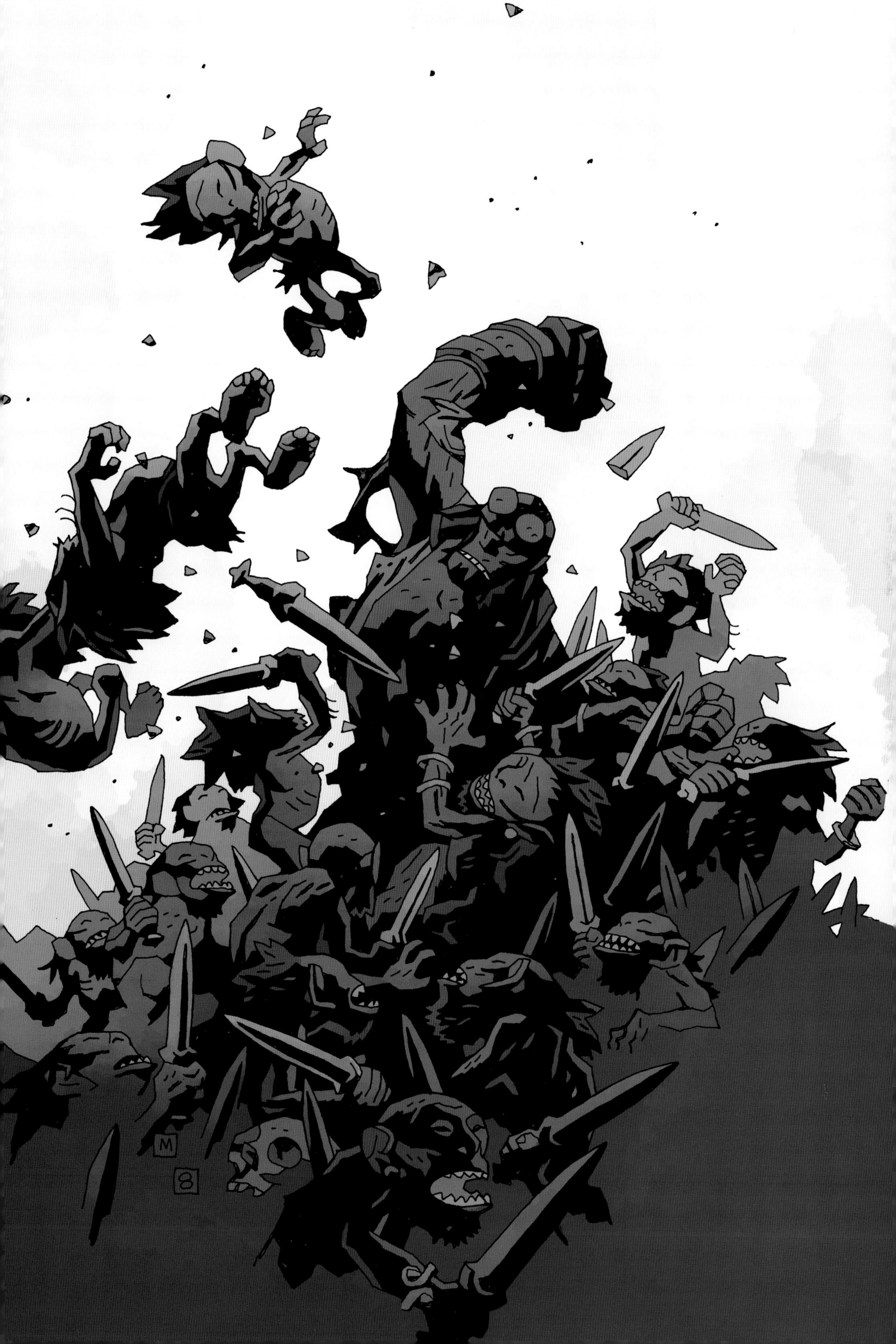

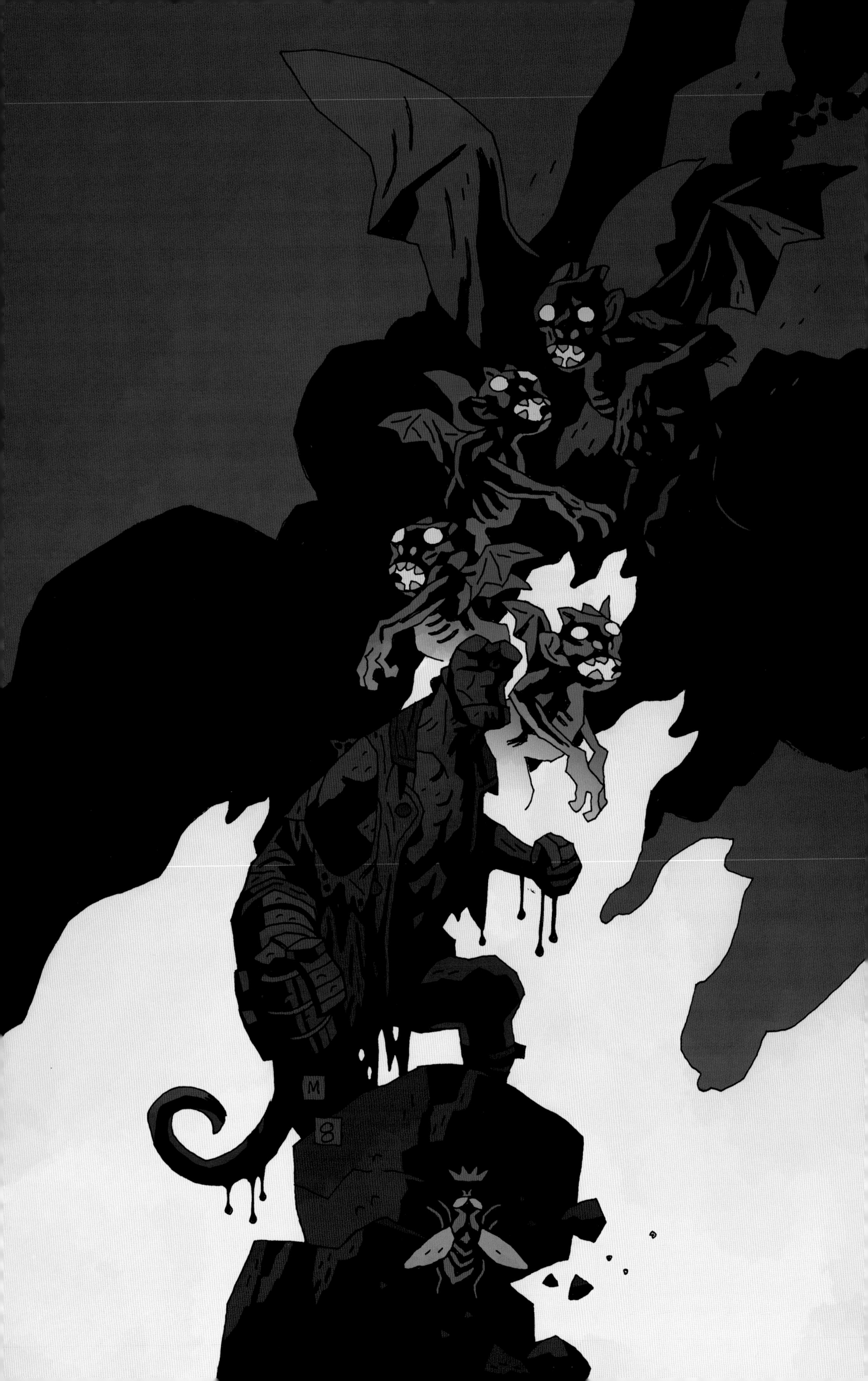

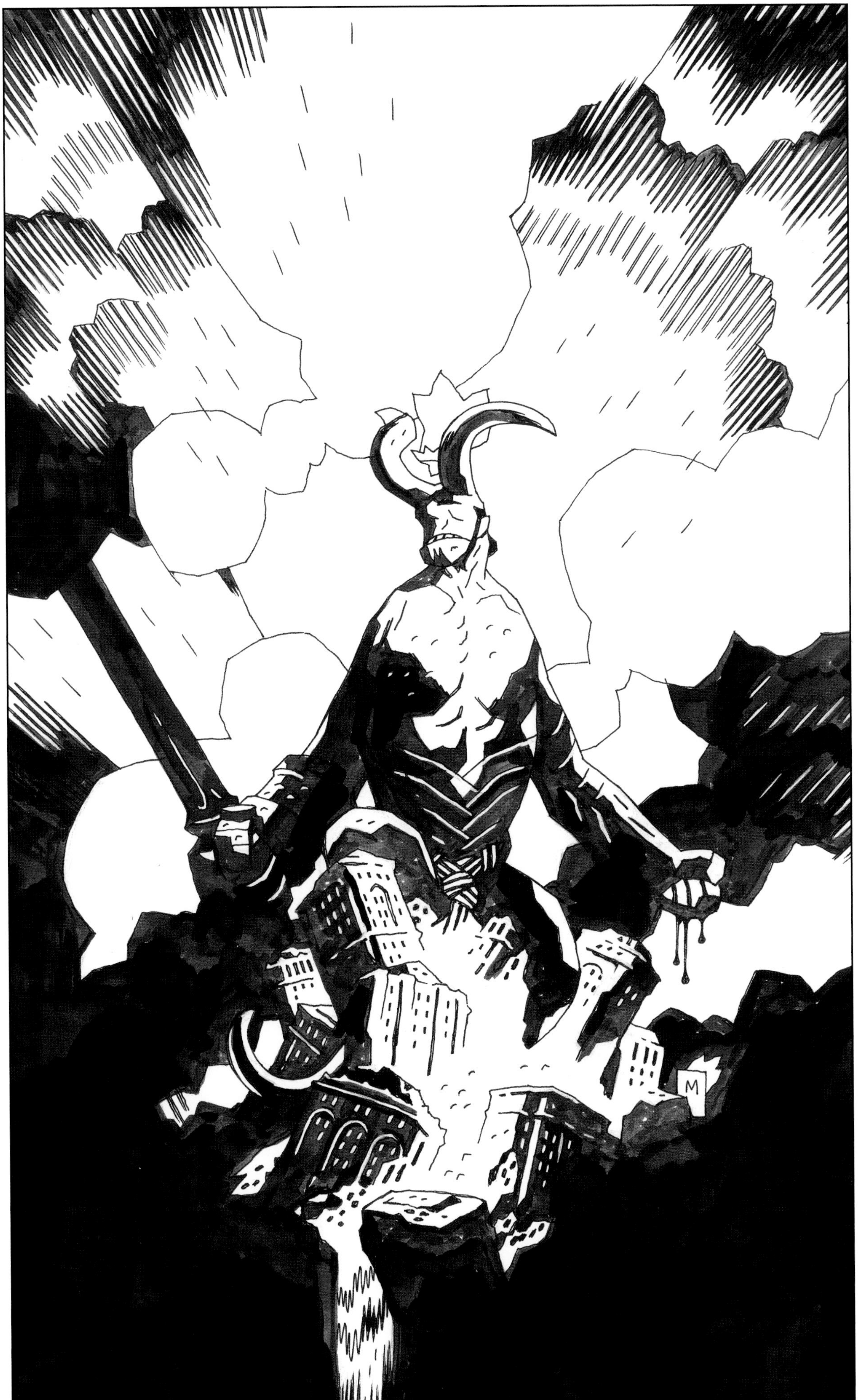

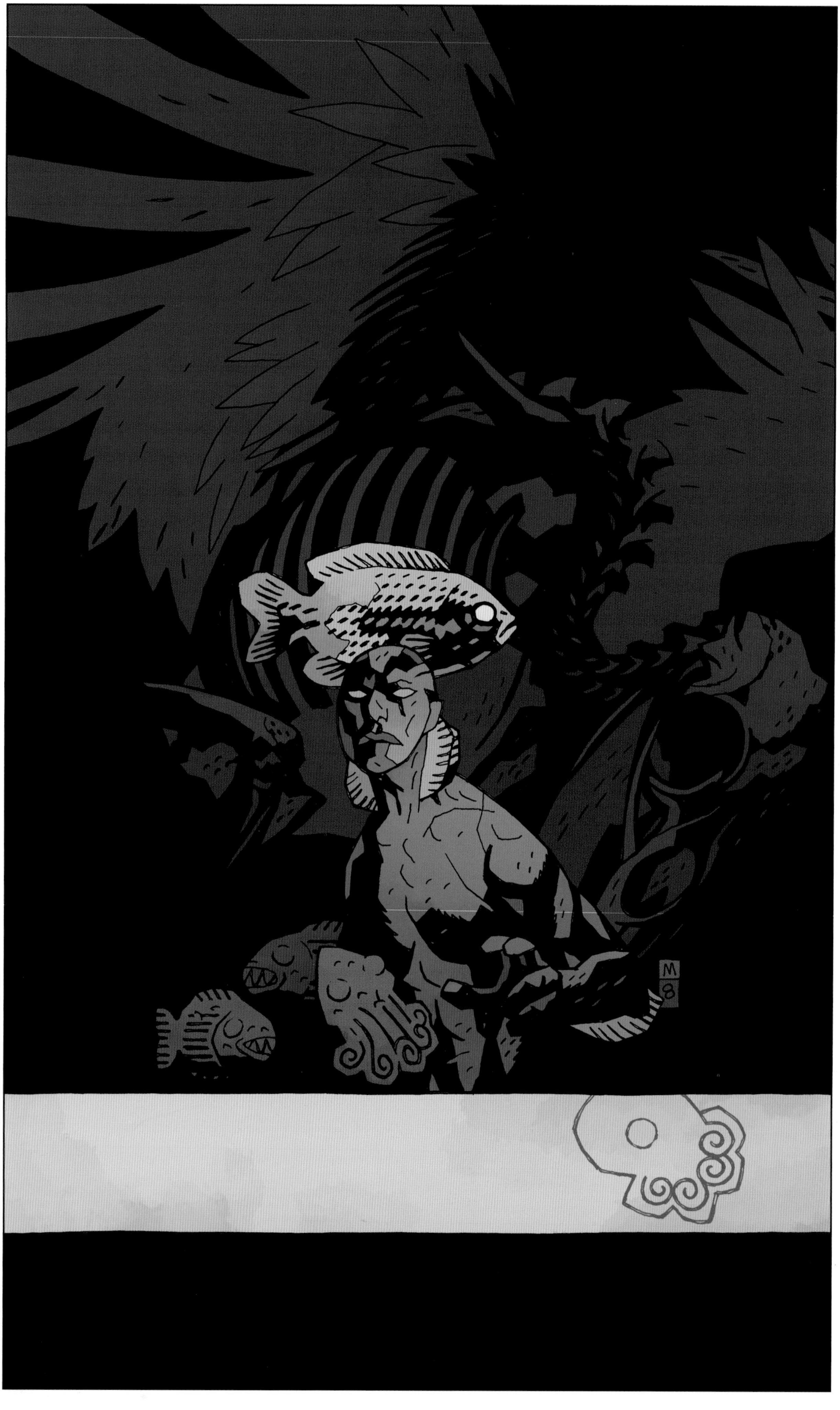

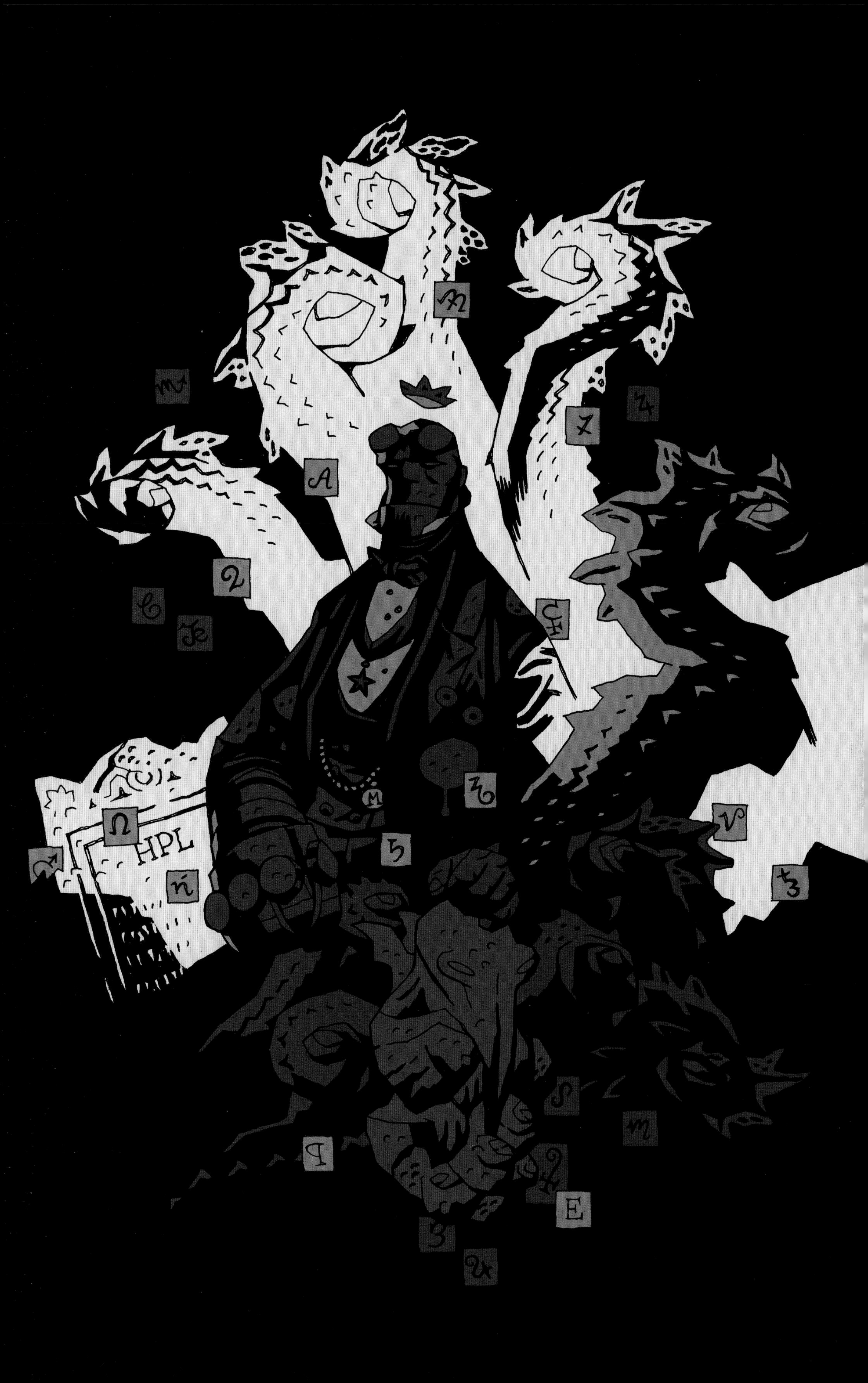
HPL

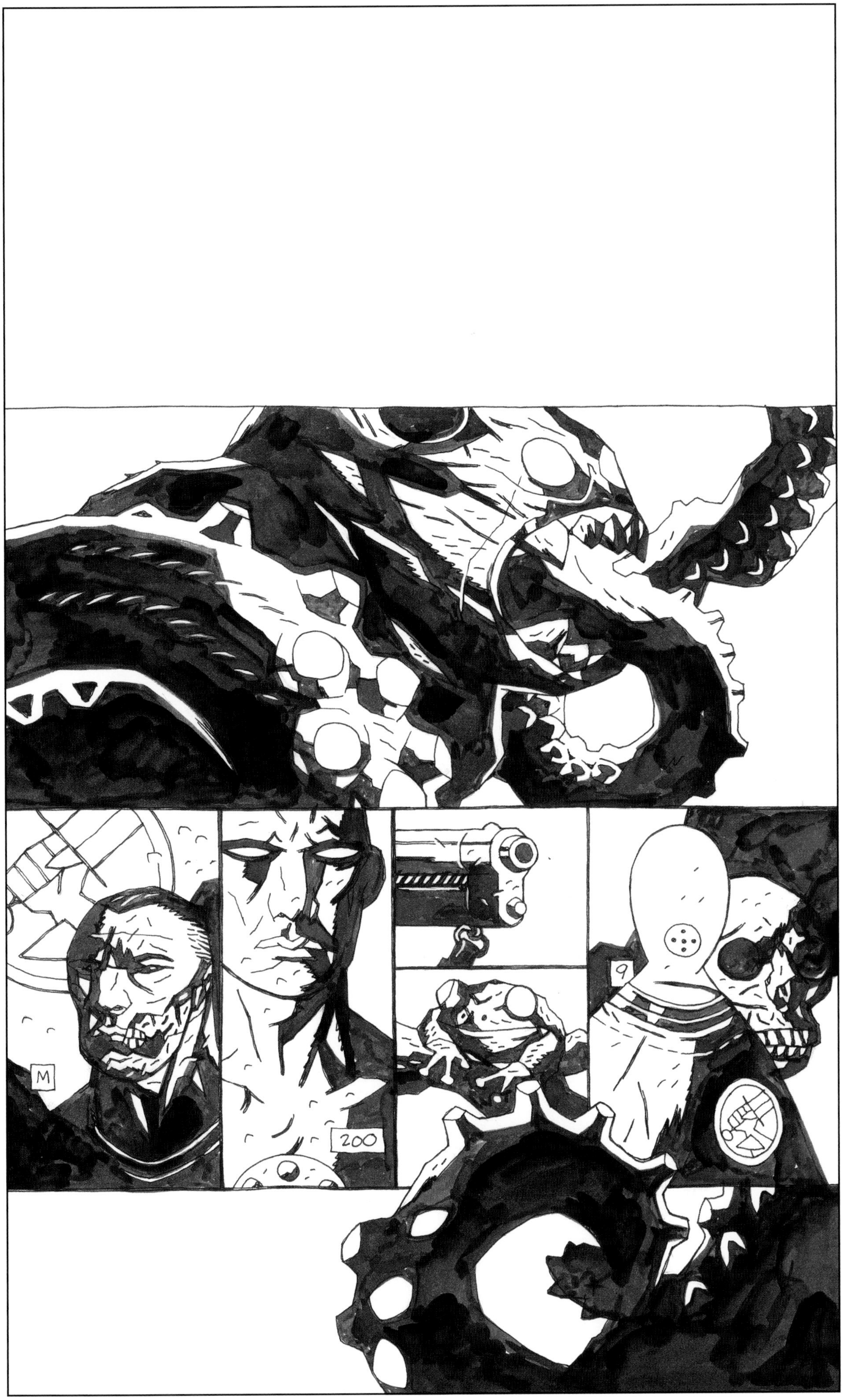
M
200
9

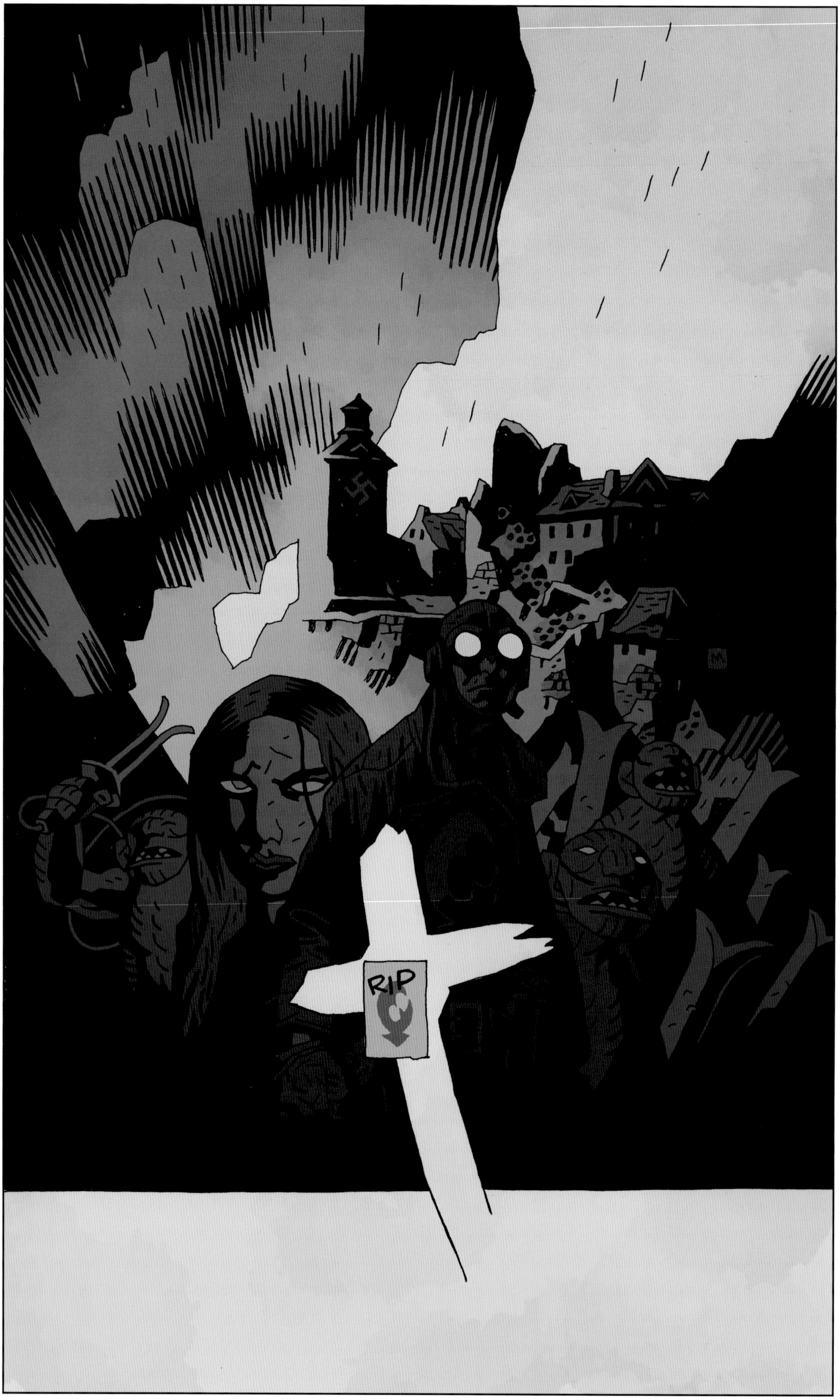
RIP

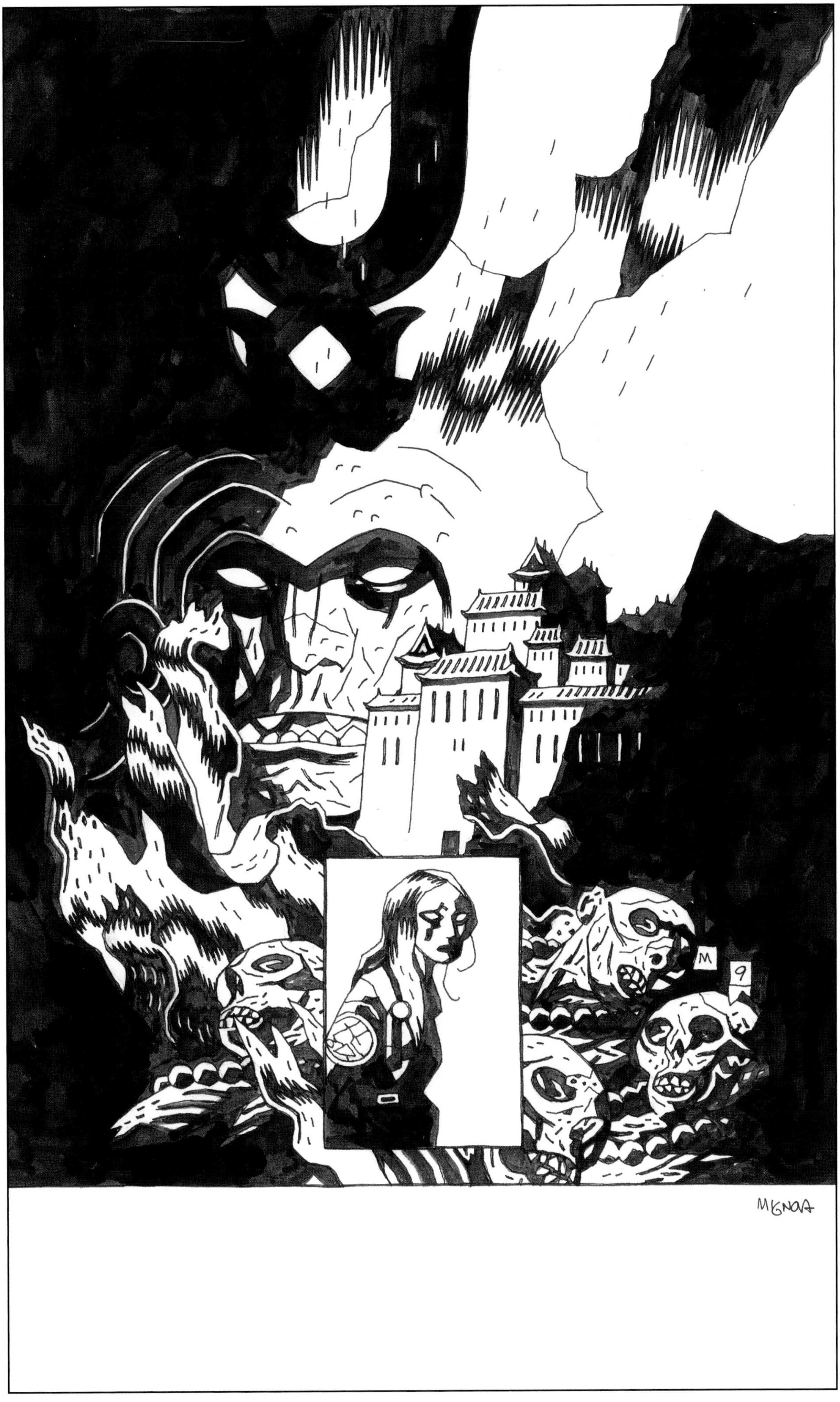
M
9
MIGNOLA

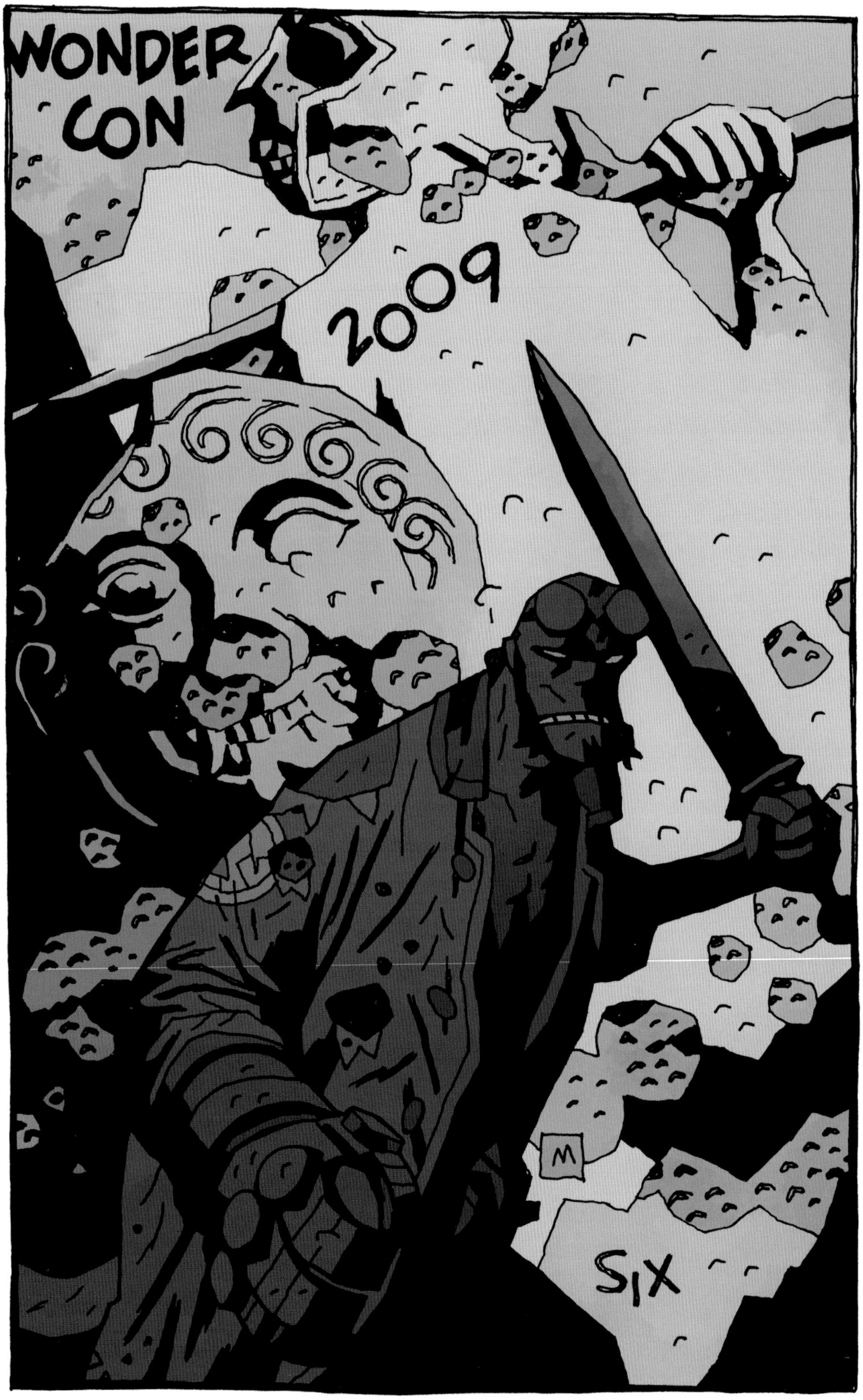
WONDER CON
2009
SIX

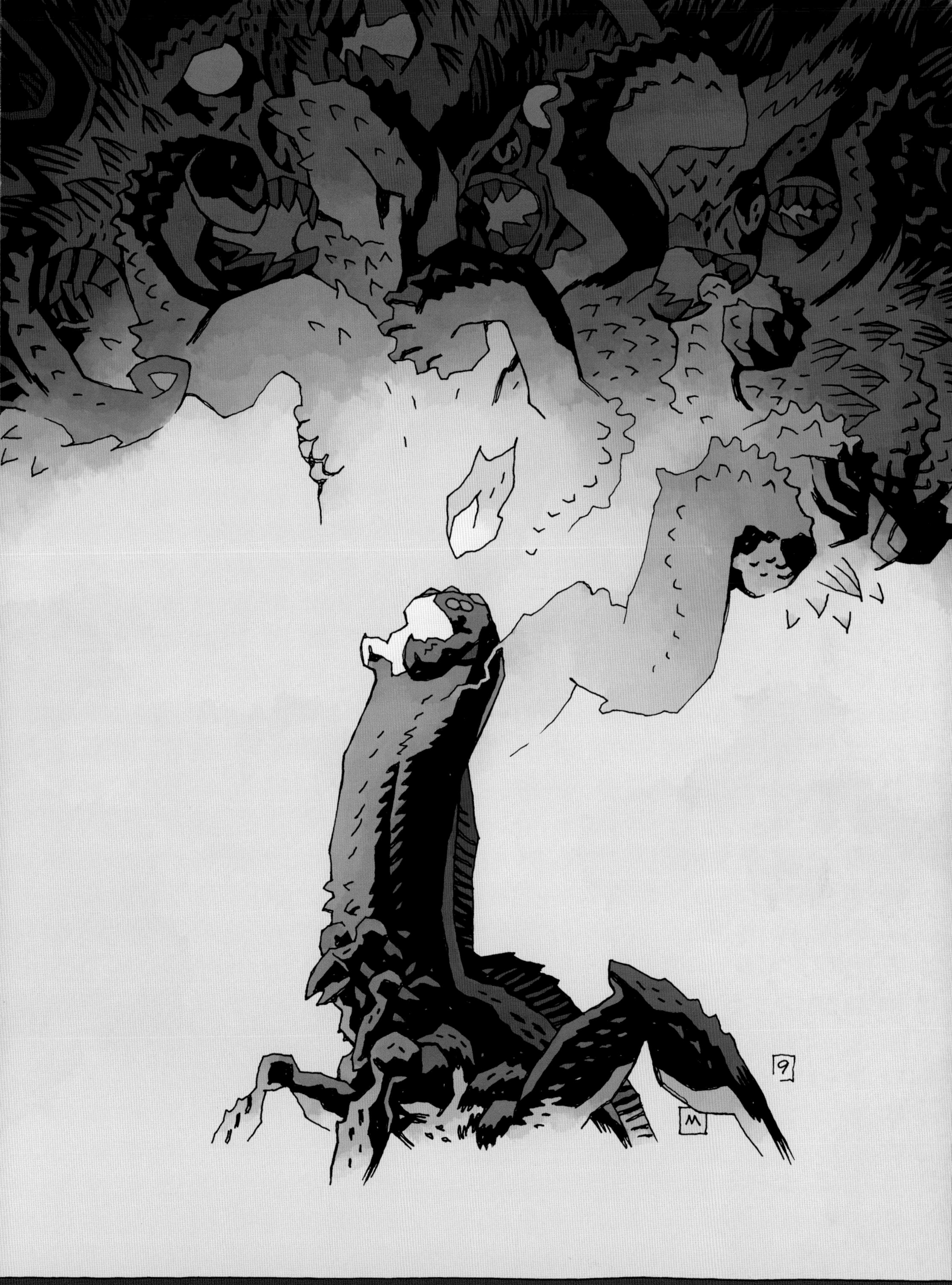

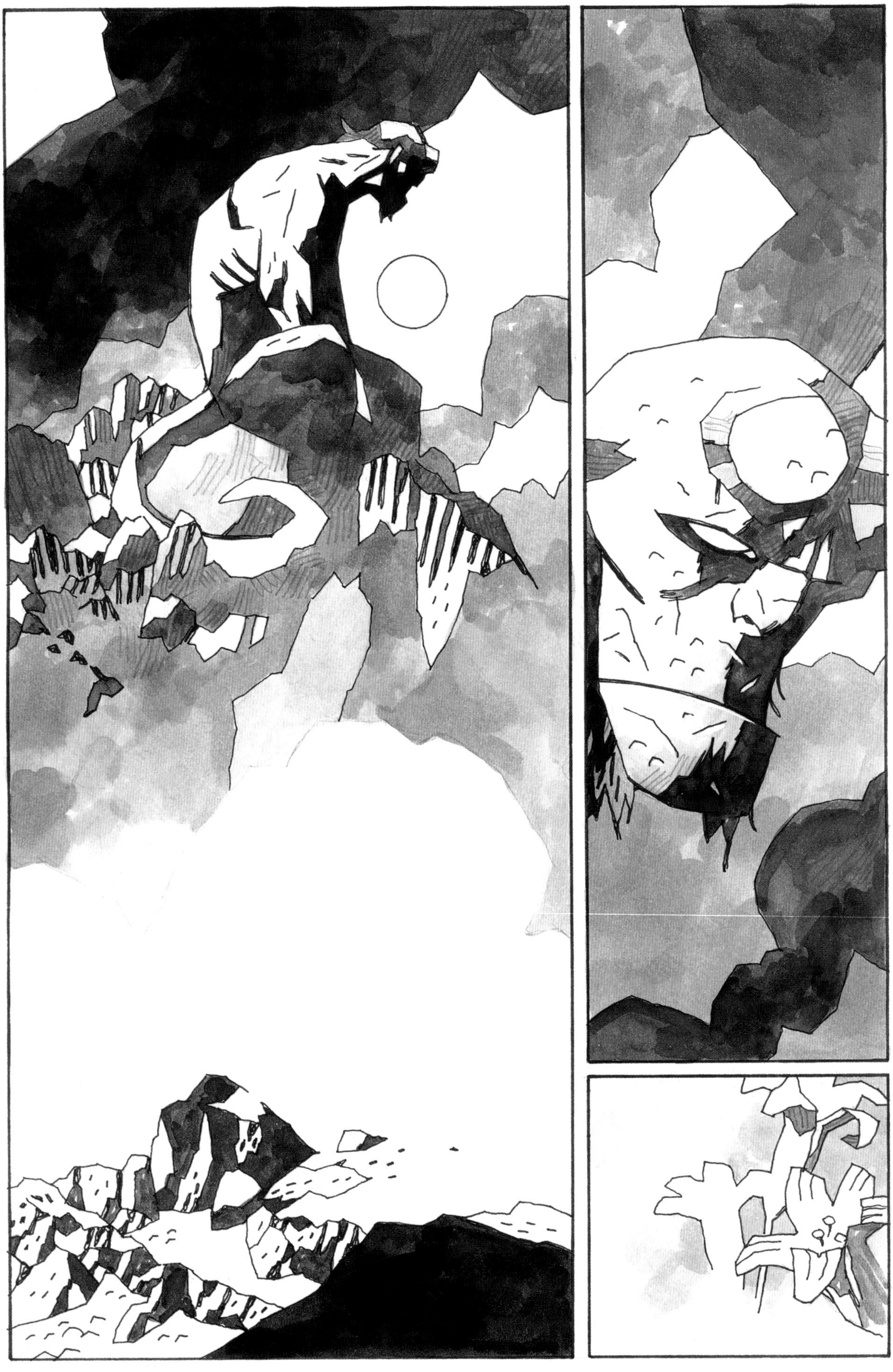

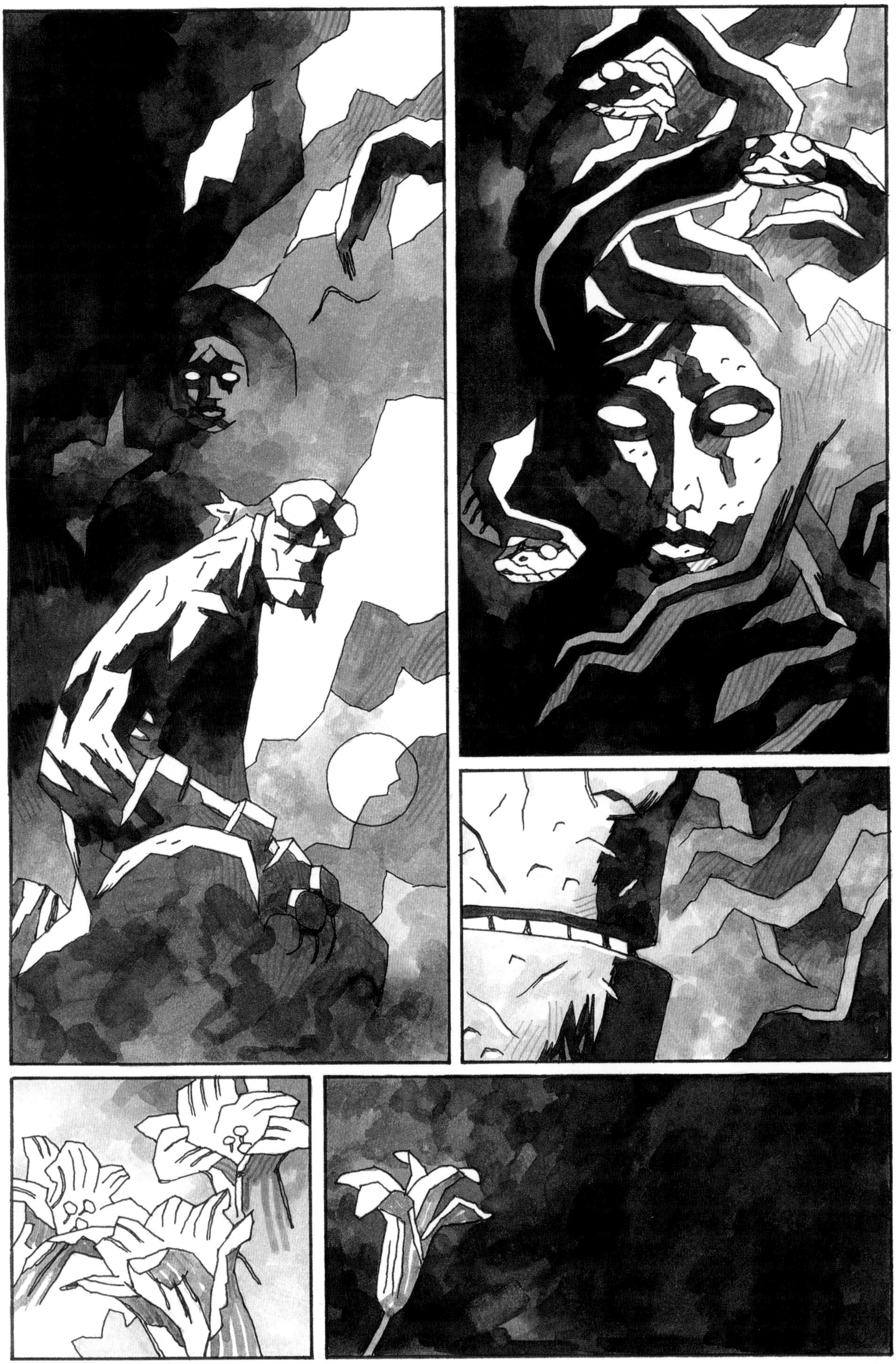

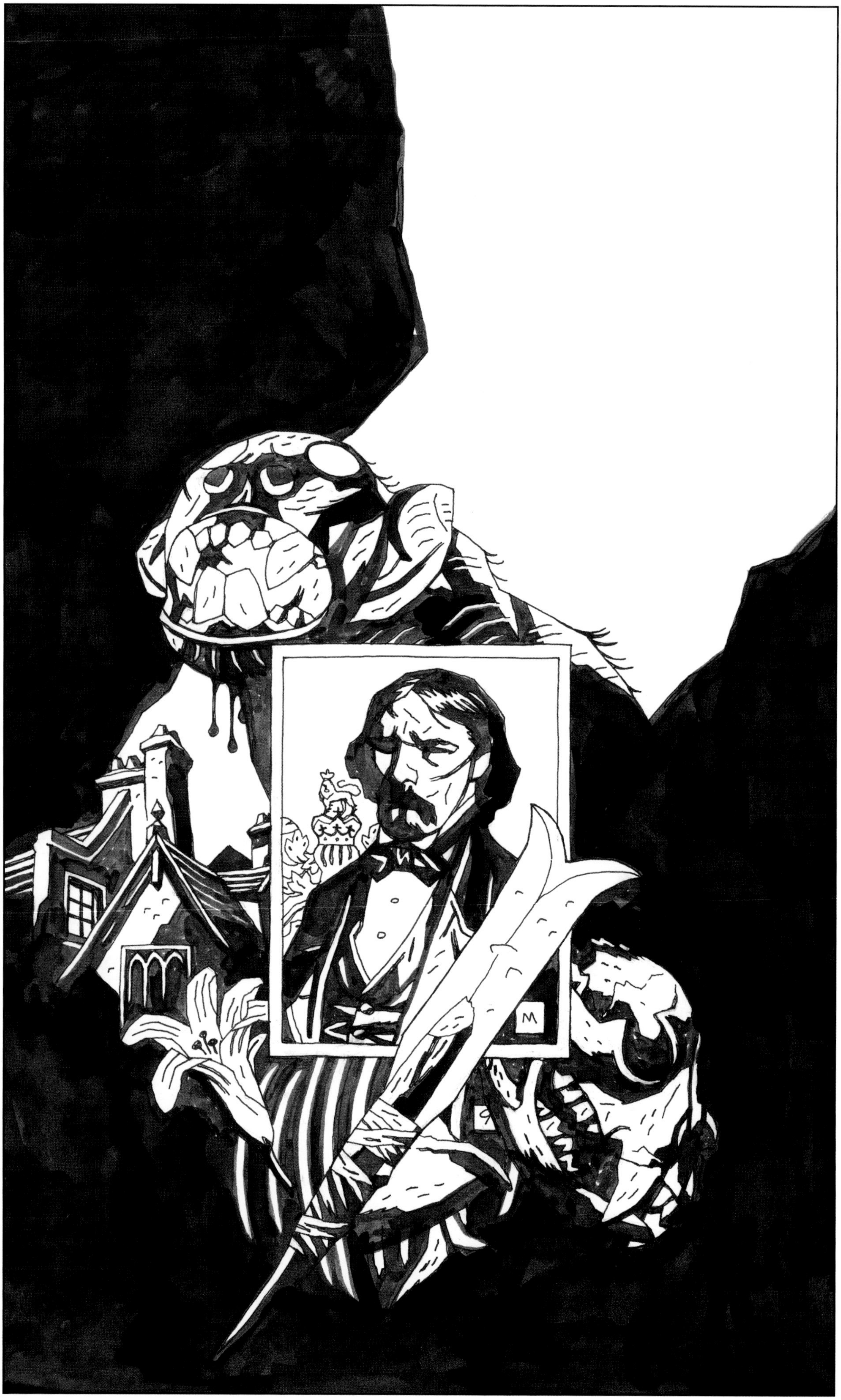

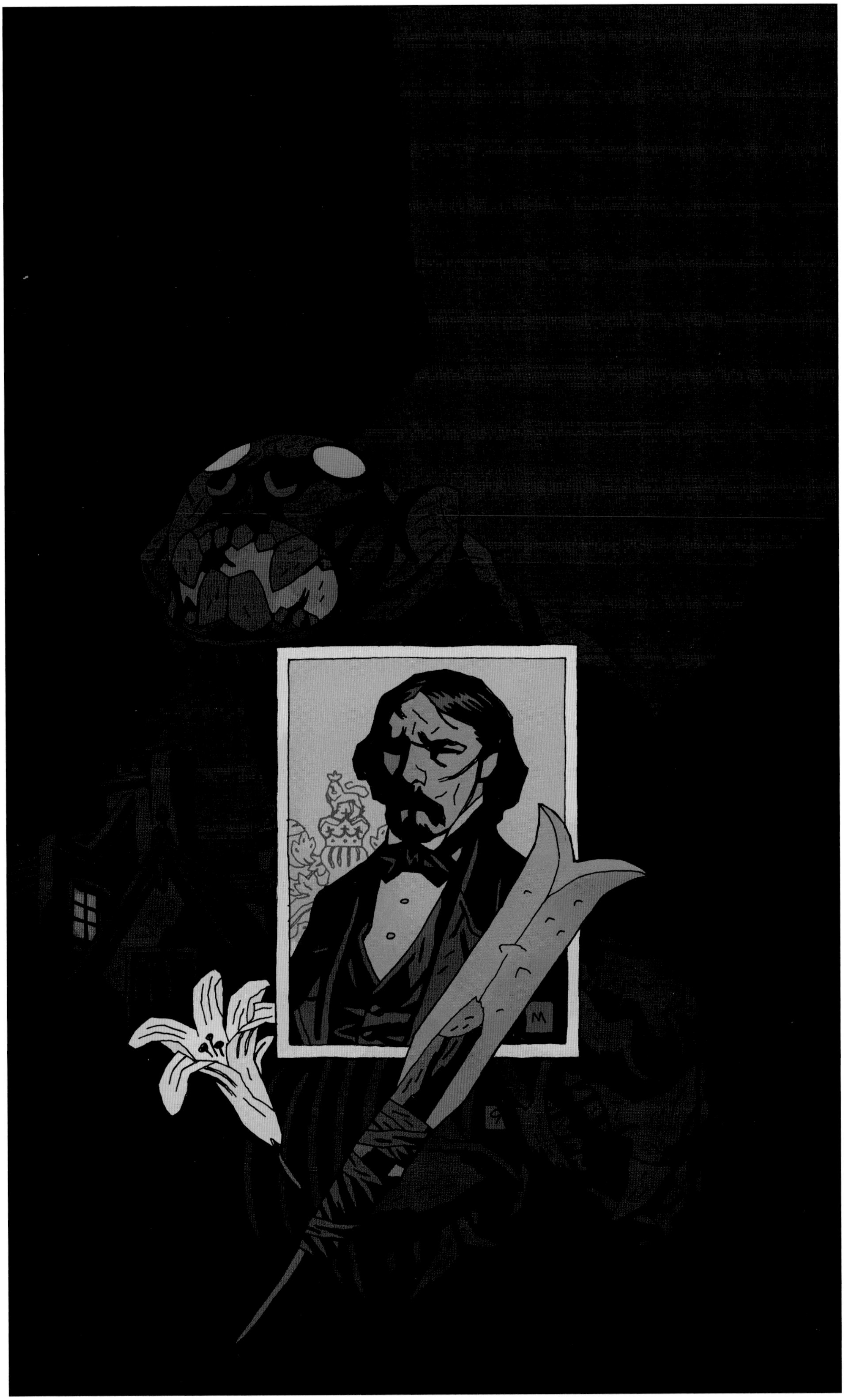

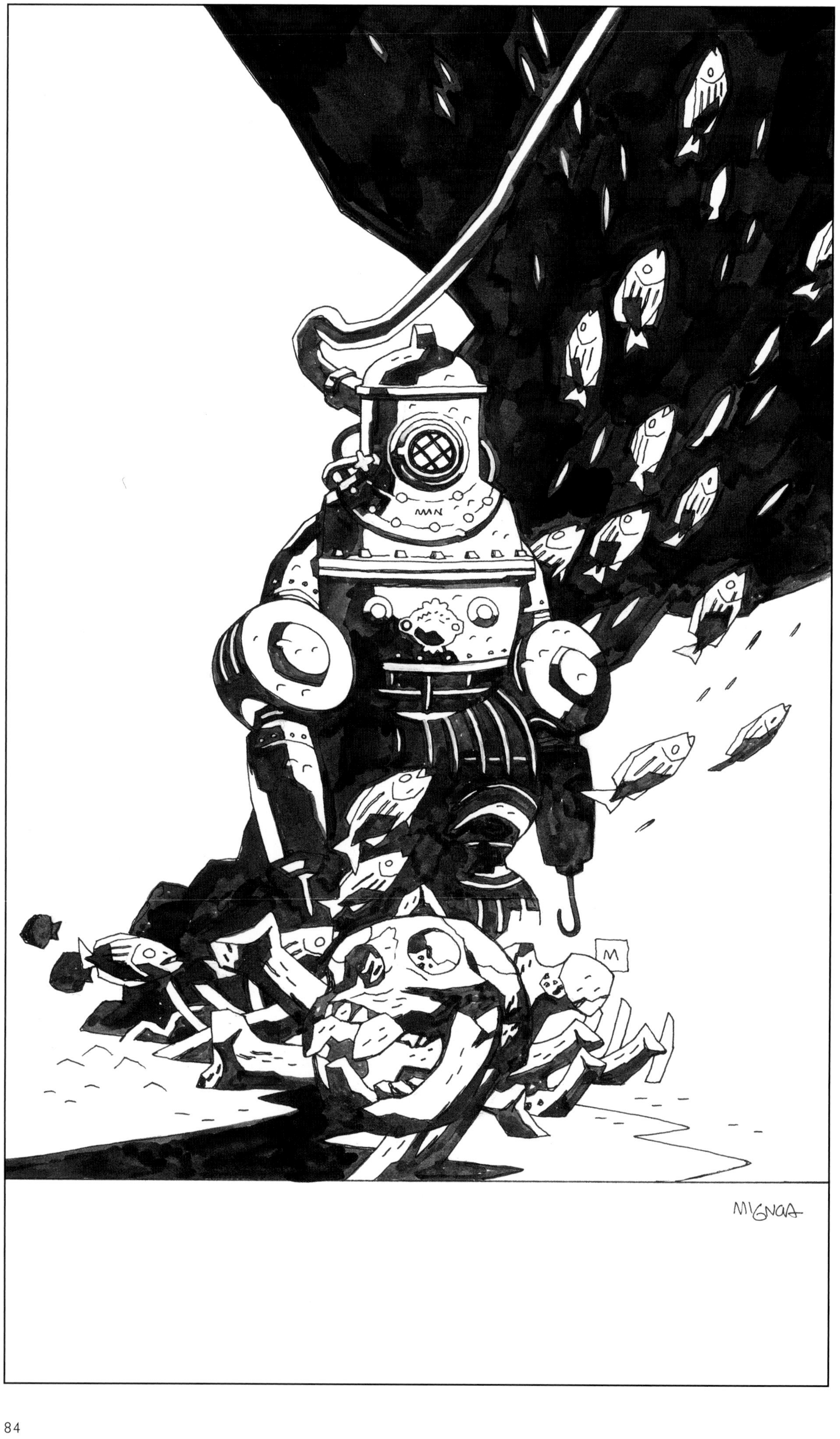

MIGNOLA

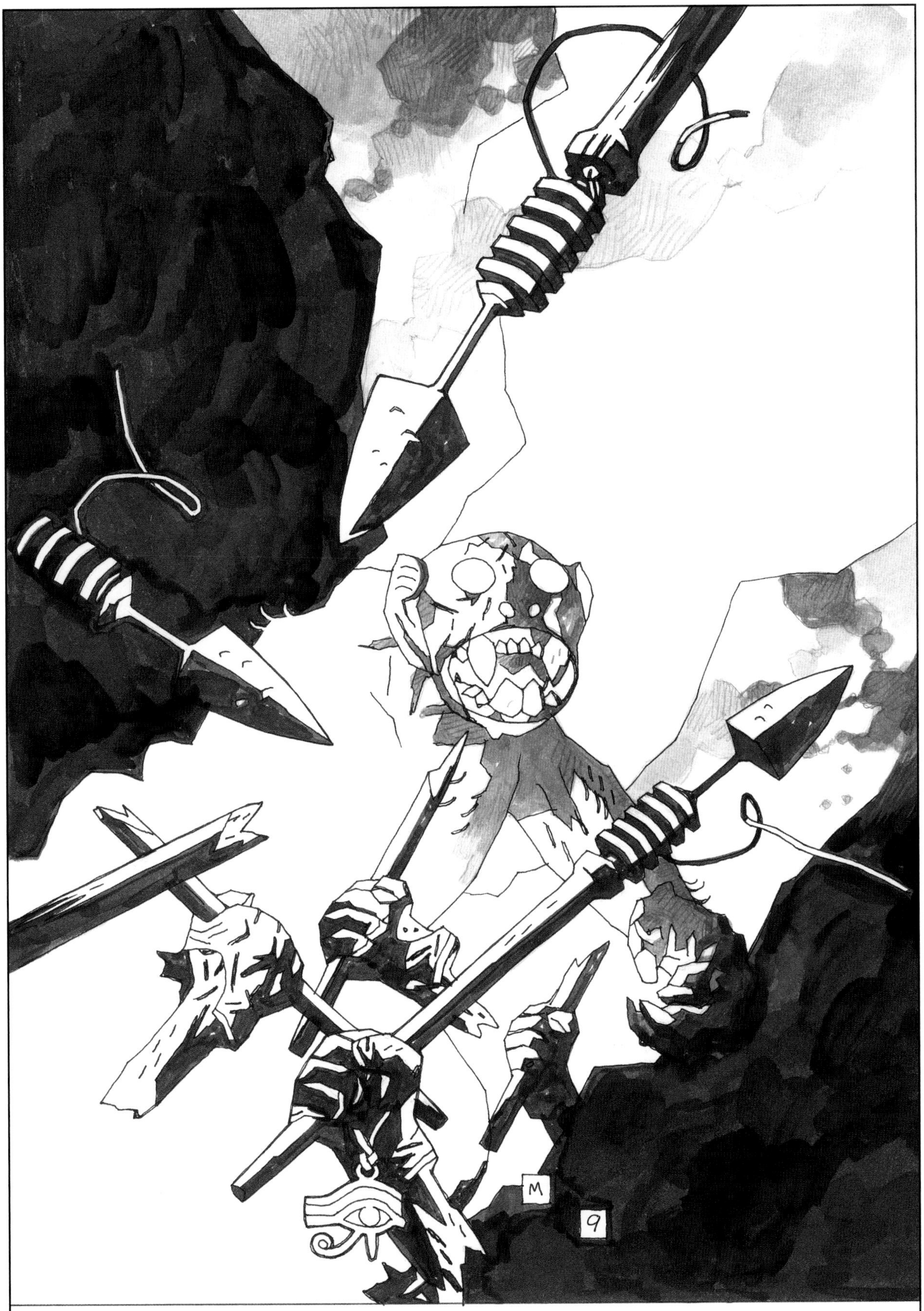
MIGNOLA

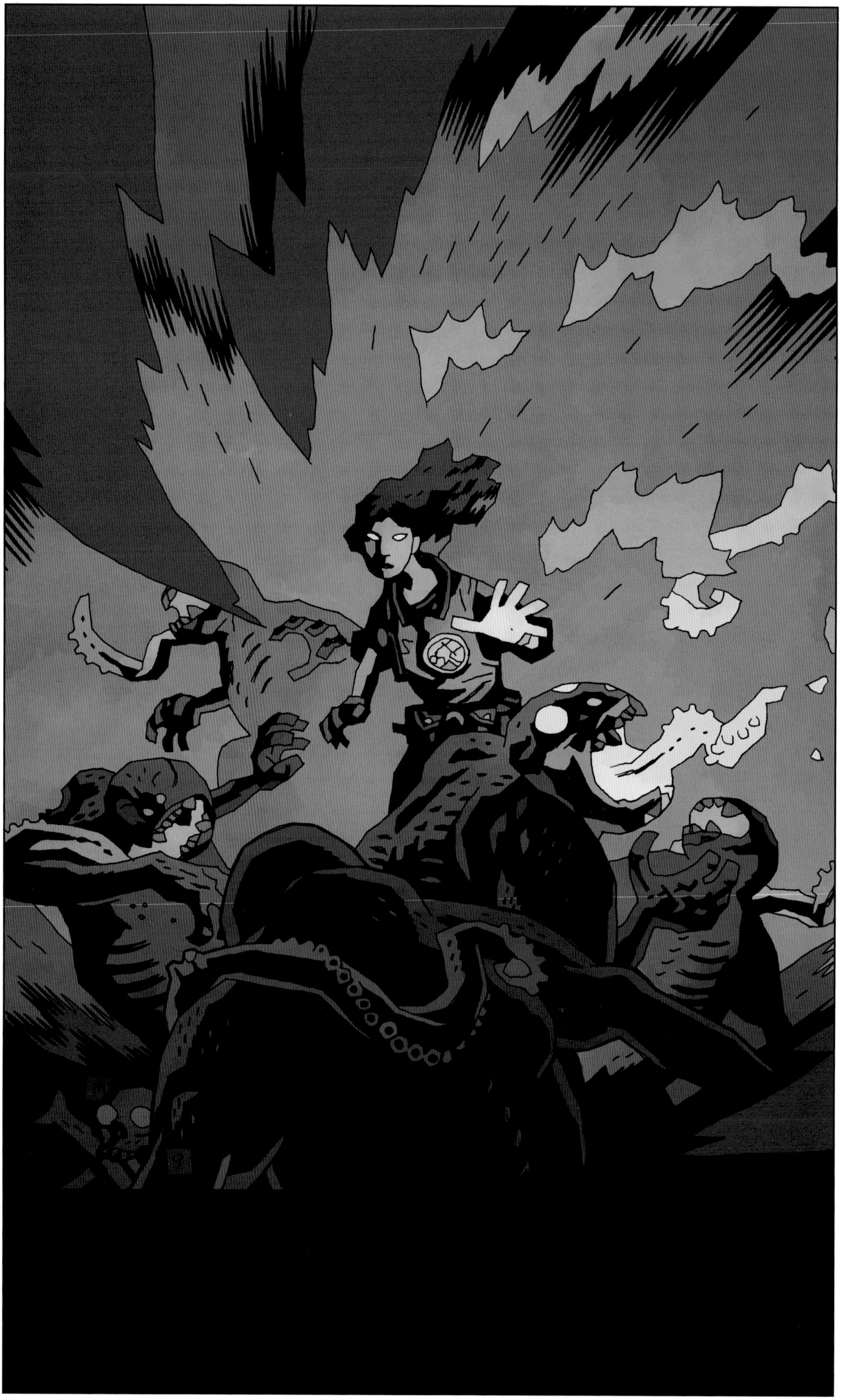

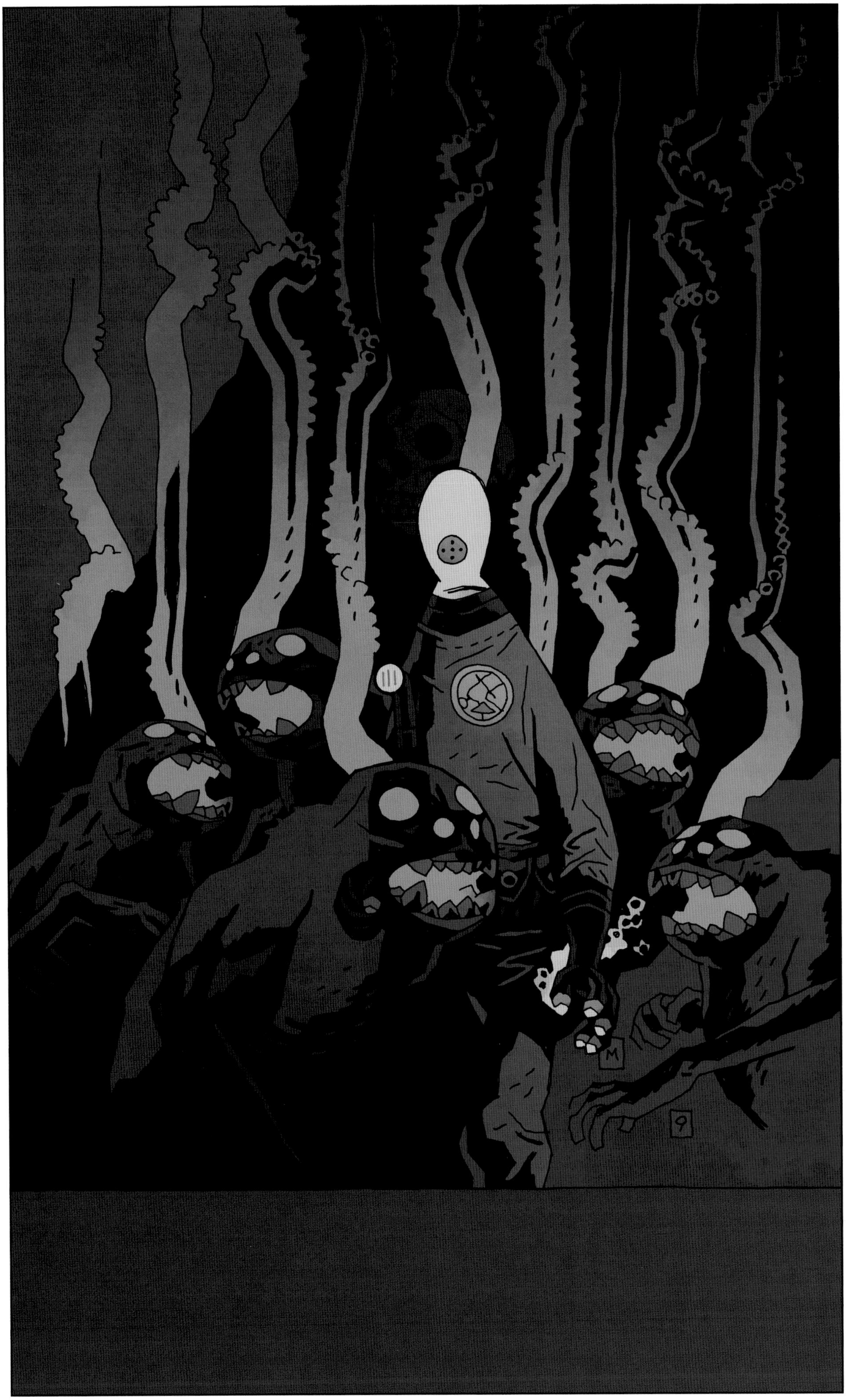

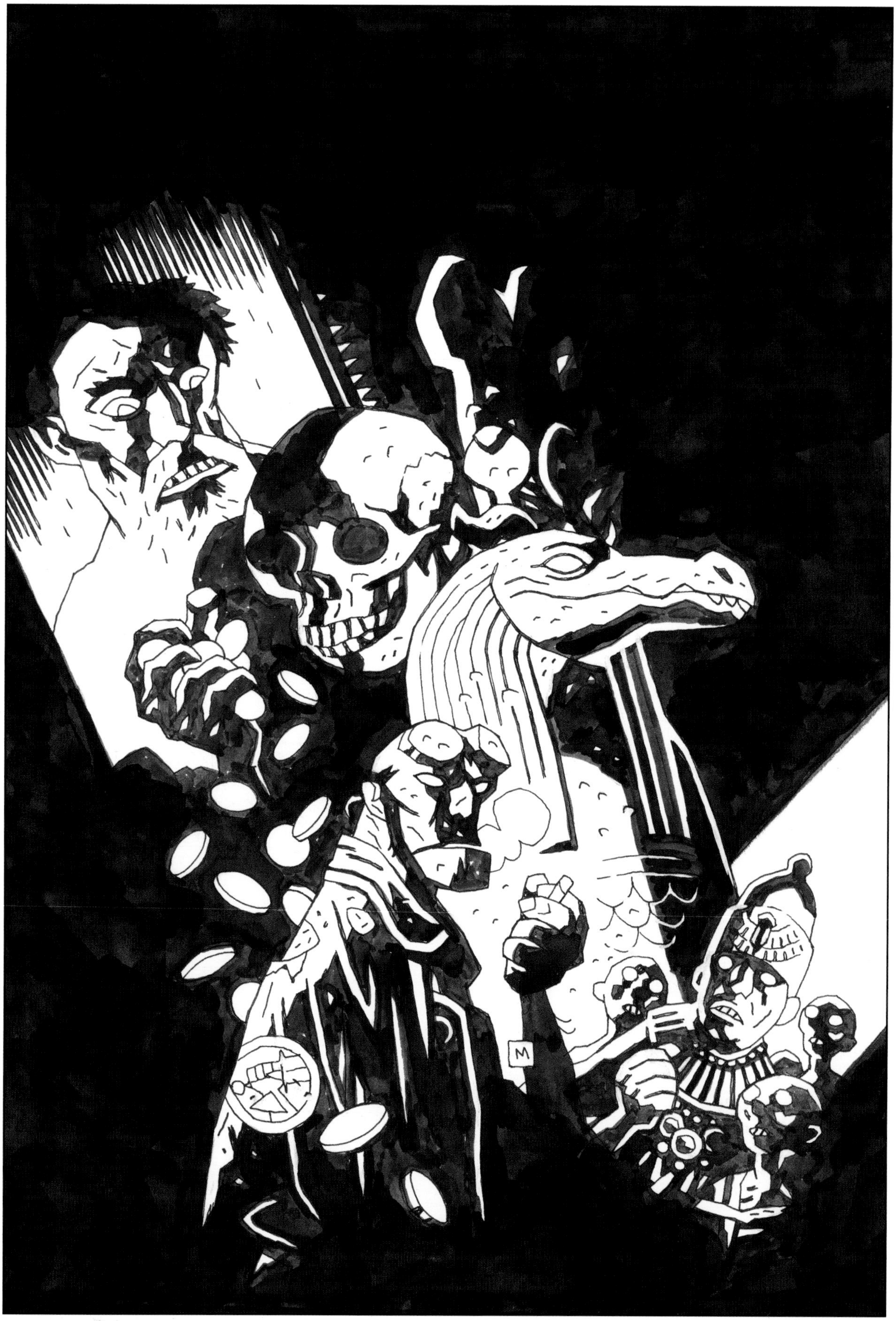
M

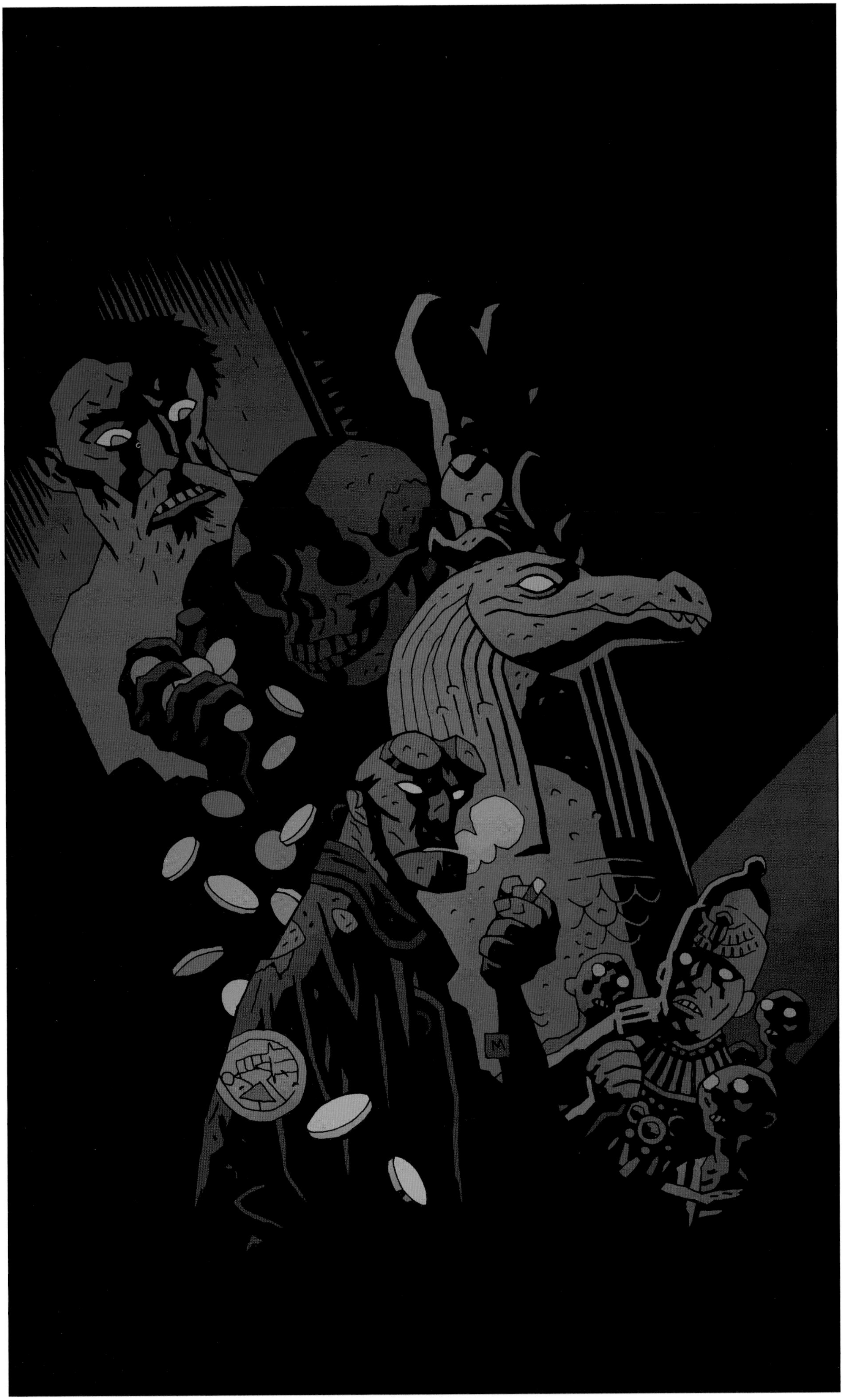

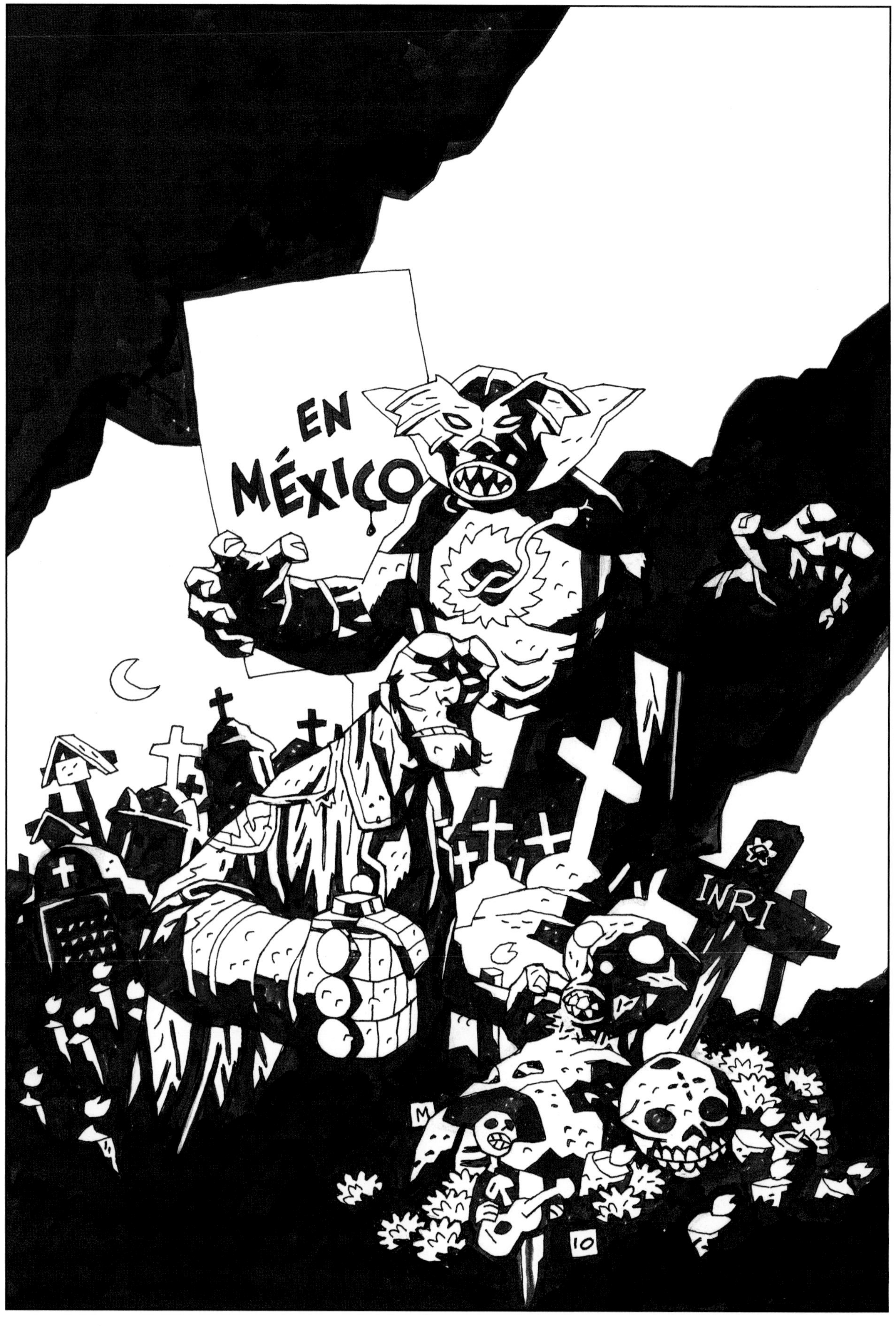
EN MÉXICO
INRI
M
10

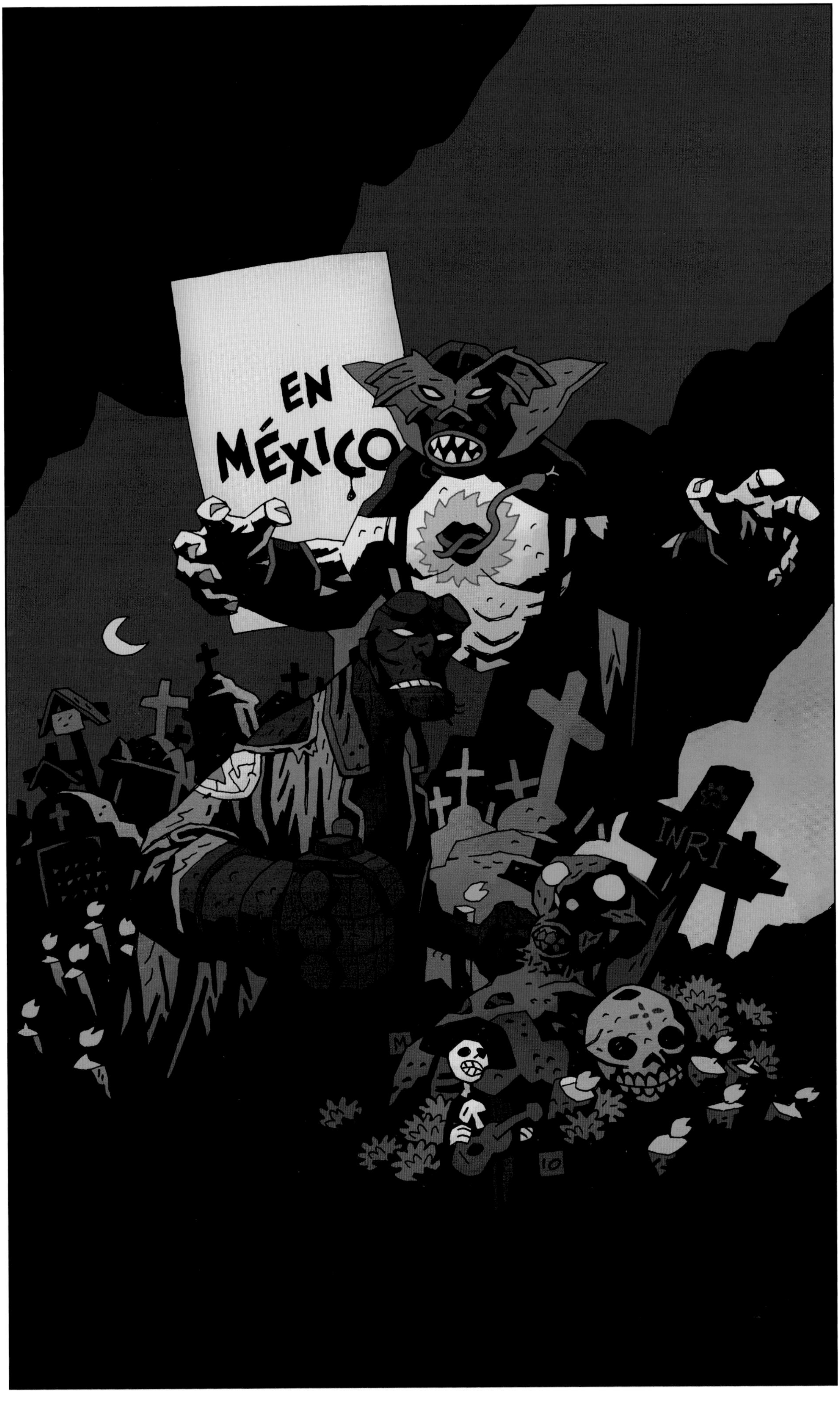
EN MÉXICO
INRI

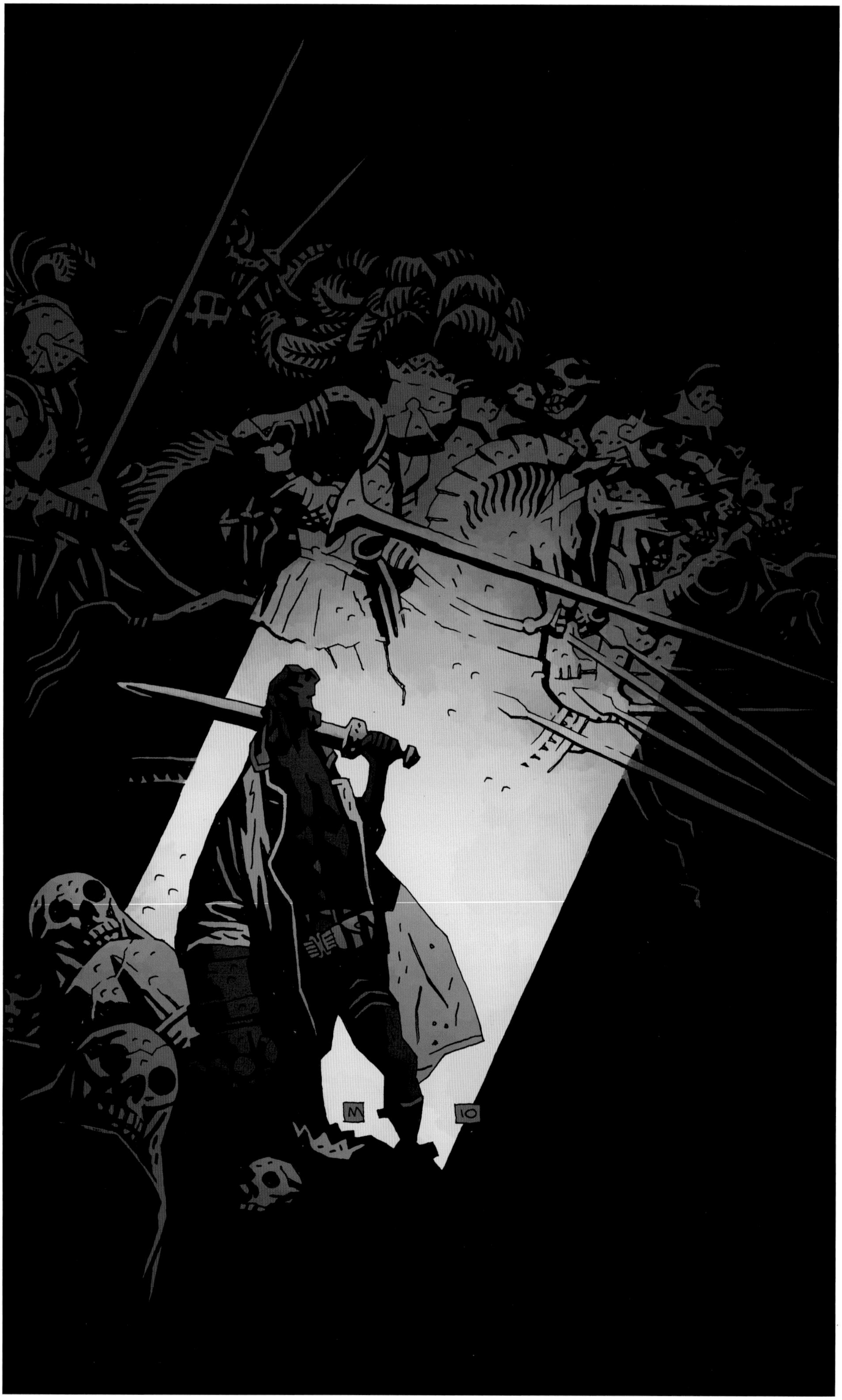

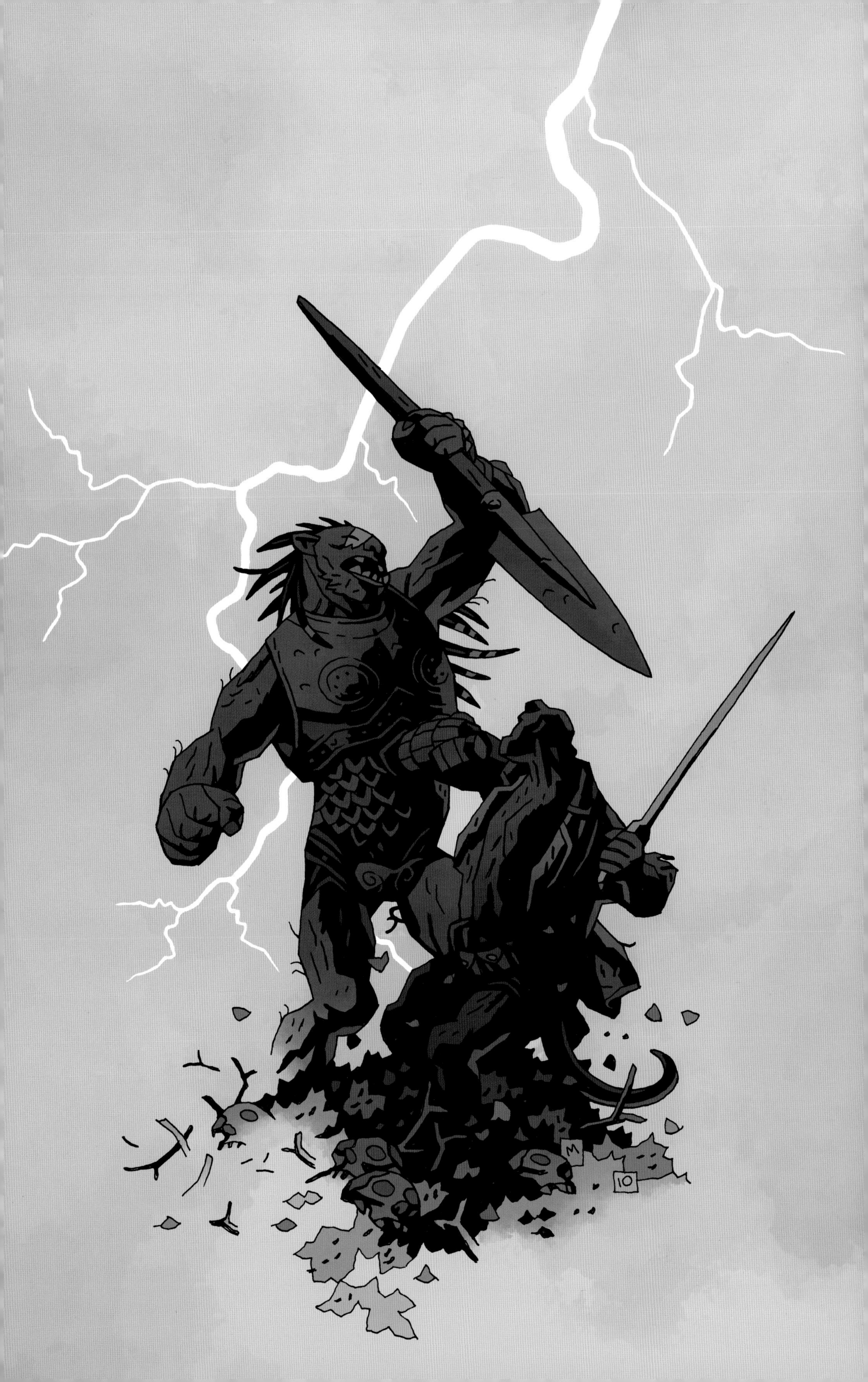

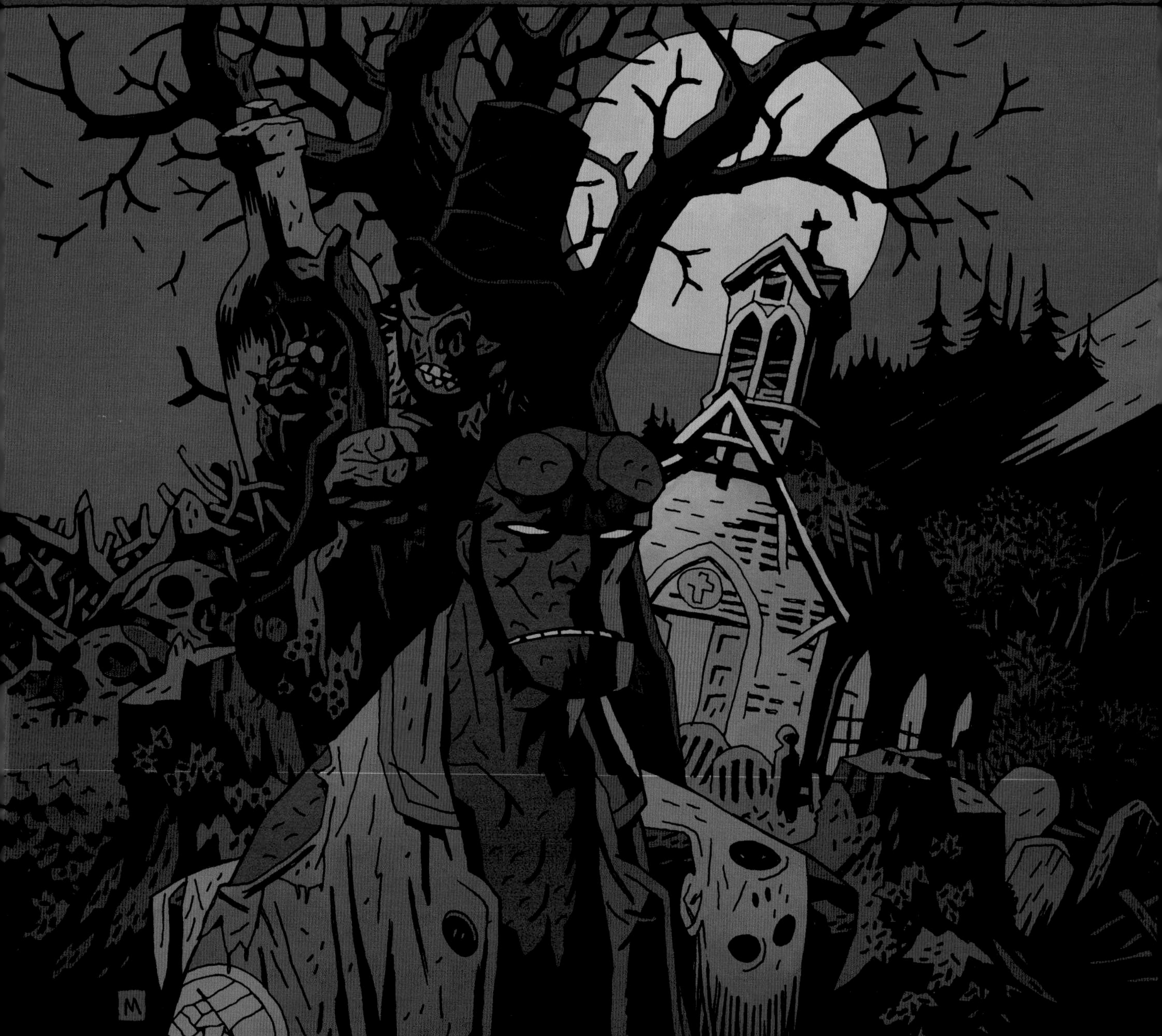

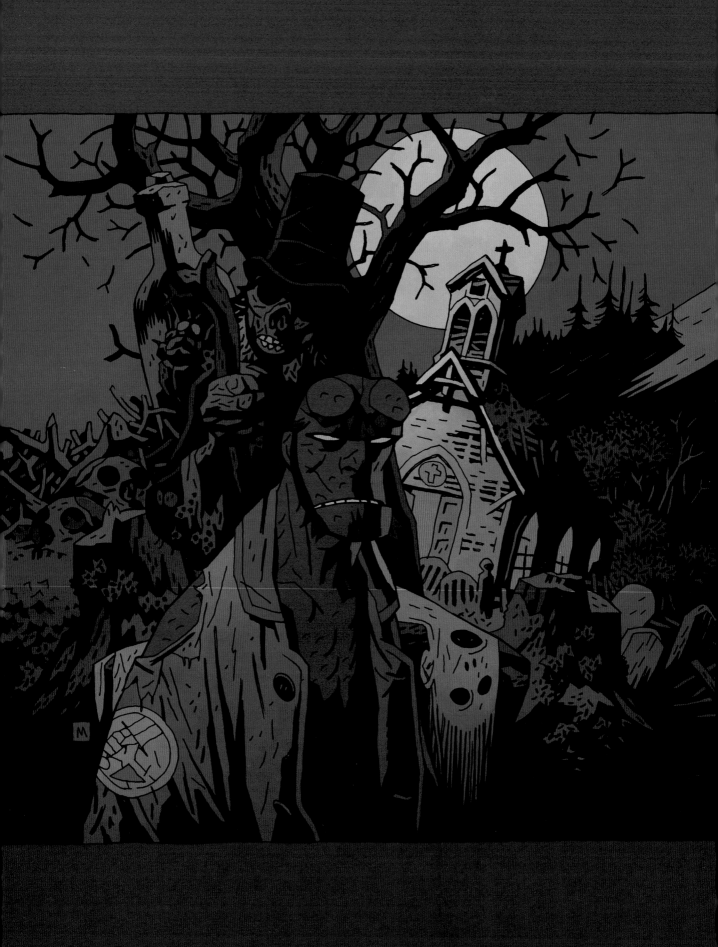

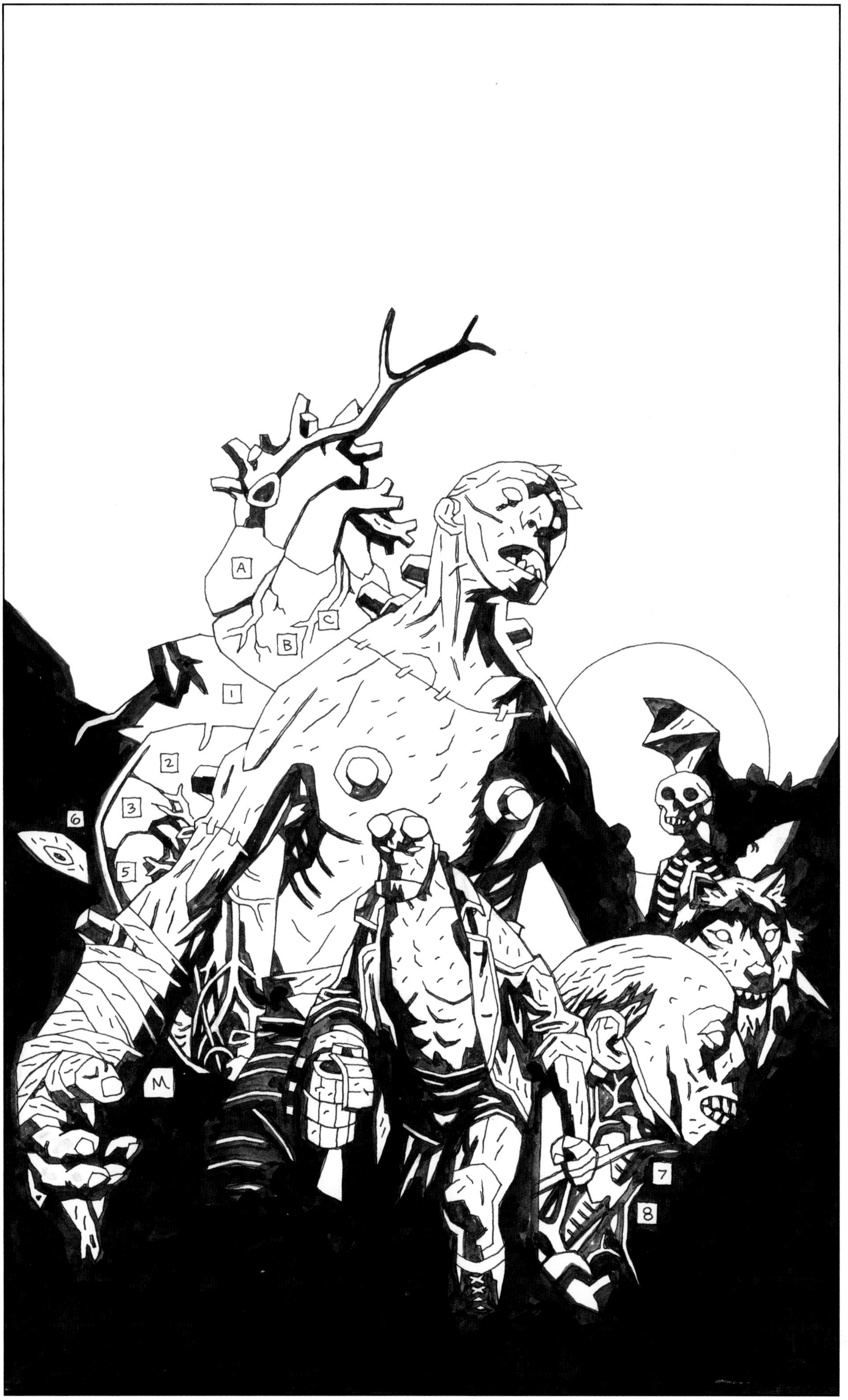
A
B
C
1
2
3
5
6
M
7
8

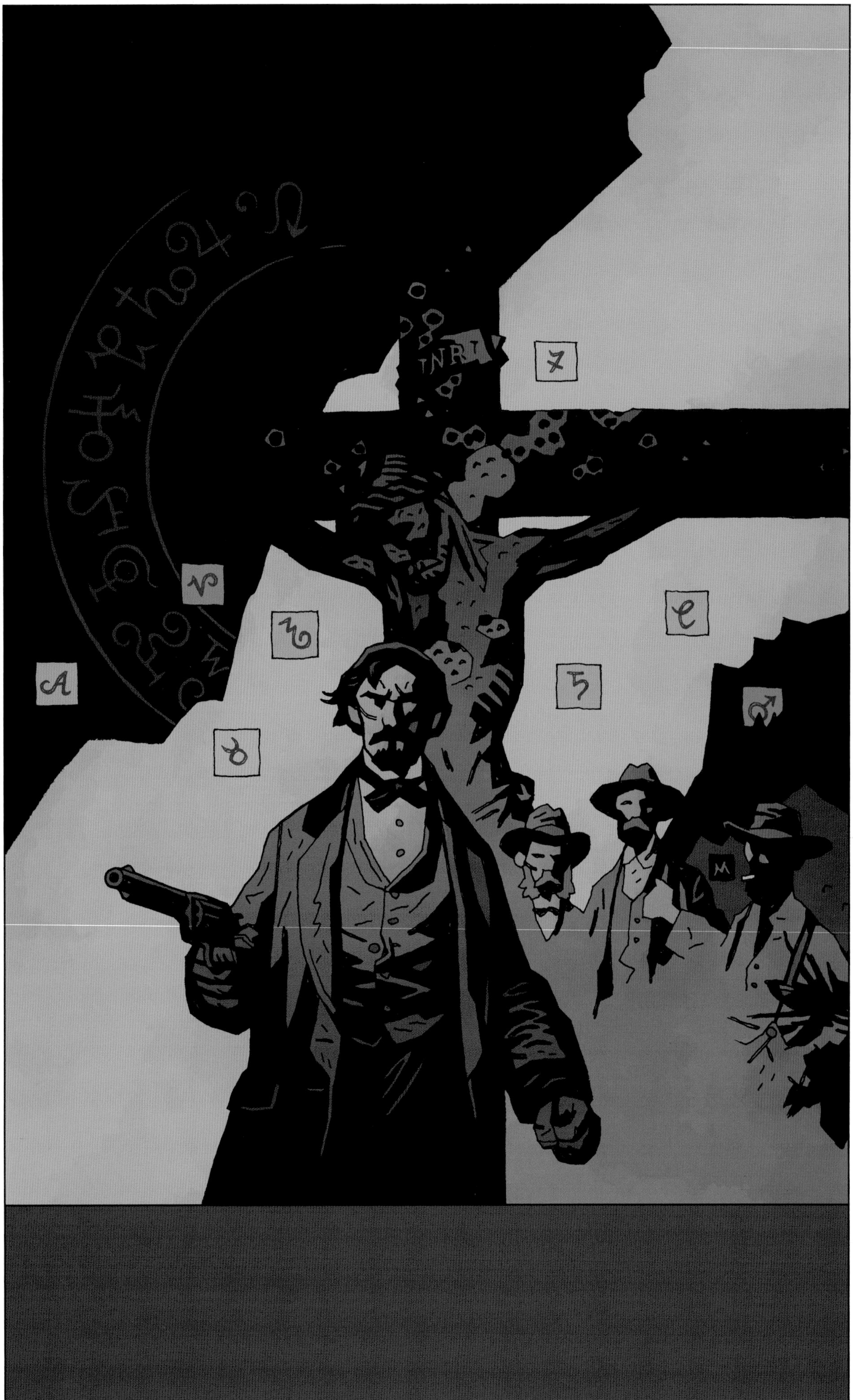
INRI

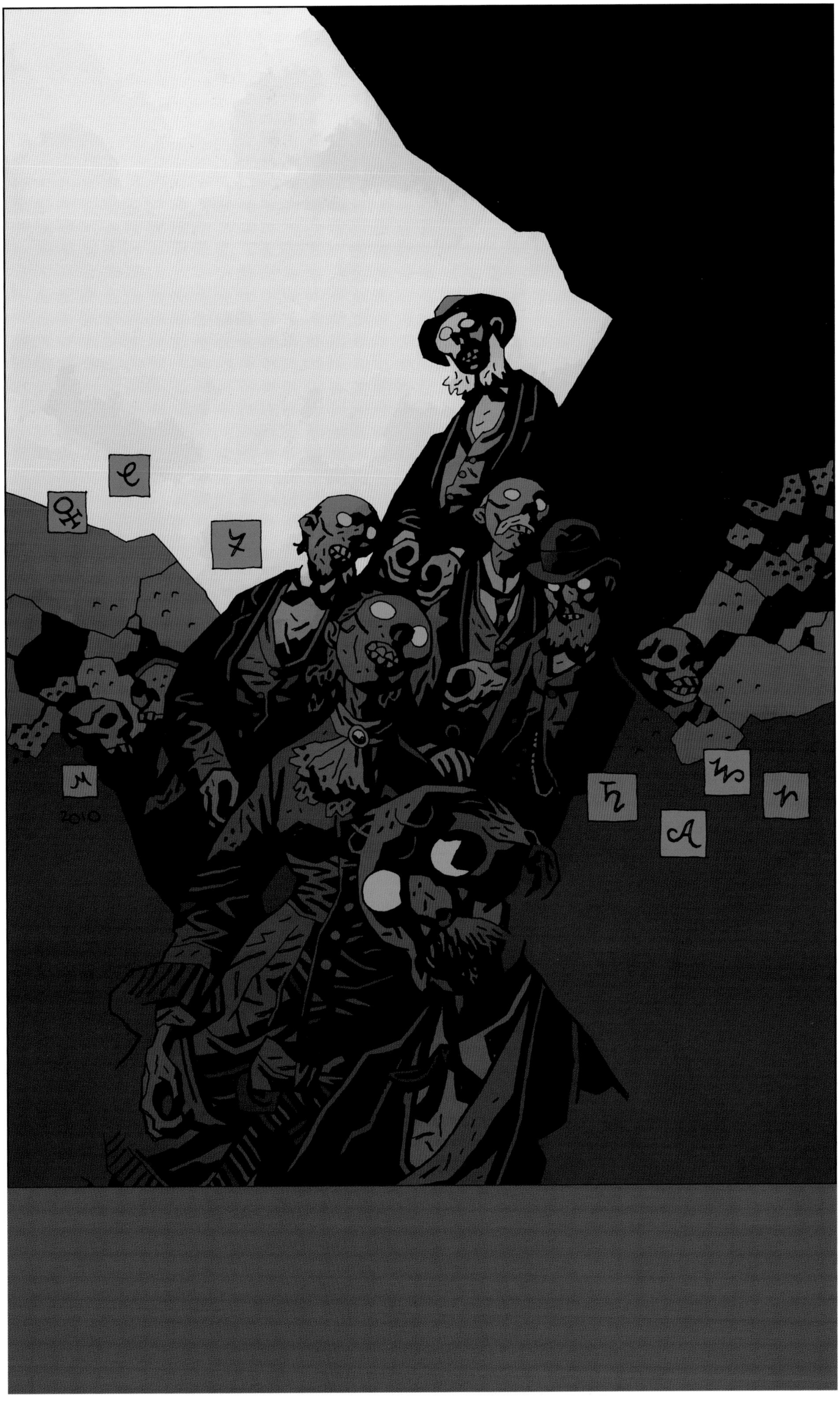

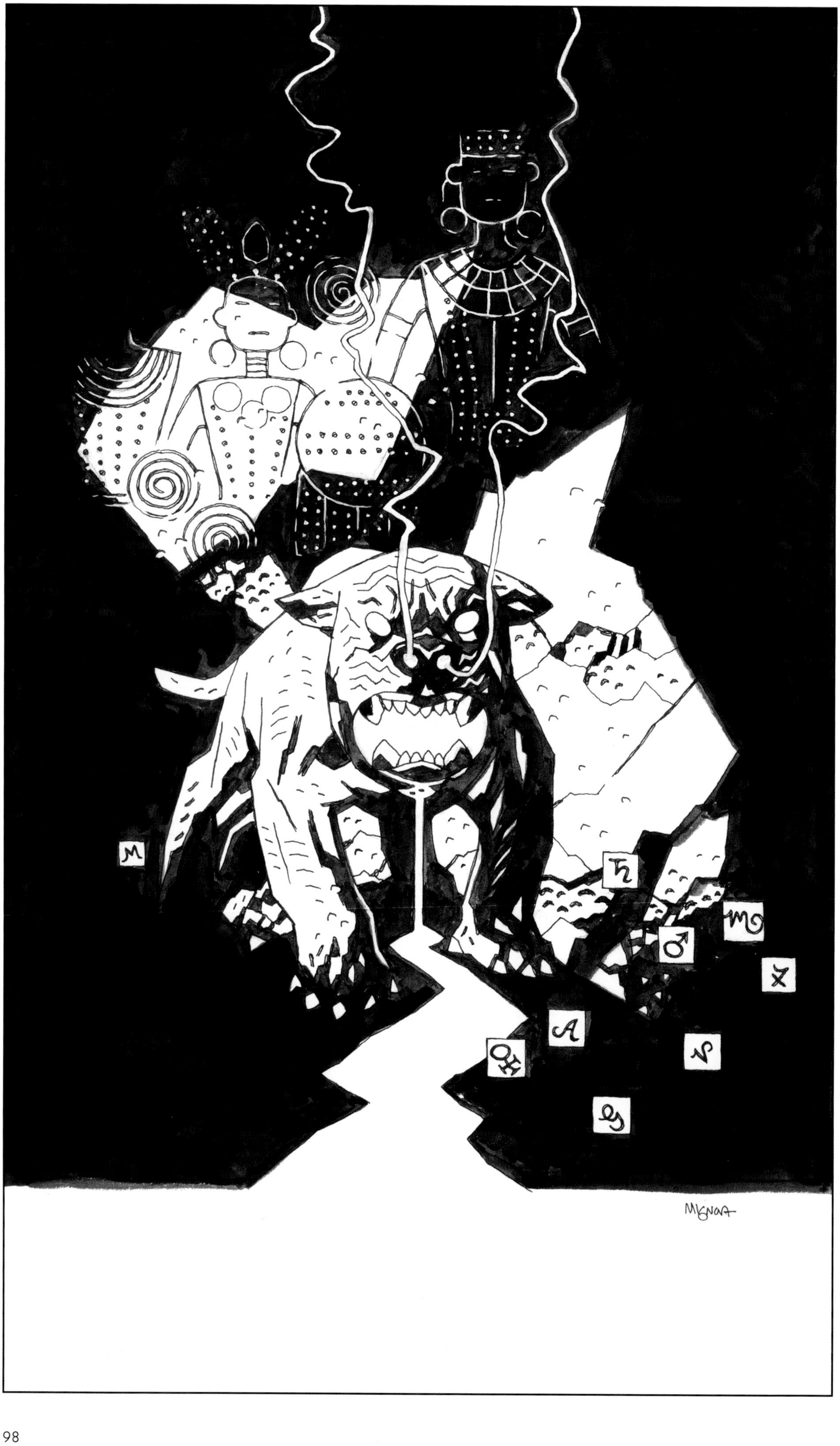

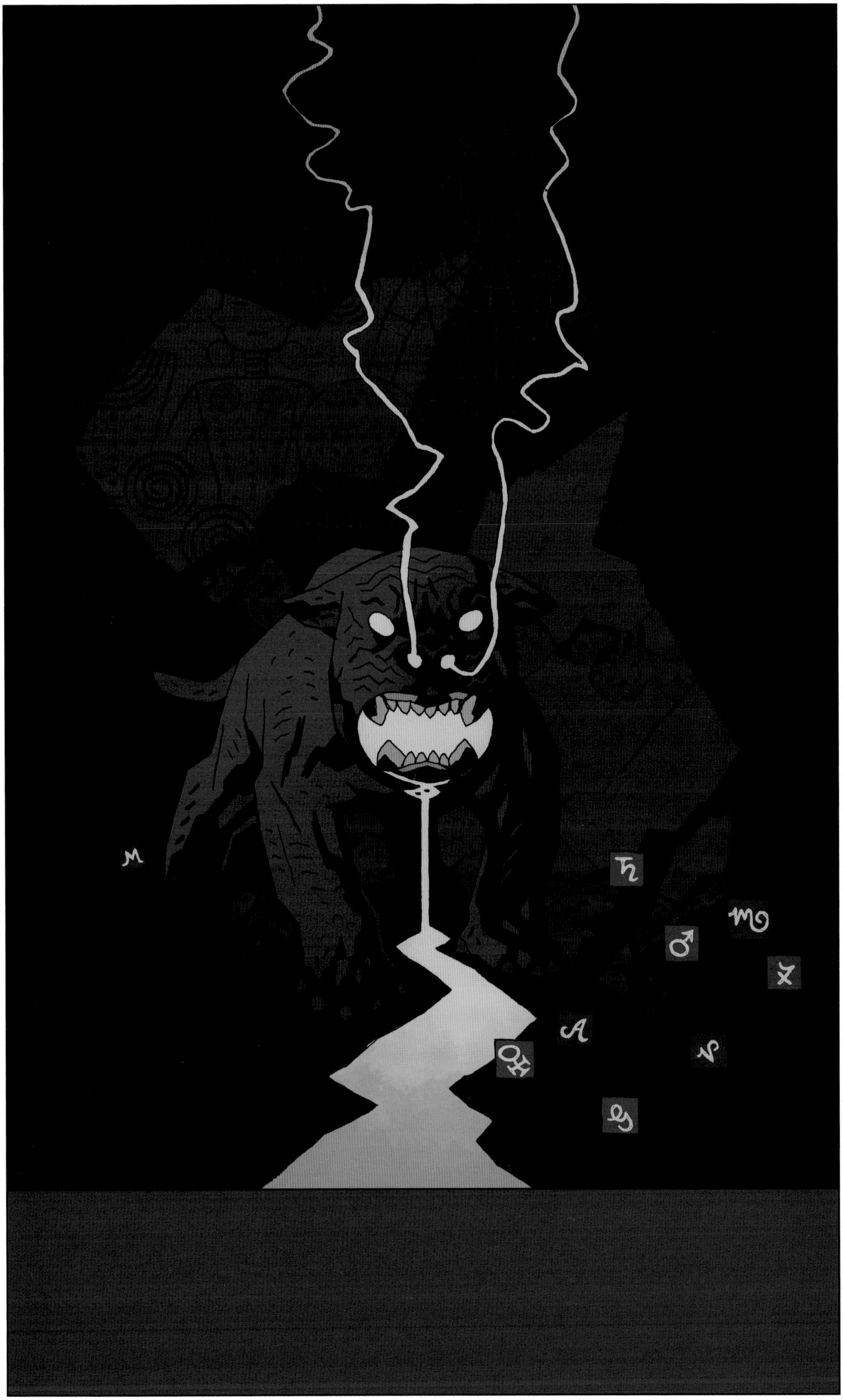

100

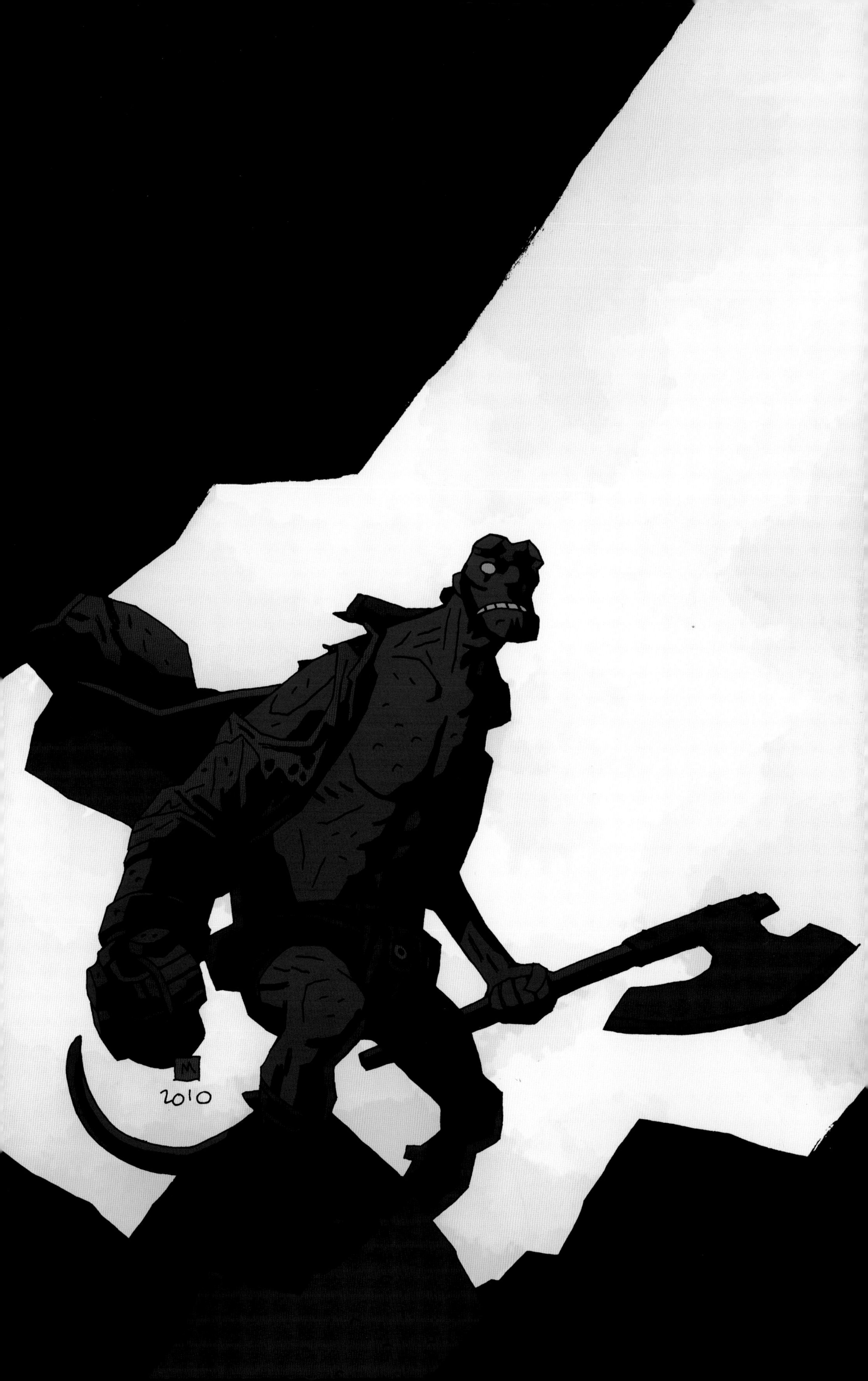
2010

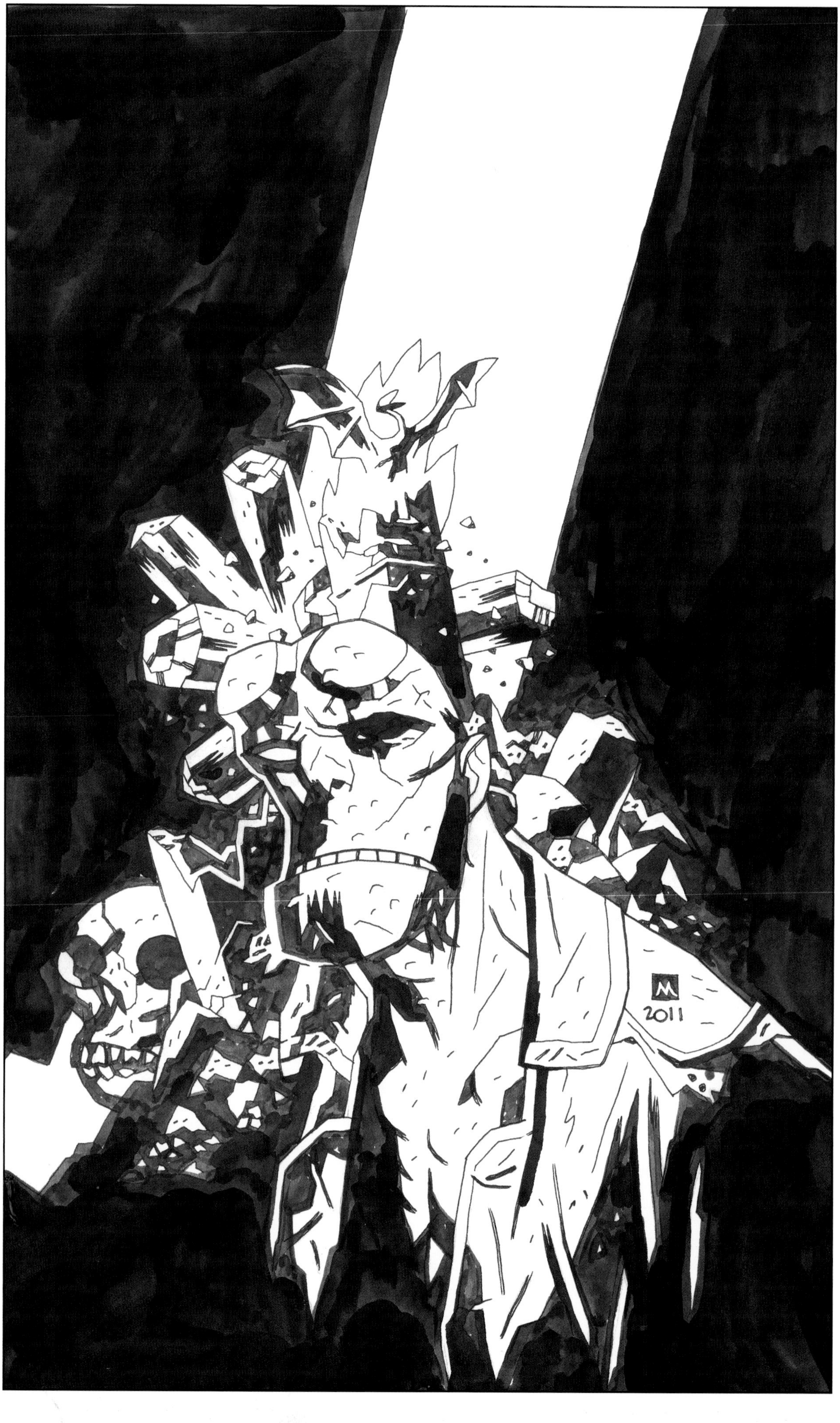
2011

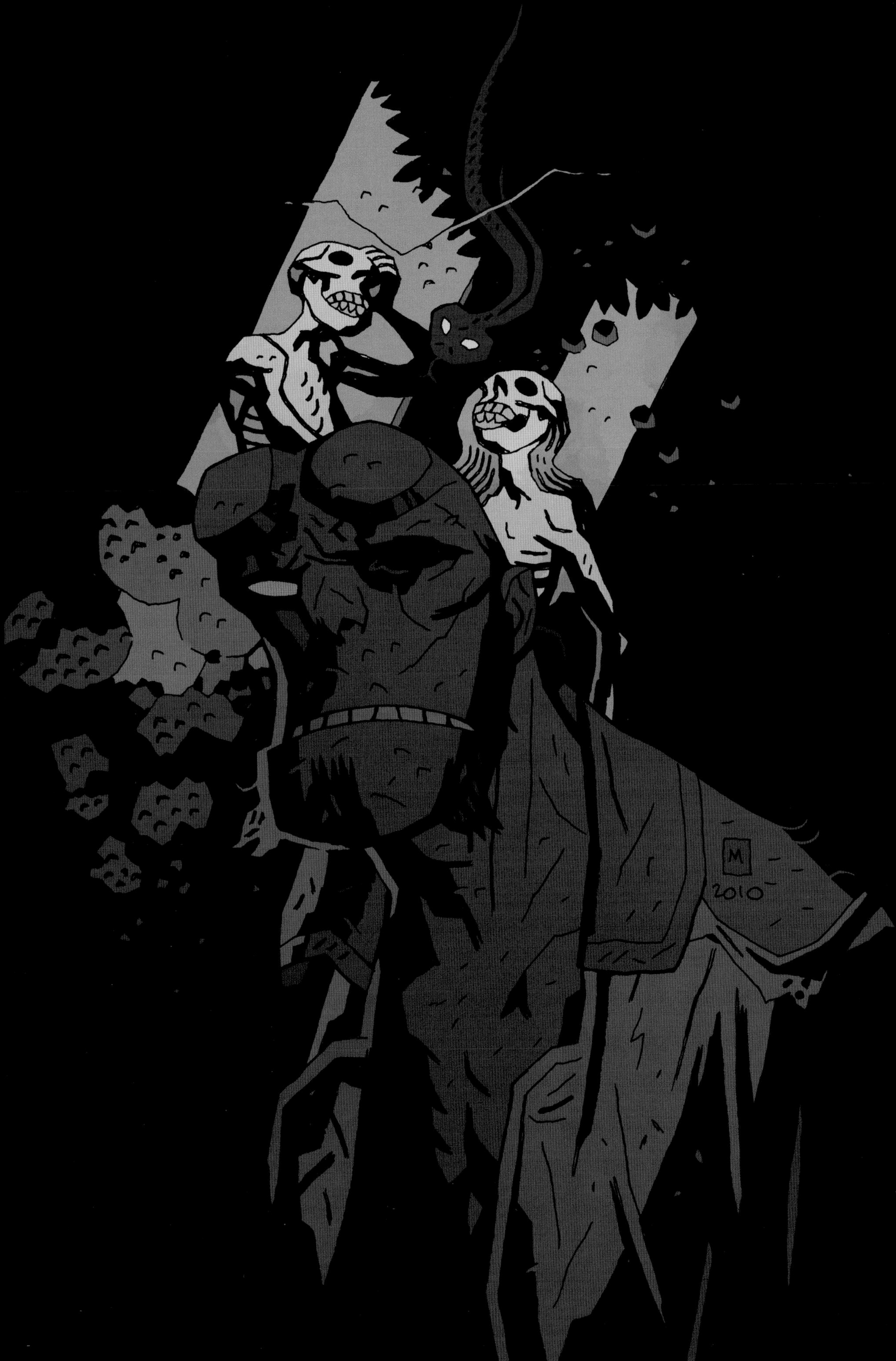

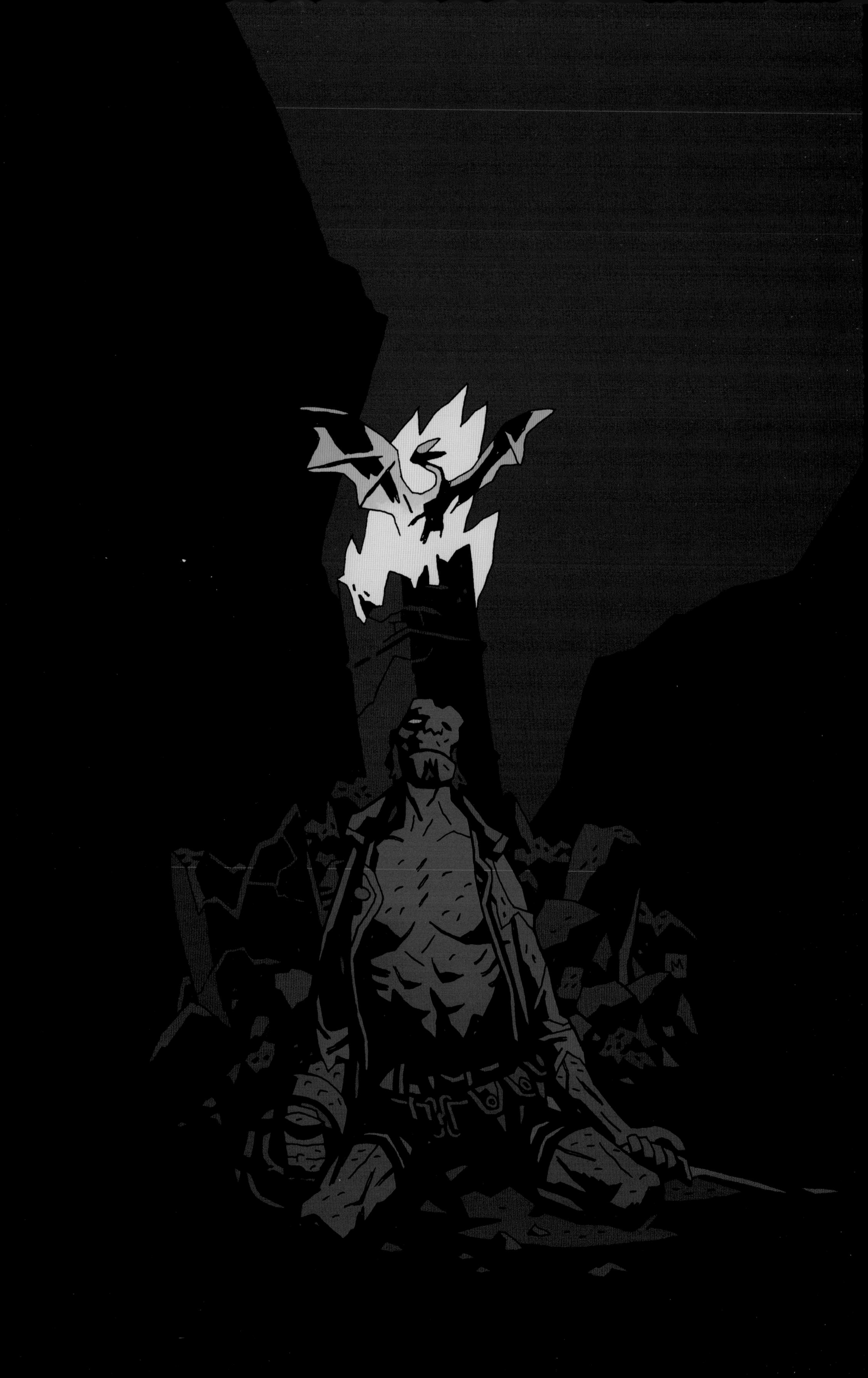

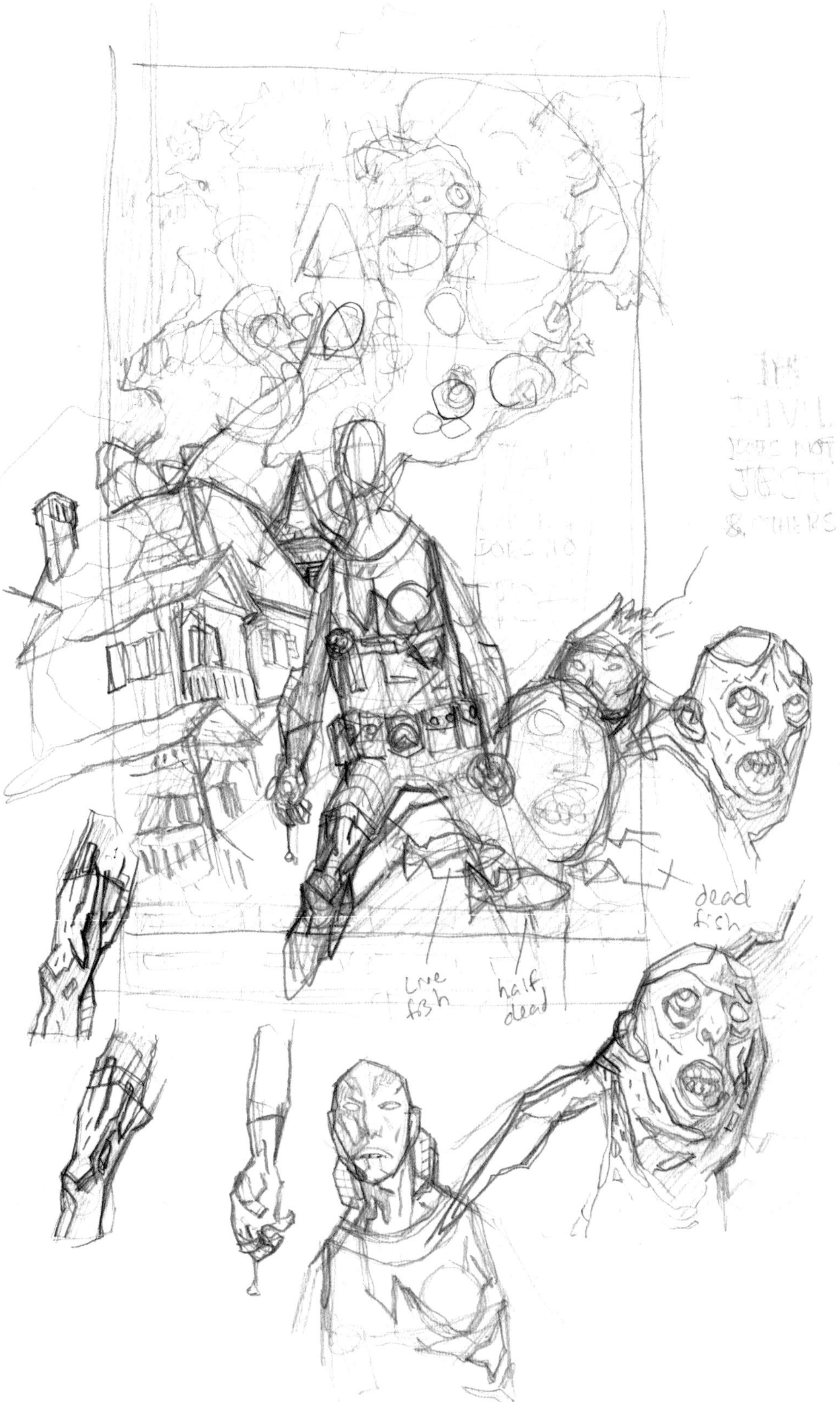
dead fish
live fish
half dead

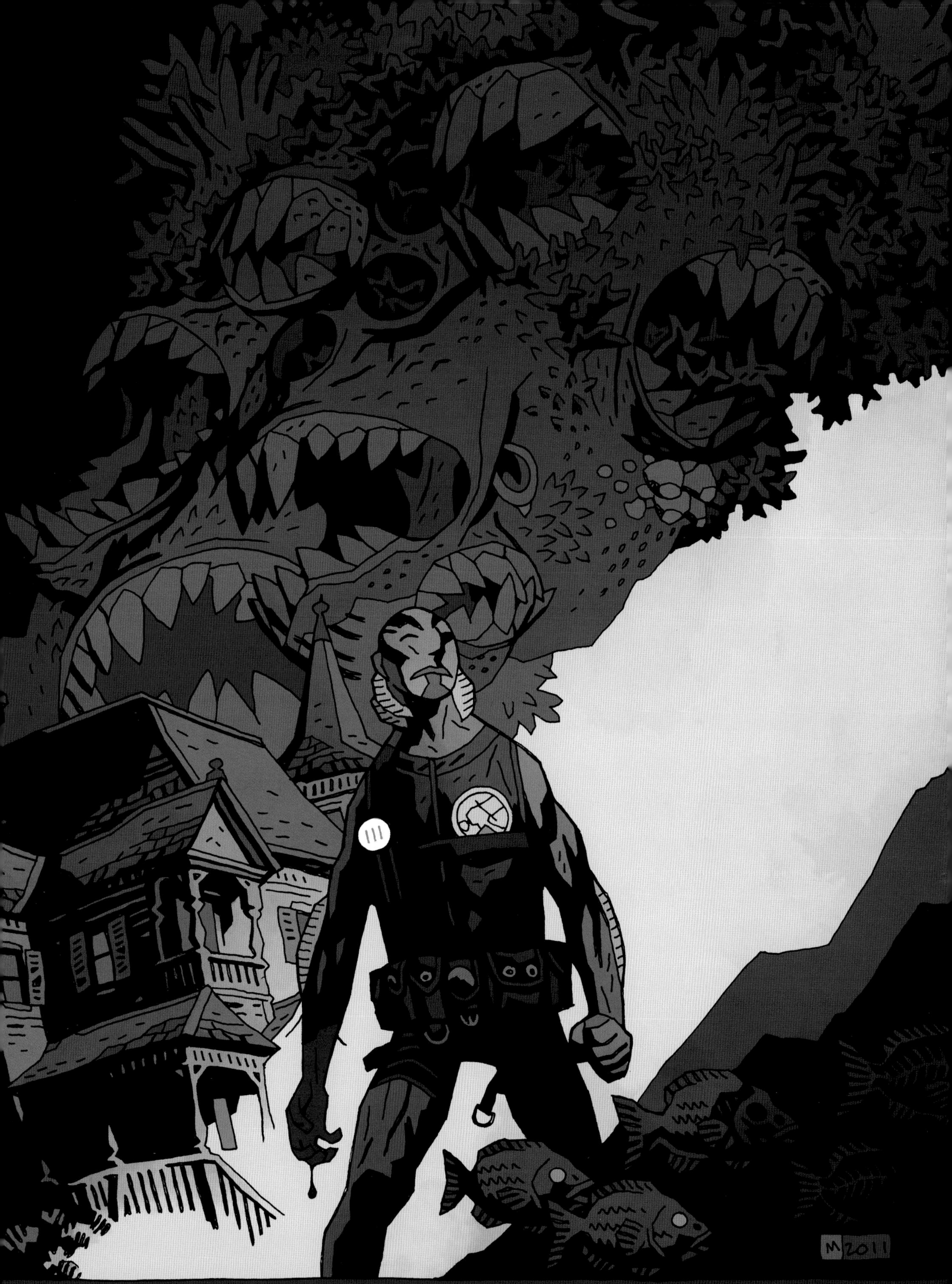
III
M 2011

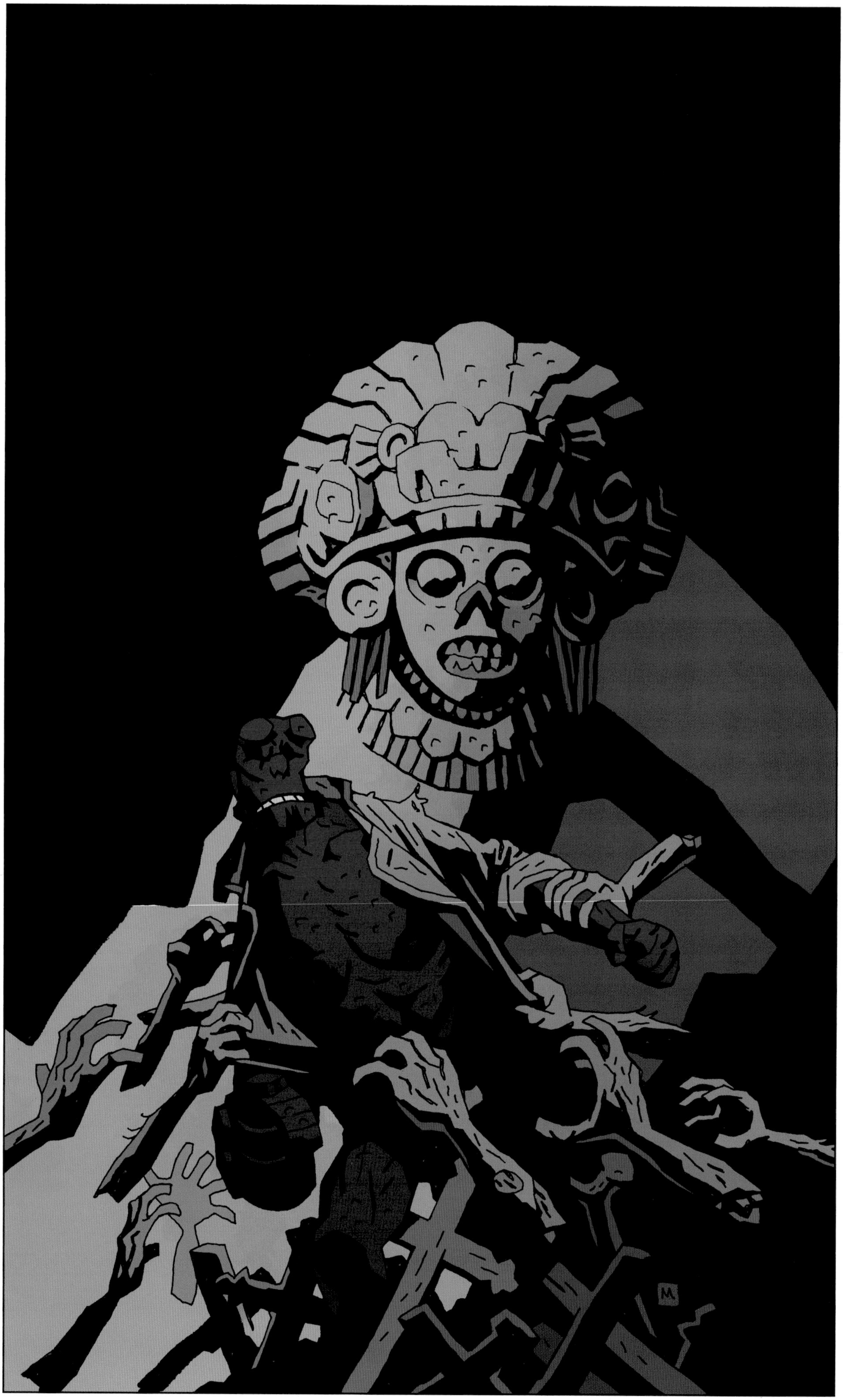

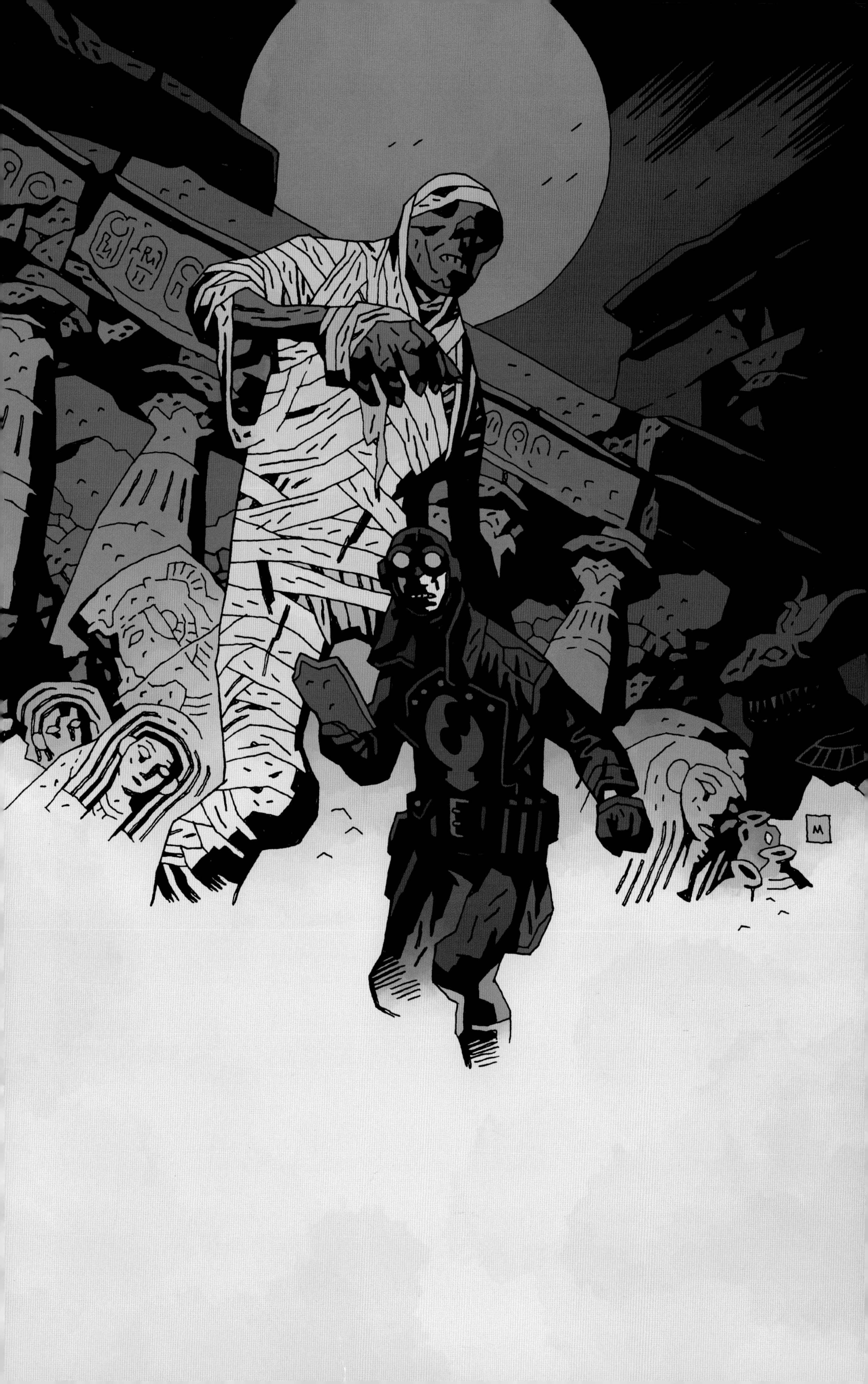

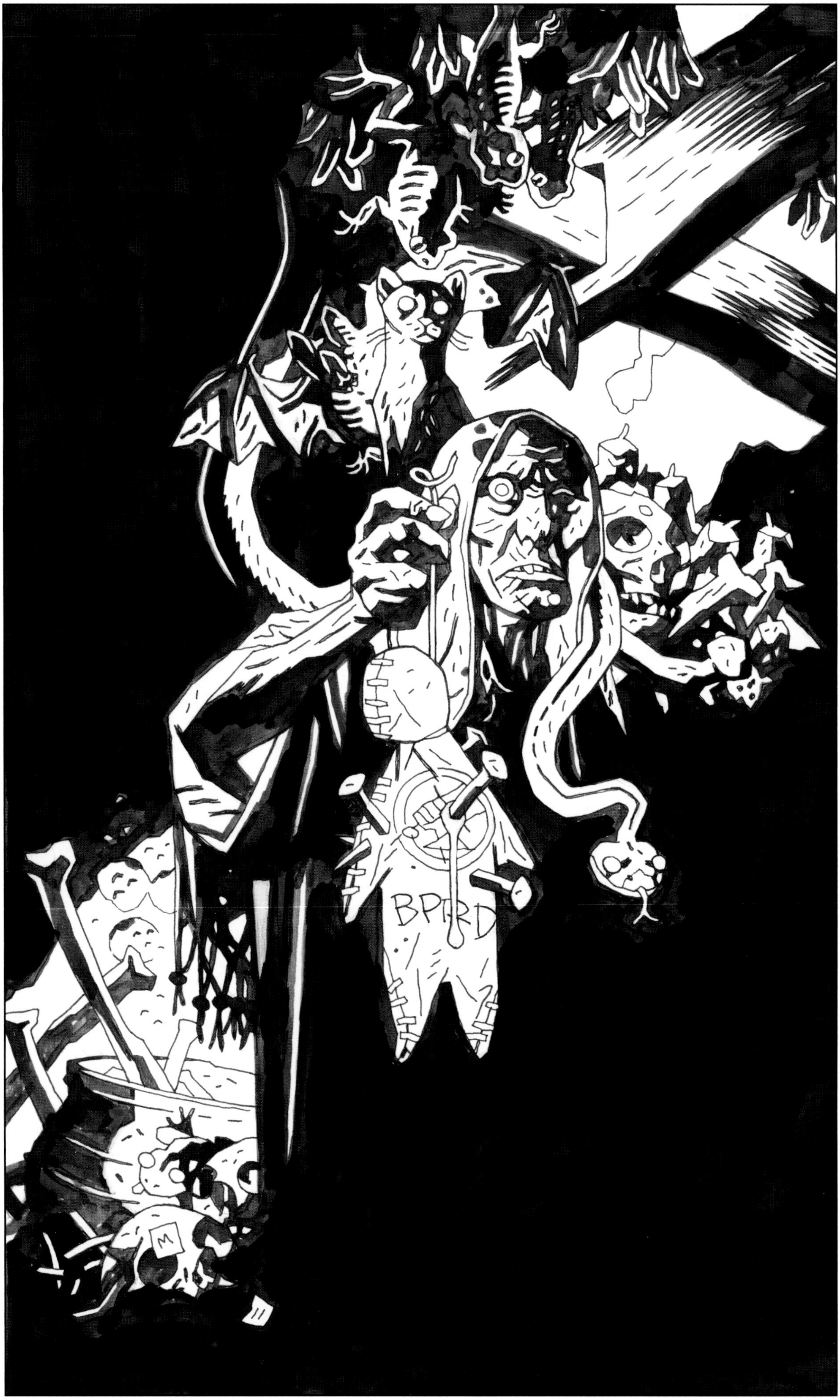
BPRD

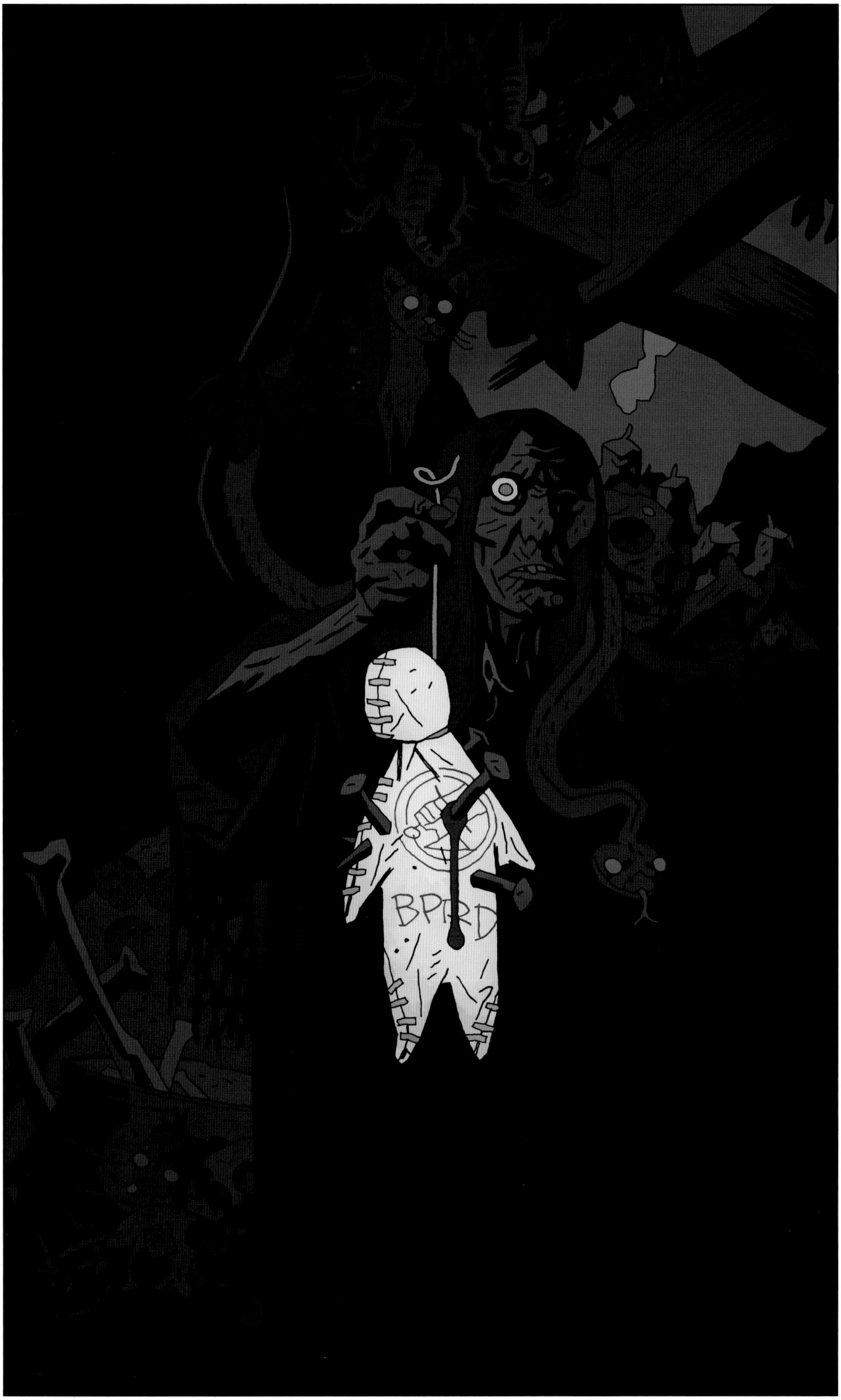
BPRD

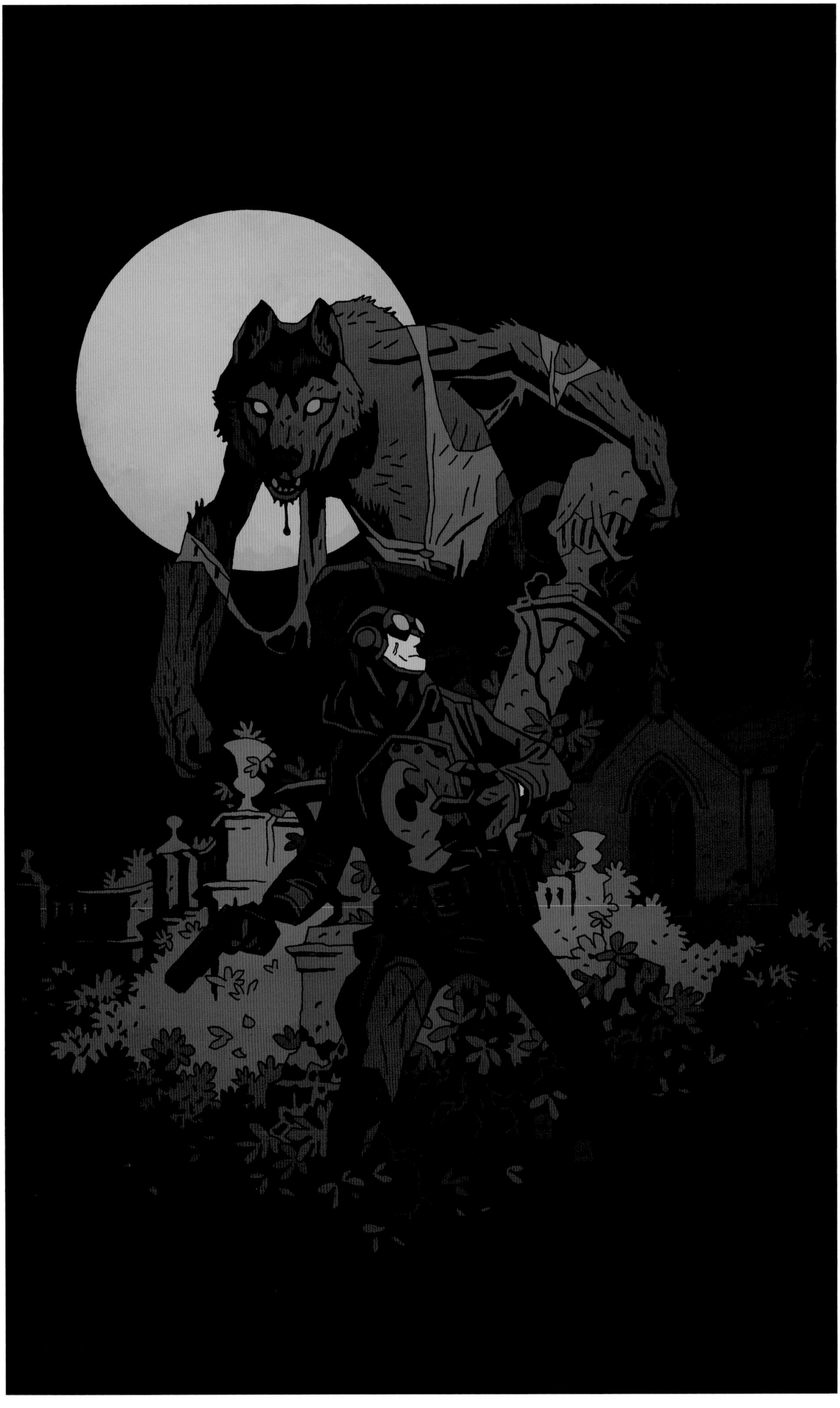

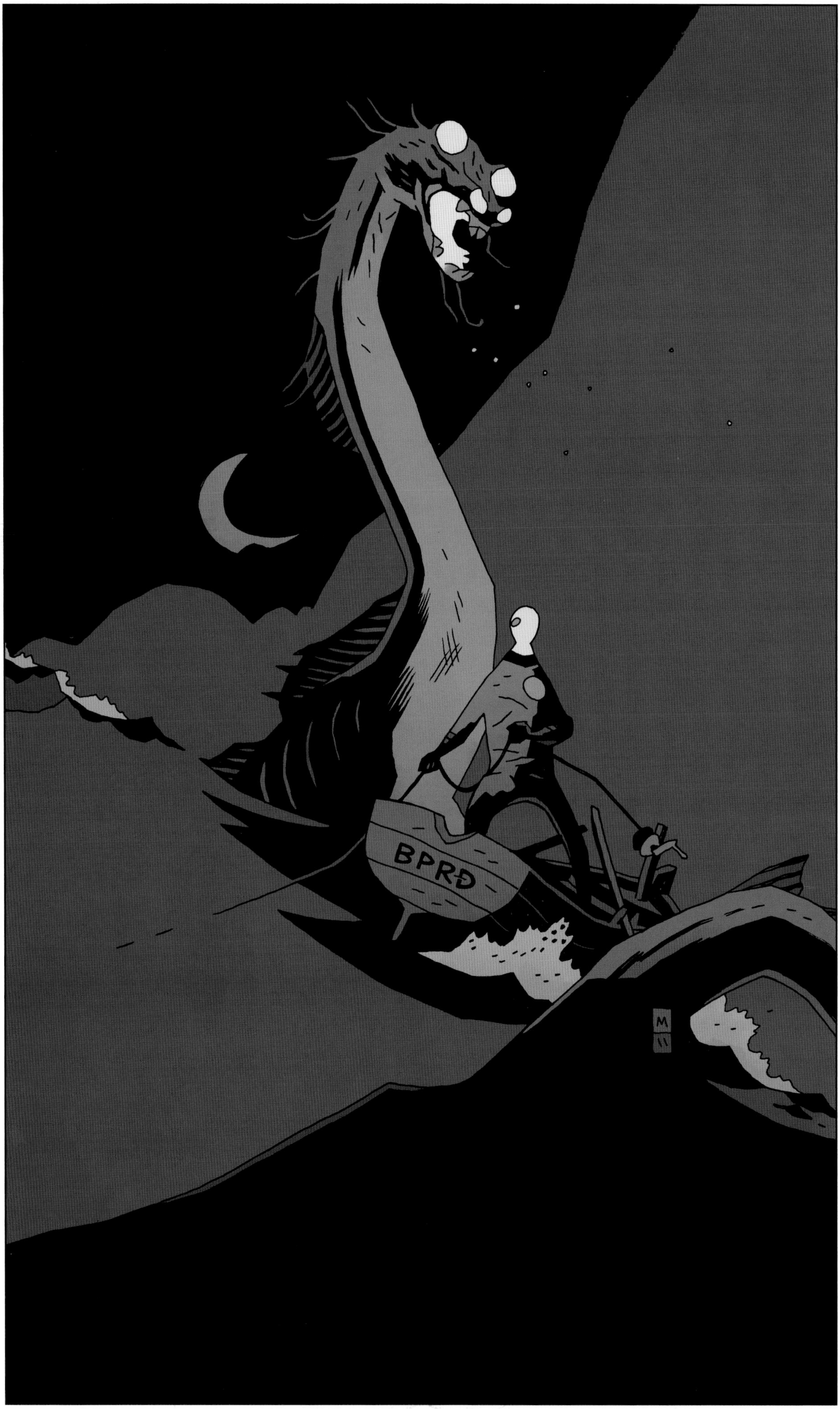
BPRD

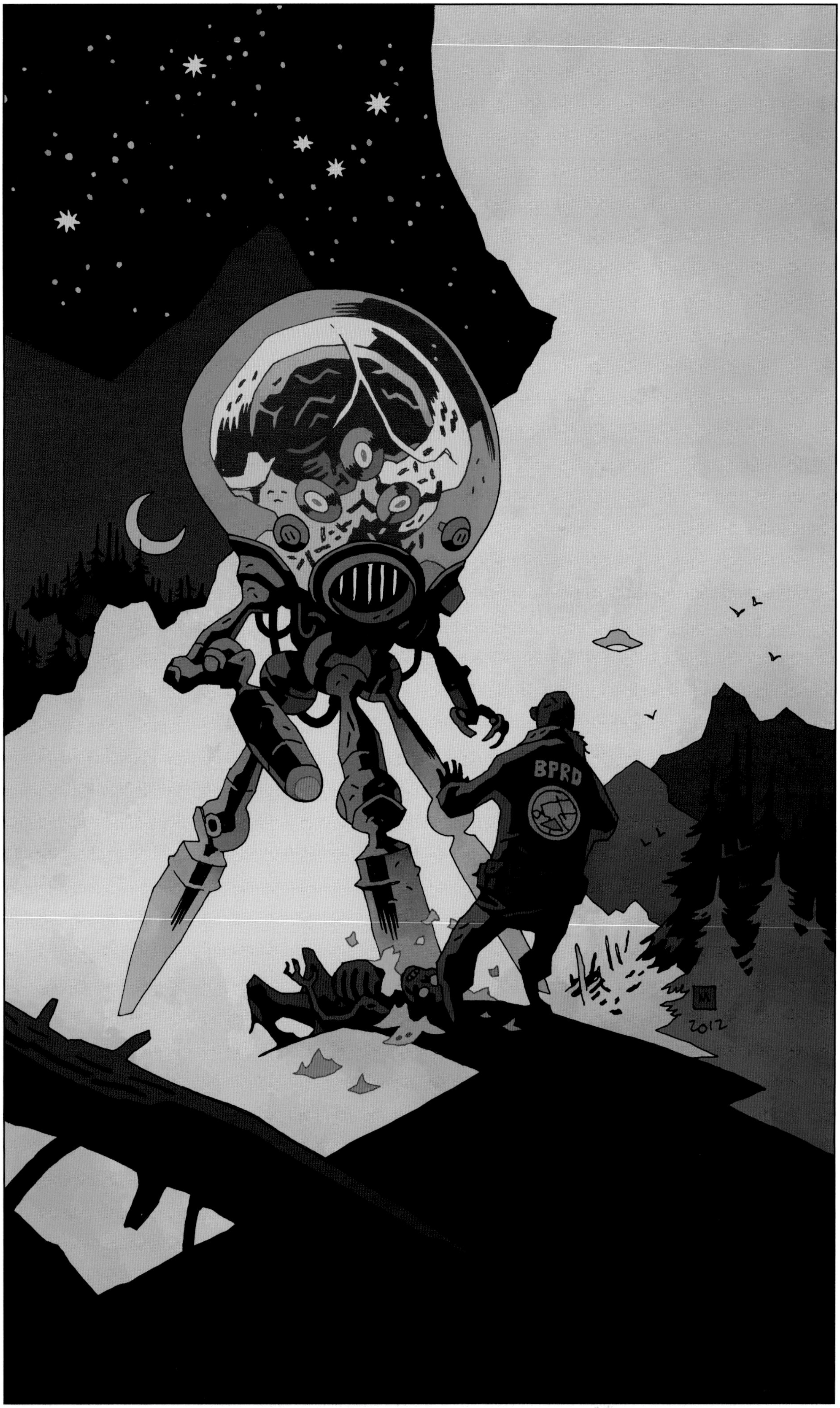
BPRD
2012

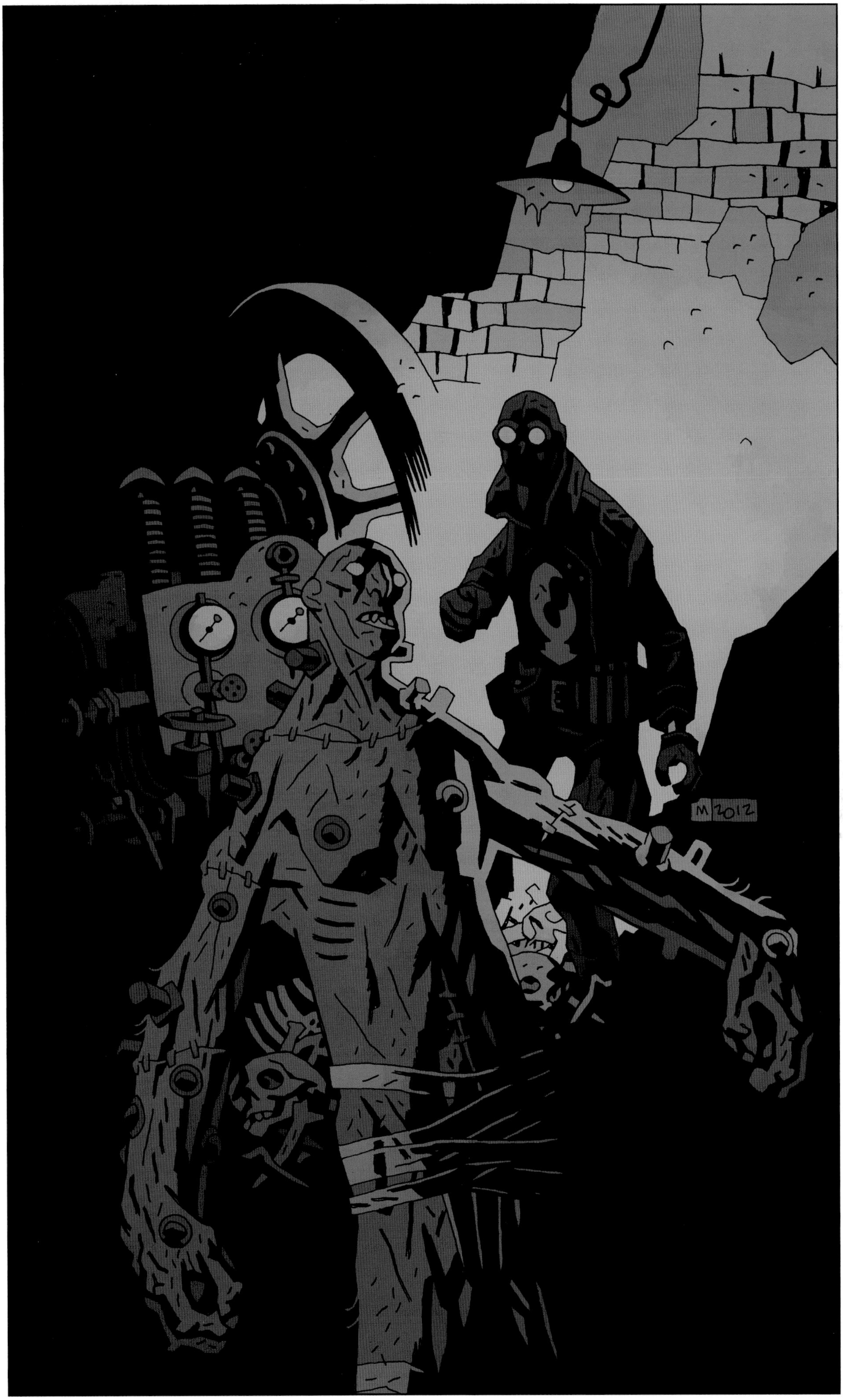
M 2012

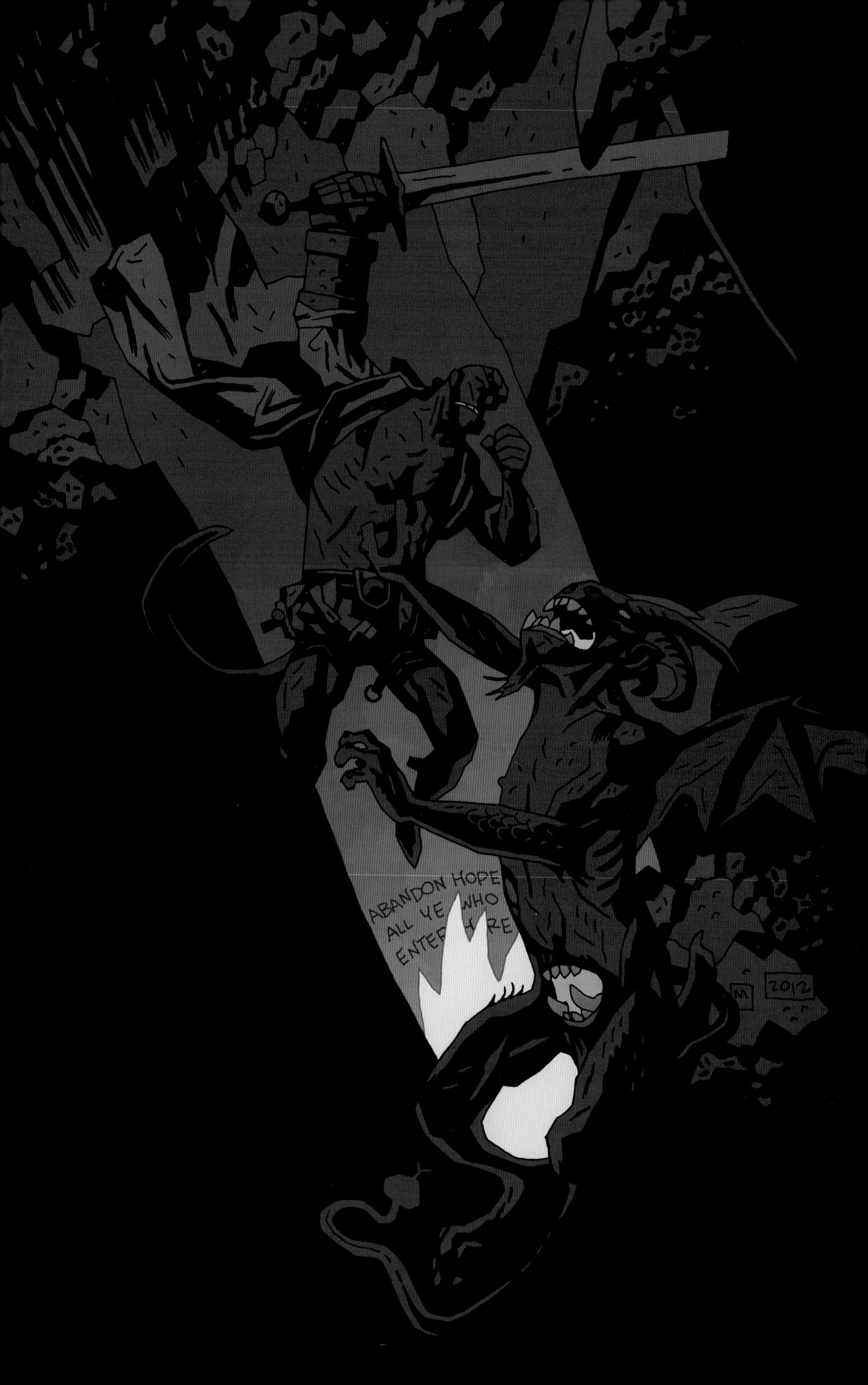
ABANDON HOPE
ALL YE WHO
ENTER H RE
2012

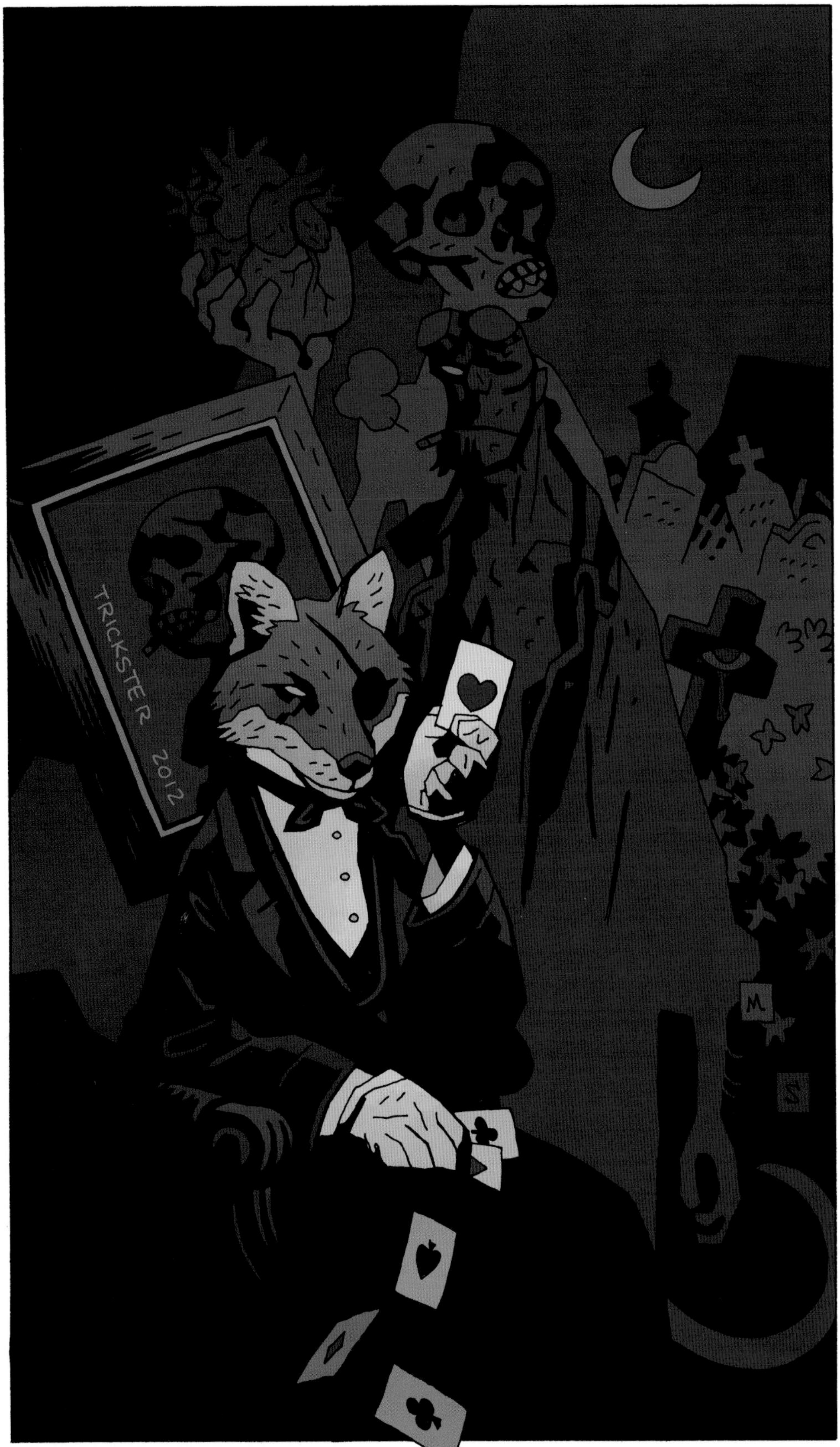
TRICKSTER 2012
M

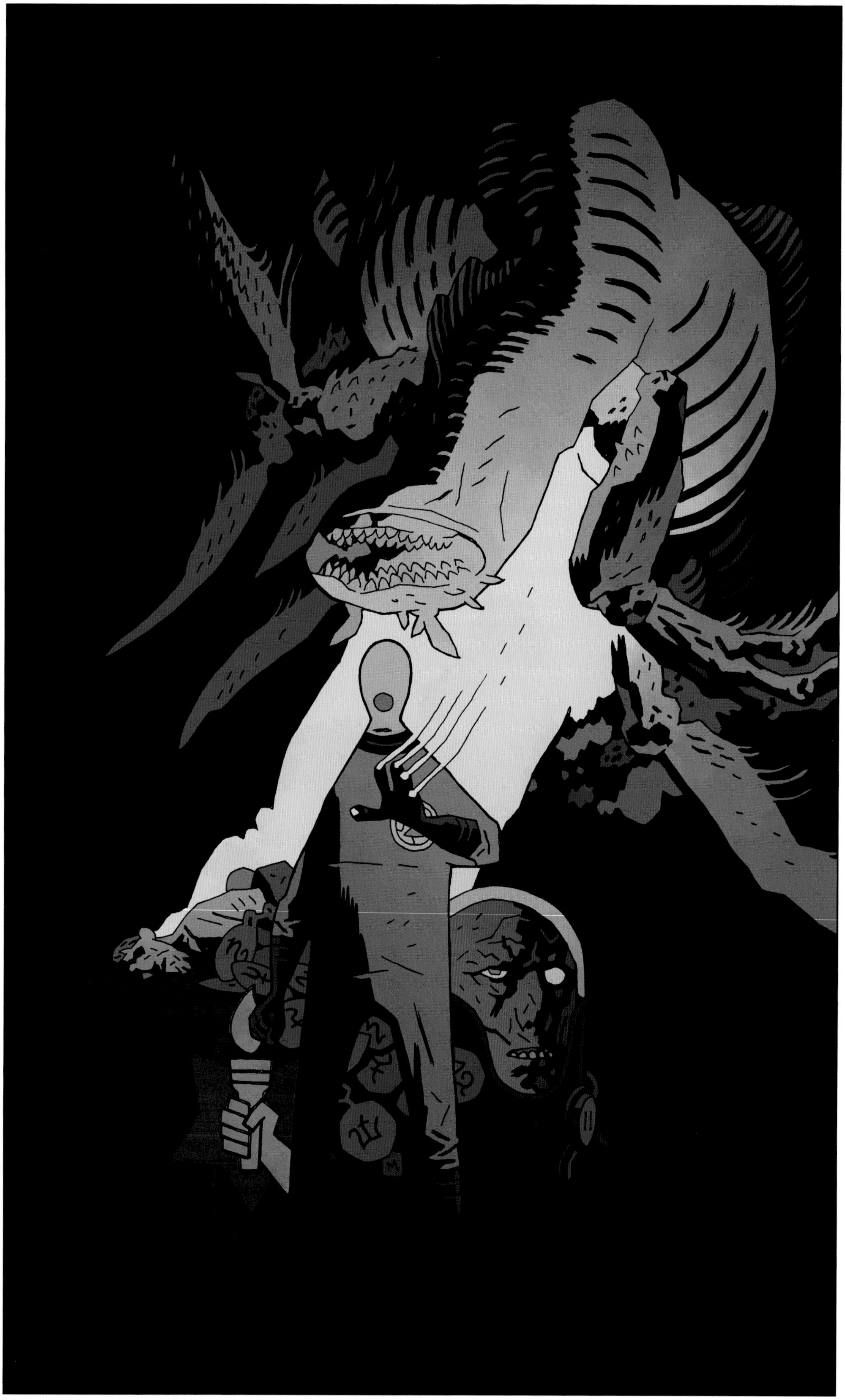

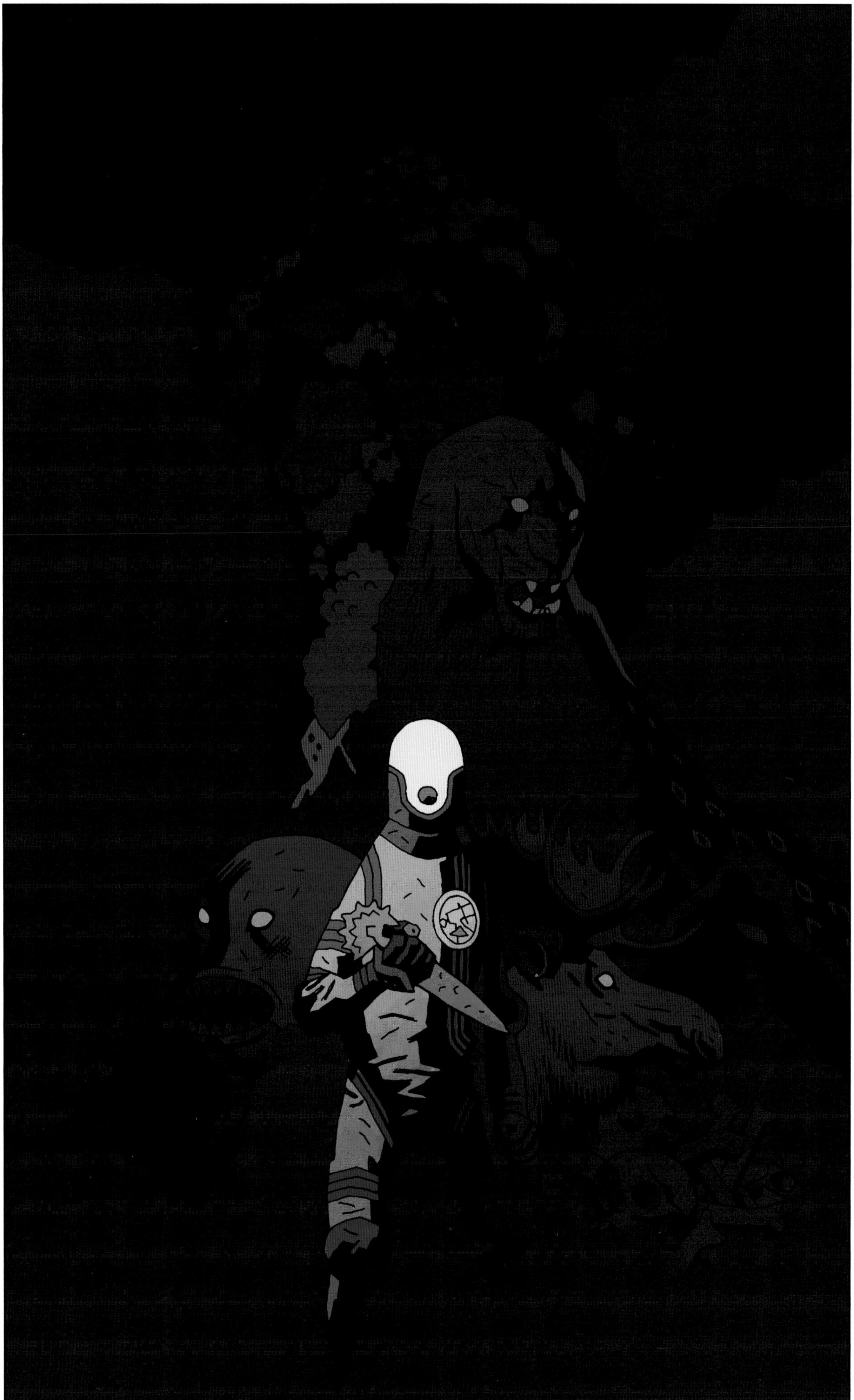

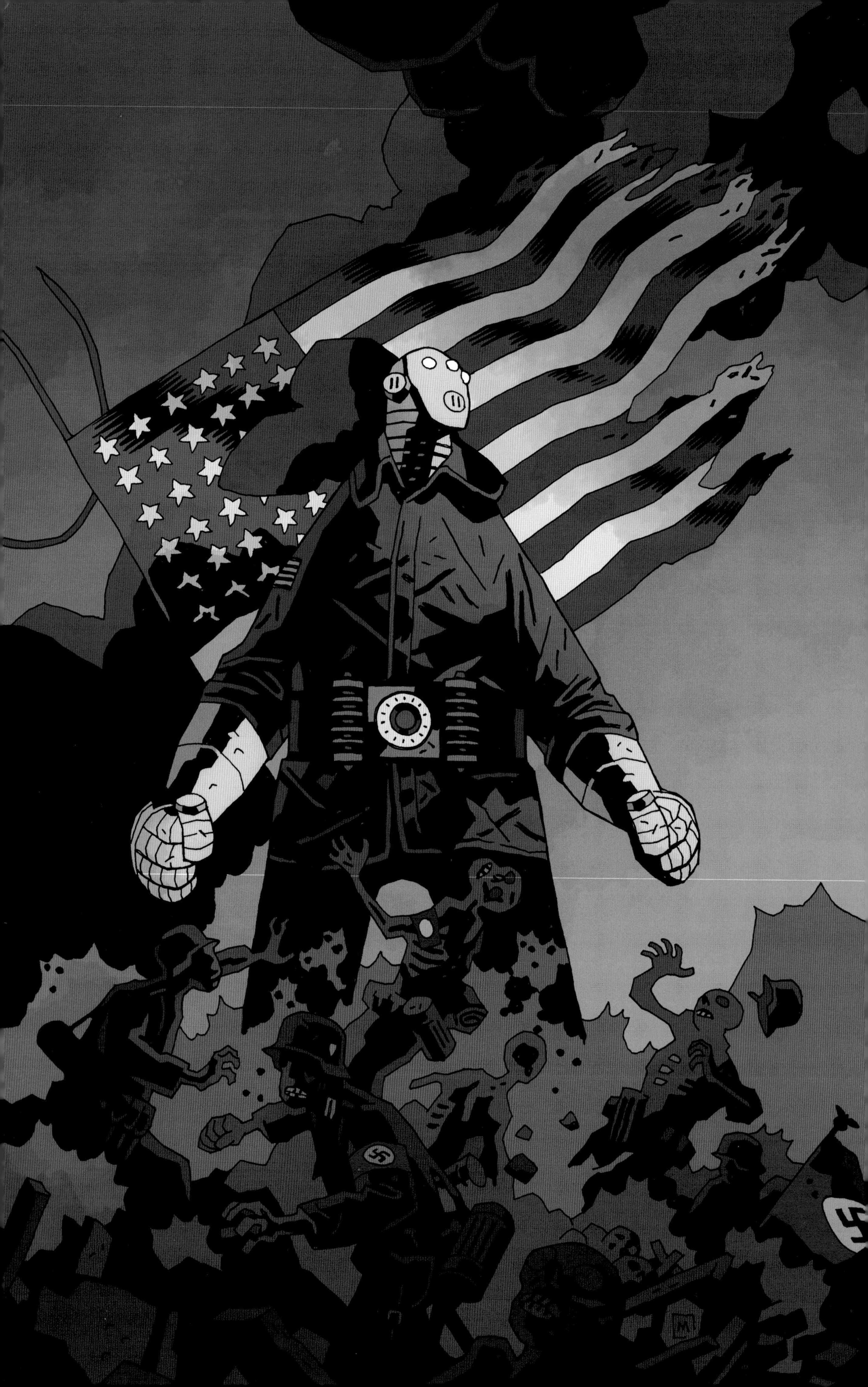

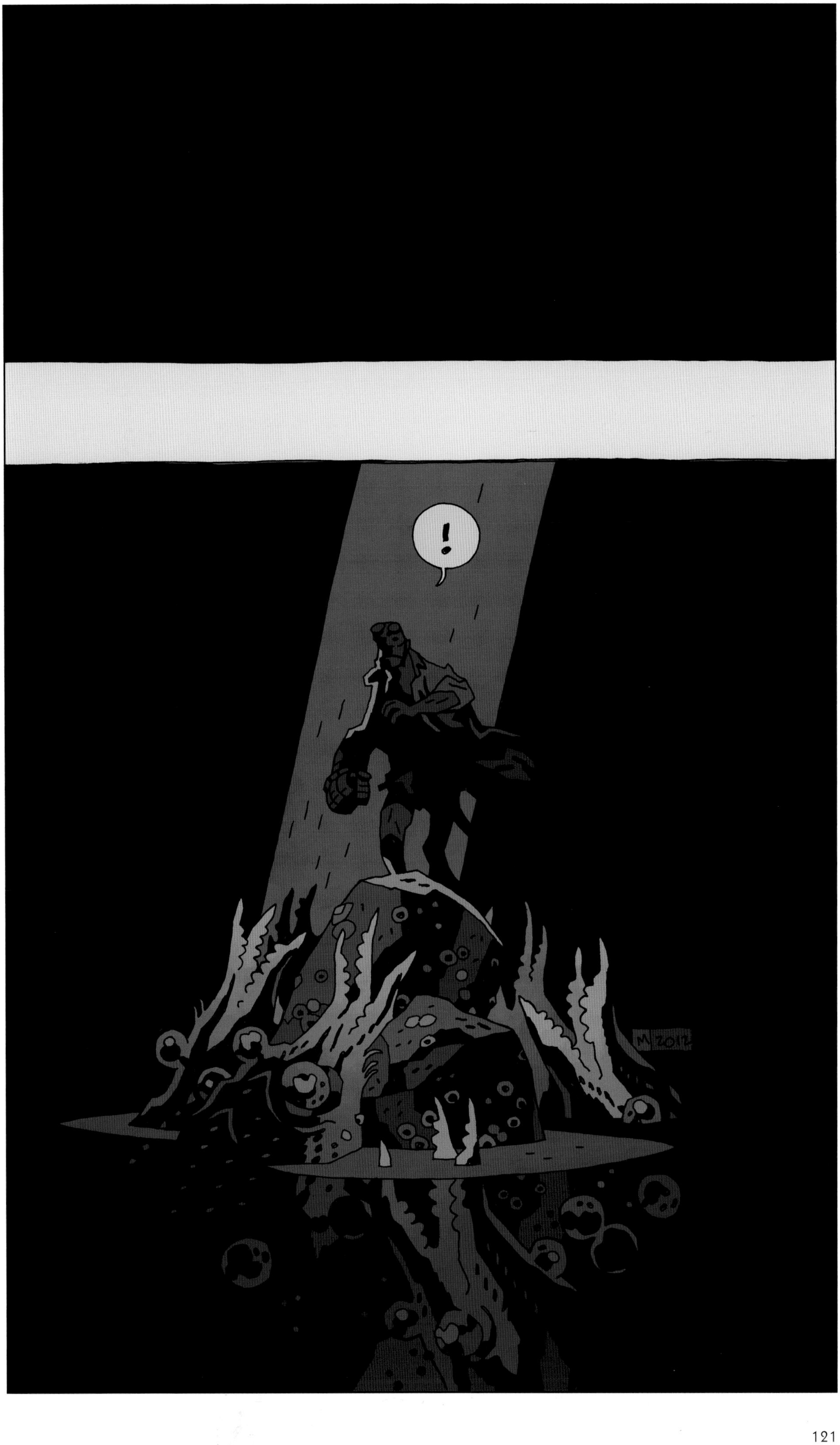
!

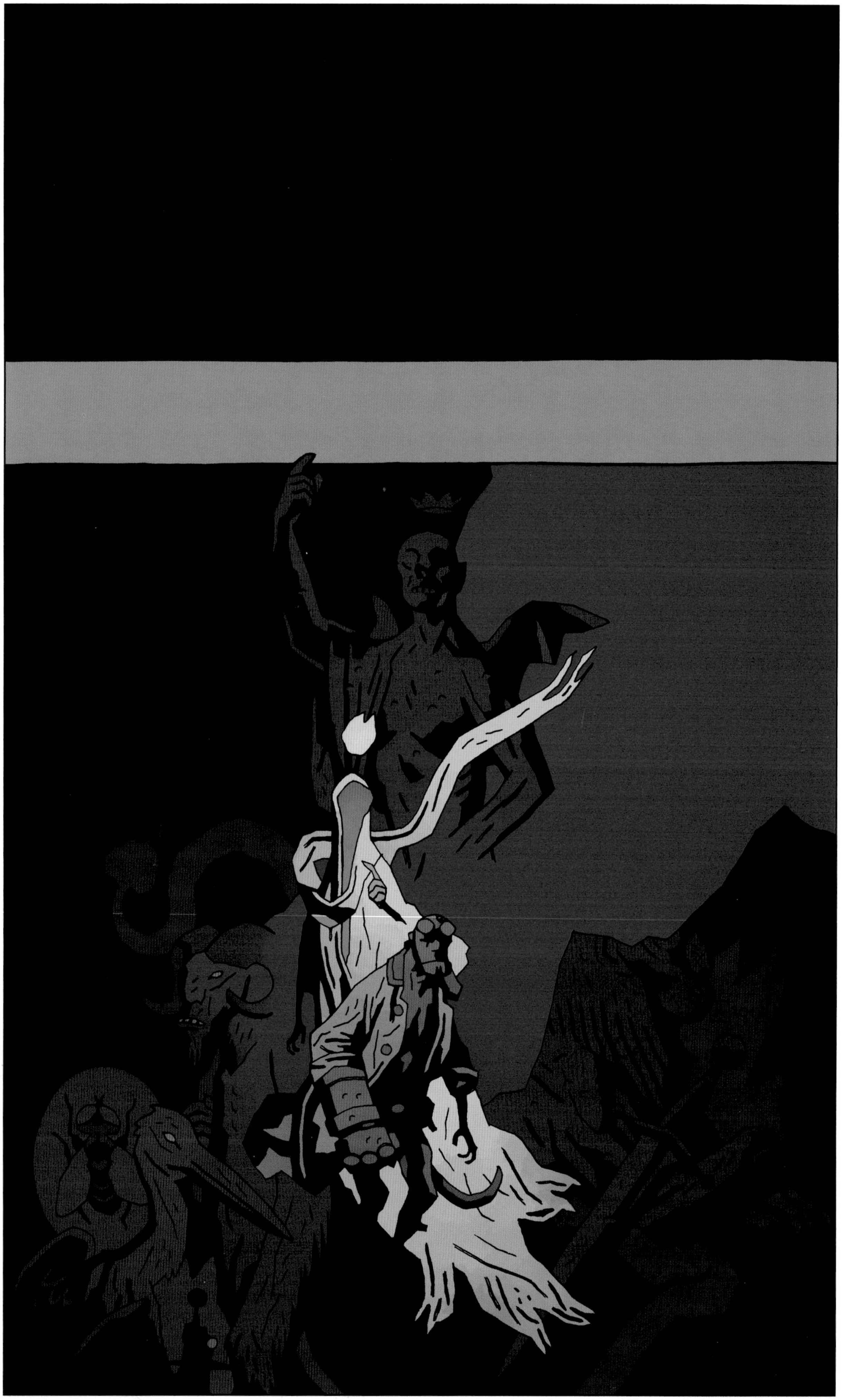

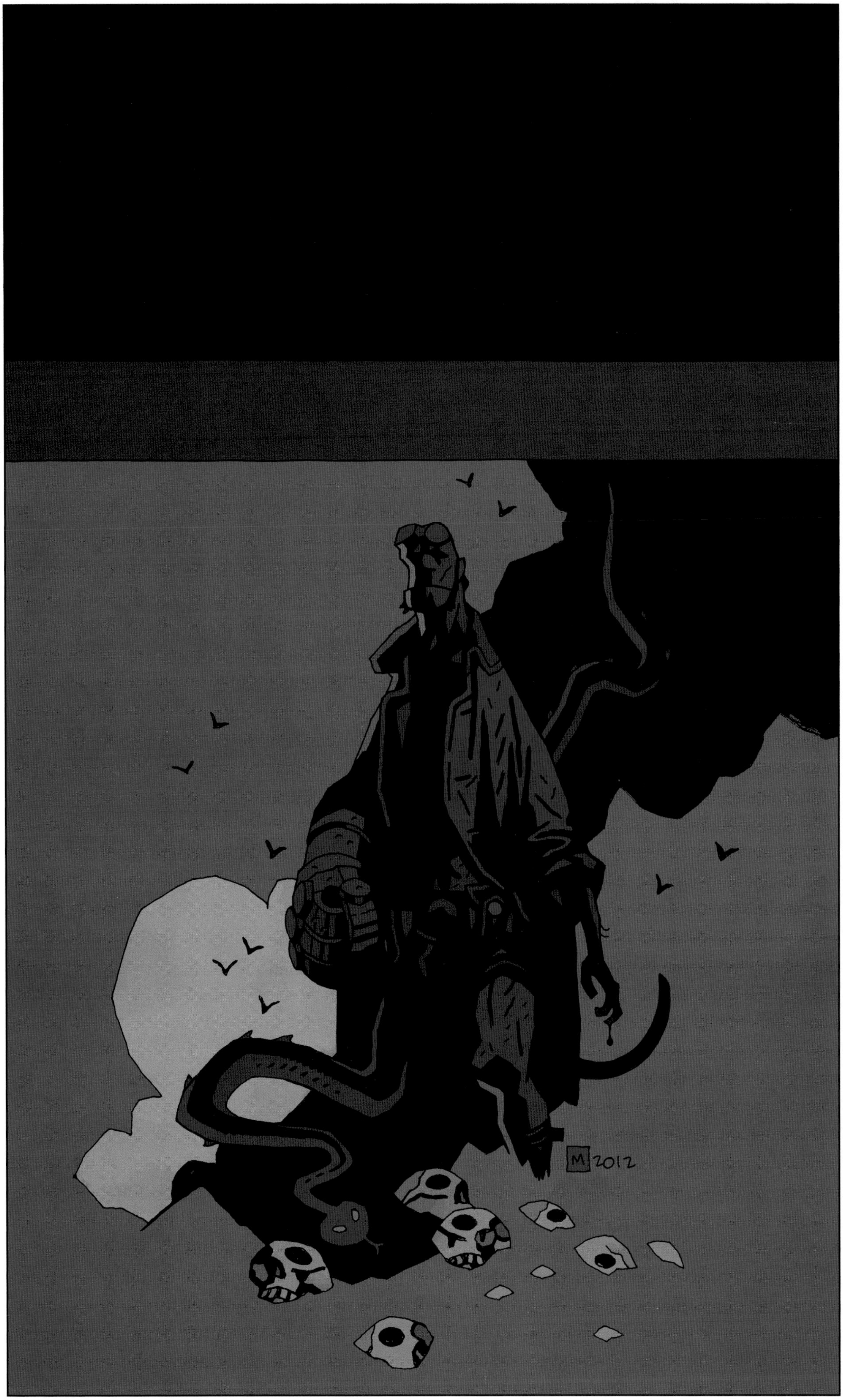
M 2012

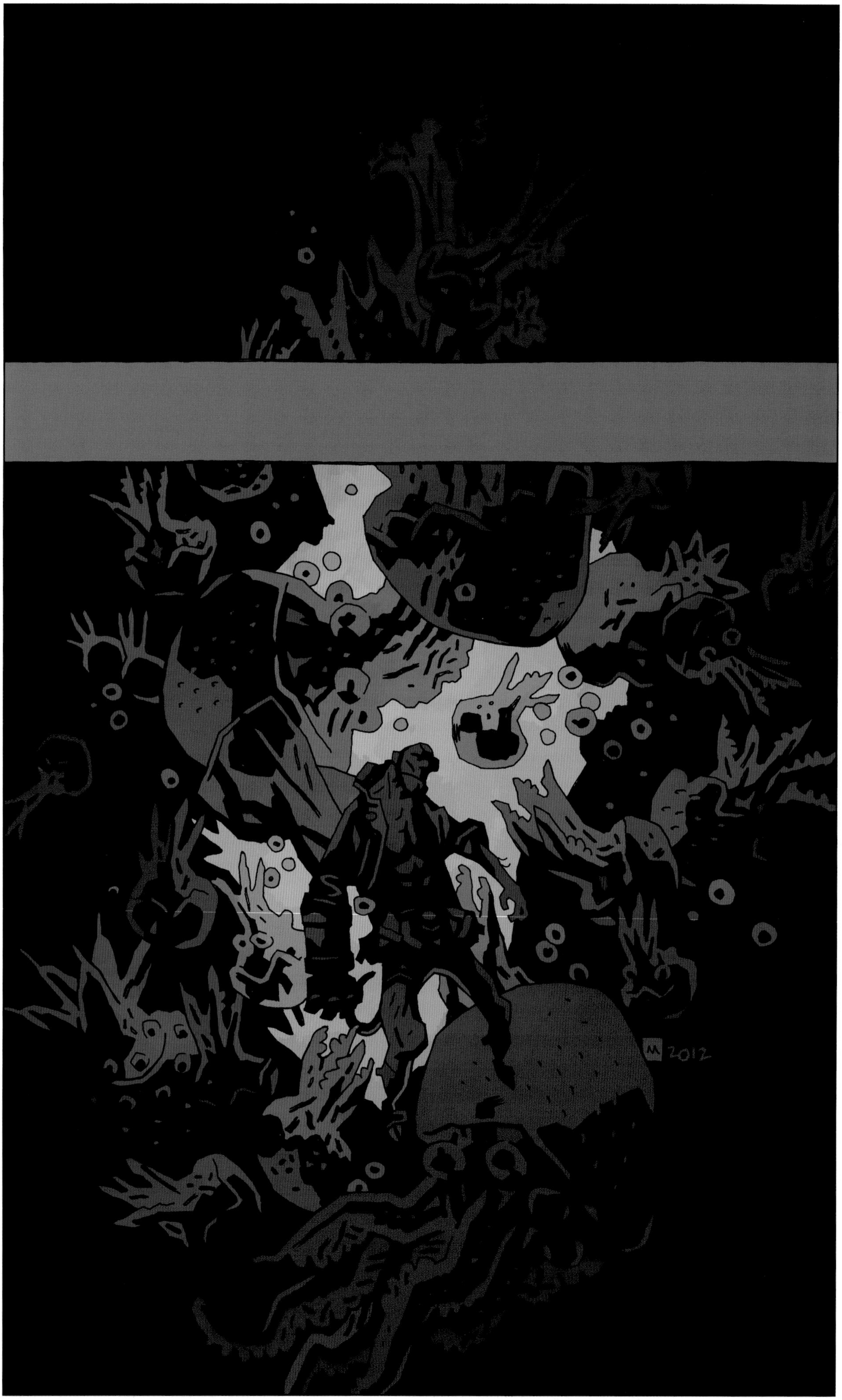

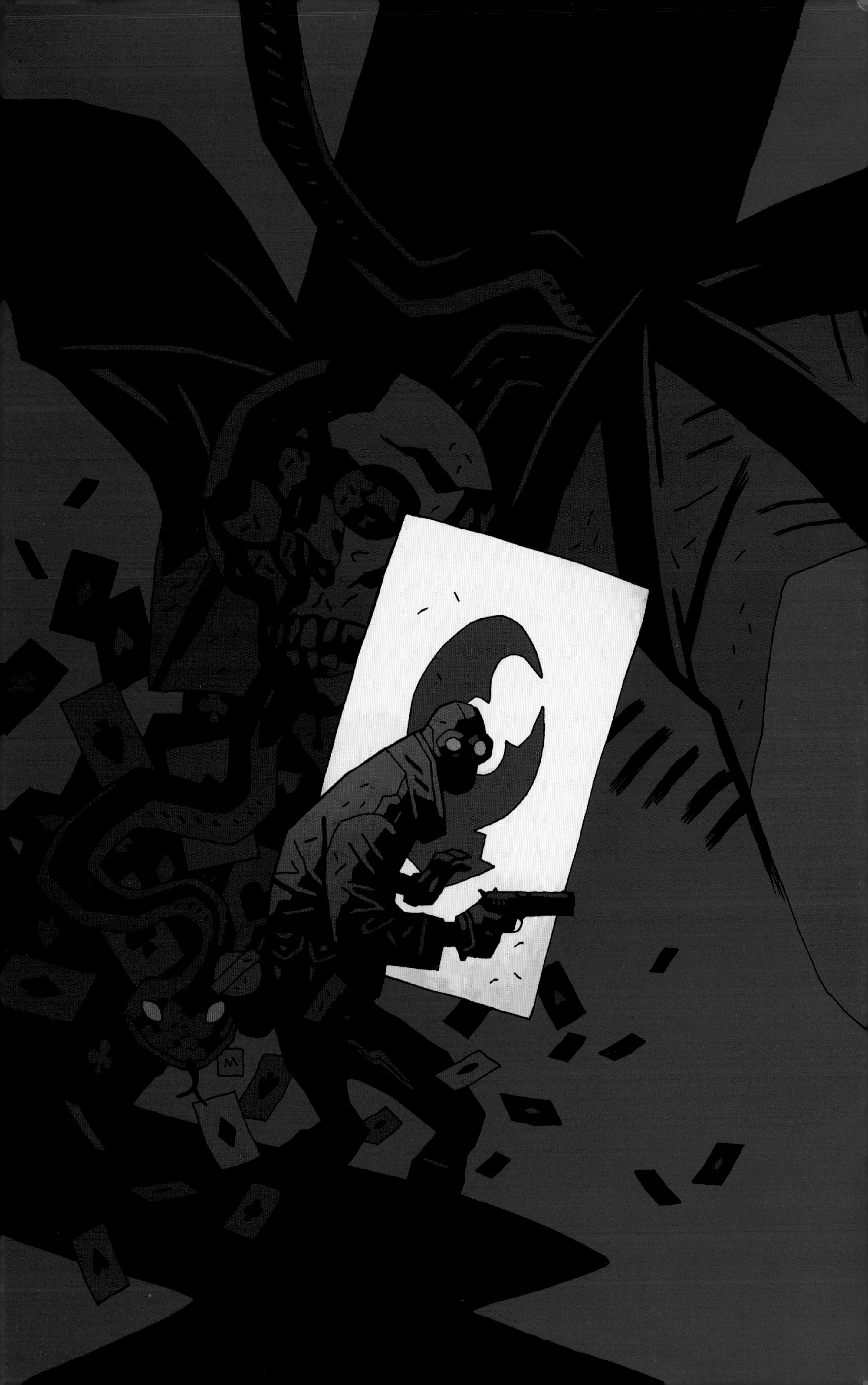

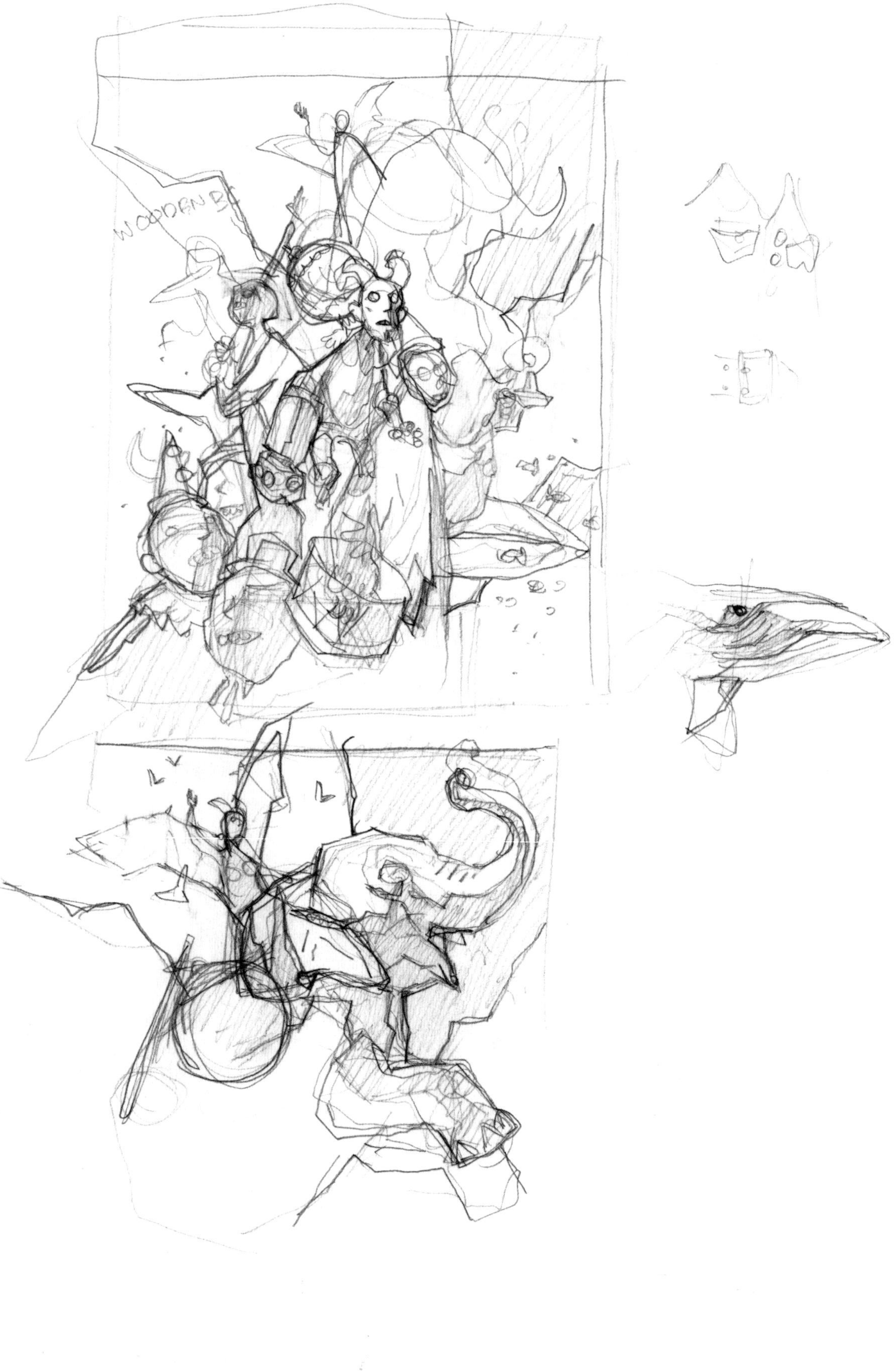

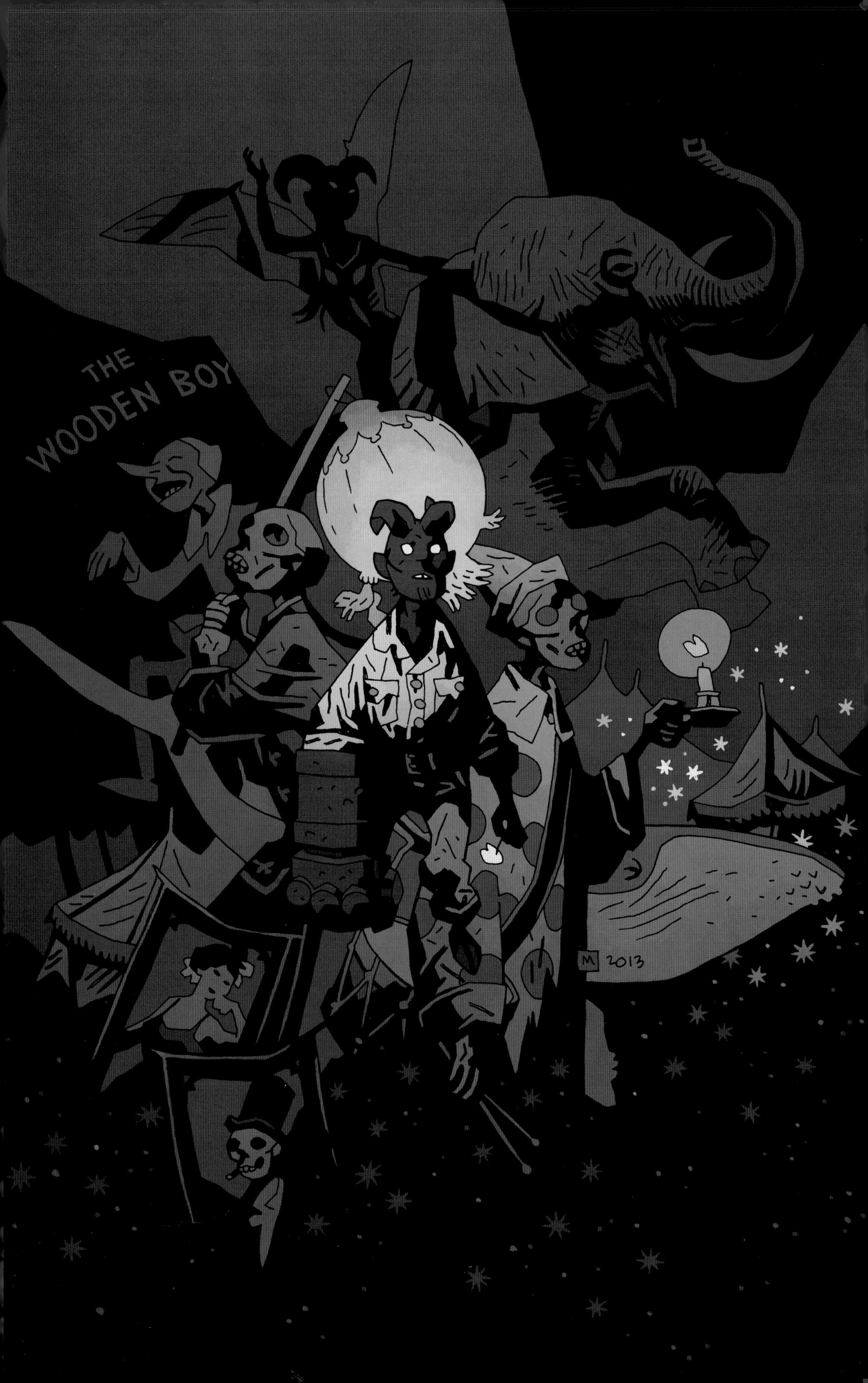
THE WOODEN BOY
M 2013

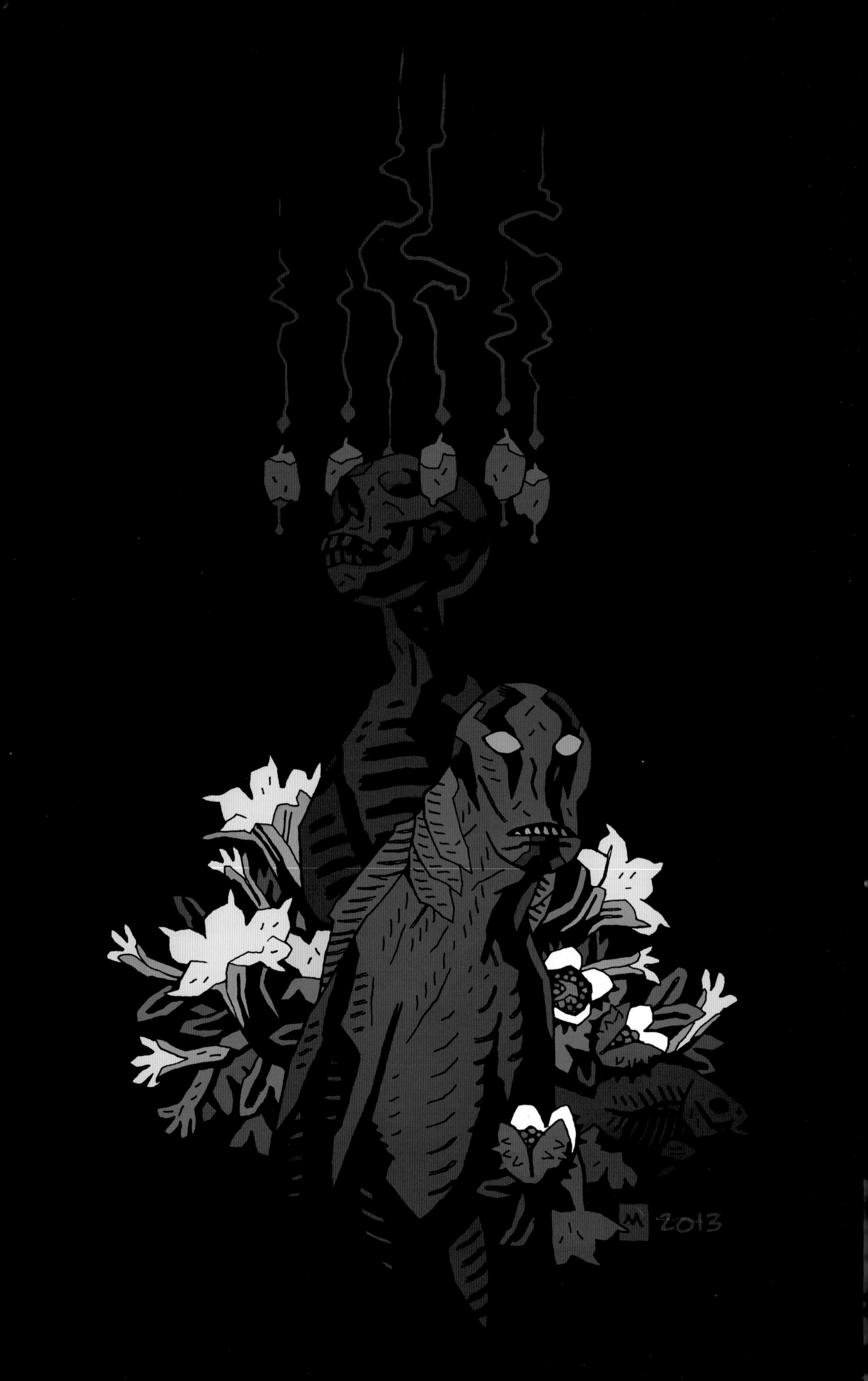
2013

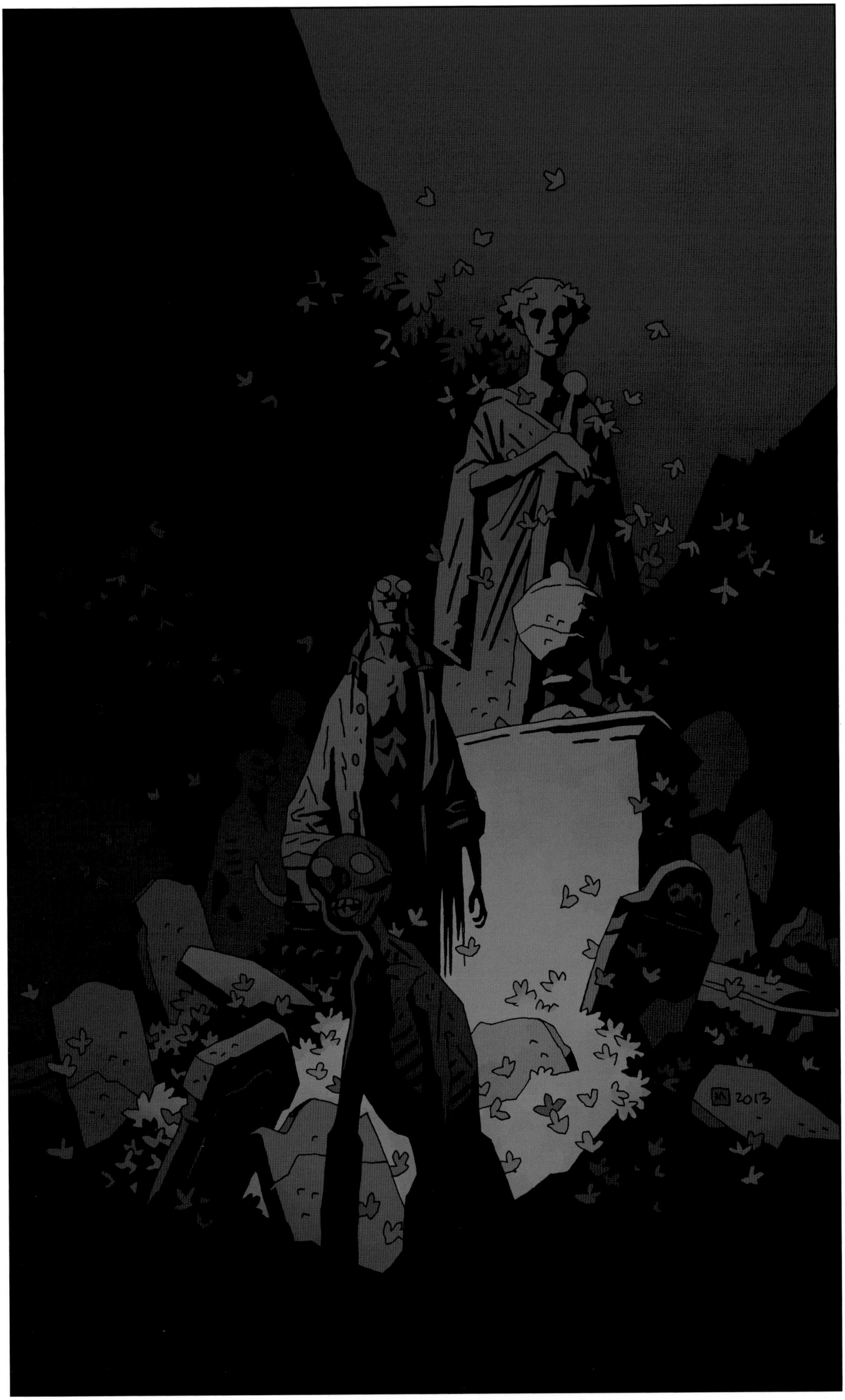

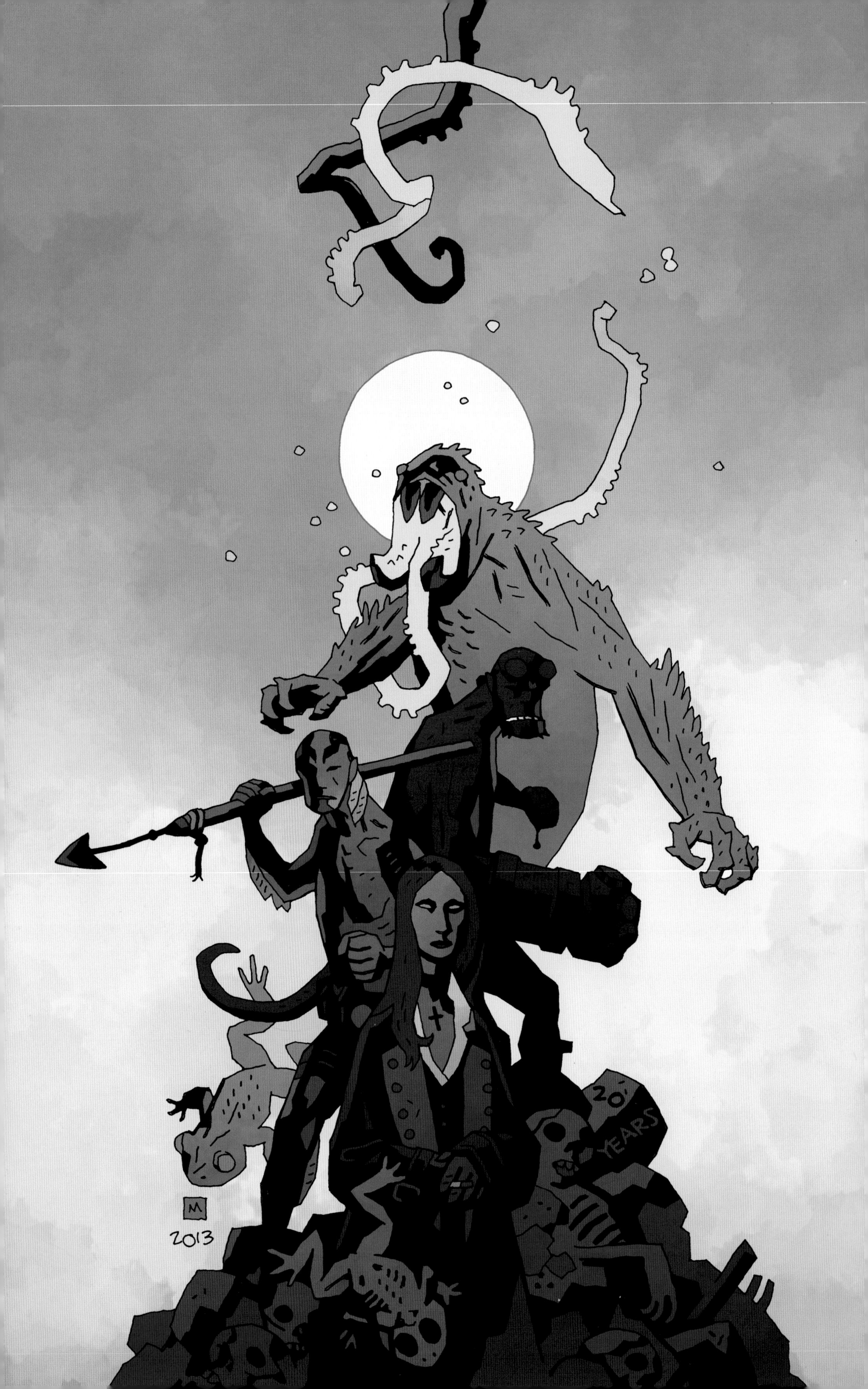
20 YEARS
M
2013

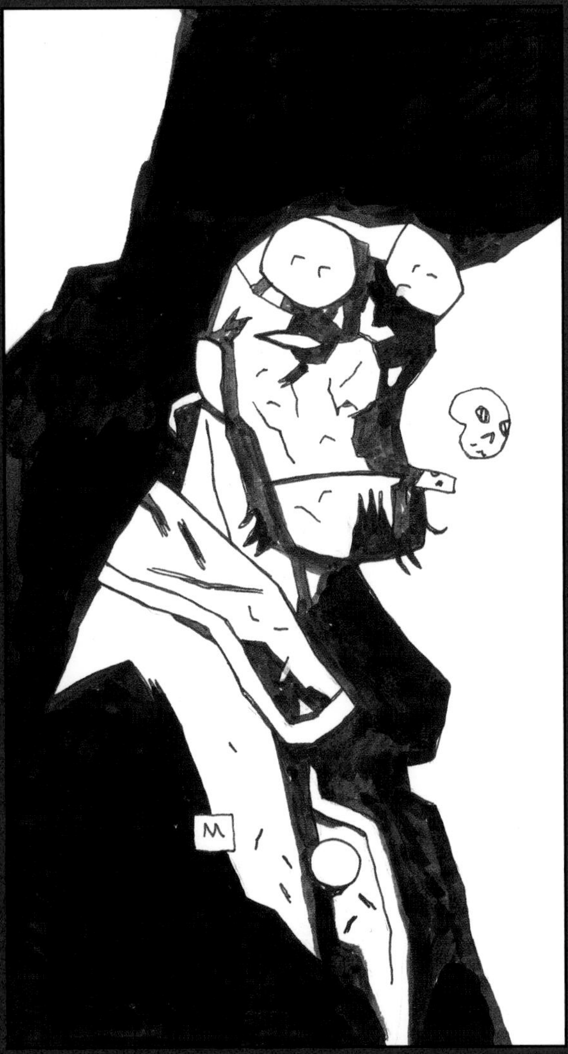
M

Index of Images

PAGE 69: *Hellboy: The Wild Hunt* #4 front cover. Colors by Dave Stewart. 2008.
PAGE 70: *Hellboy: The Wild Hunt* #5 front cover. Colors by Dave Stewart. 2008.
PAGE 71: *Hellboy: The Wild Hunt* #7 original front cover line art. 2009.
PAGE 72: *Abe Sapien: The Drowning* collection front cover. Colors by Dave Stewart. 2008.
PAGE 73: H. P. Lovecraft Film Festival & Cthulhucon poster art. Colors by Dave Stewart. 2008.
PAGE 74: *B.P.R.D.: War on Frogs* #1 front cover. Colors by Dave Stewart. 2008.
PAGE 75: *B.P.R.D.: War on Frogs* collection original front cover line art. 2010.
PAGE 76: *B.P.R.D.: King of Fear* #1 front cover. Colors by Dave Stewart. 2010.
PAGE 77: *B.P.R.D.: King of Fear* #2 original front cover line art. 2009.
PAGE 78: WonderCon print. Colors by Dave Stewart. 2009.
PAGE 79: *B.P.R.D.: King of Fear* #5 front cover. Colors by Dave Stewart. 2009.
PAGE 80: *B.P.R.D.: King of Fear* #4 original line art, page 14. 2009.
PAGE 81: *B.P.R.D.: King of Fear* #4 original line art, page 15. 2009.
PAGE 82: *Witchfinder: In the Service of Angels* collection original front cover line art. 2009.
PAGE 83: *Witchfinder: In the Service of Angels* collection front cover. Colors by Dave Stewart. 2009.
PAGE 84: *Witchfinder: In the Service of Angels* #3 original front cover line art. 2009.
PAGE 85: *Witchfinder: In the Service of Angels* #4 original front cover line art. 2009.
PAGE 86: *B.P.R.D.: War on Frogs* #3 front cover. Colors by Dave Stewart. 2009.
PAGE 87: *B.P.R.D.: War on Frogs* #4 front cover. Colors by Dave Stewart. 2009.
PAGE 88: *Hellboy: Double Feature of Evil* original front cover line art. 2010.
PAGE 89: *Hellboy: Double Feature of Evil* front cover. Colors by Dave Stewart. 2010.
PAGE 90: *Hellboy in Mexico* original front cover line art. 2010.
PAGE 91: *Hellboy in Mexico* front cover. Colors by Dave Stewart. 2010.
PAGE 92: *Hellboy: The Storm* #1 front cover. Colors by Dave Stewart. 2010.
PAGE 93: *Hellboy: The Storm* #2 front cover. Colors by Dave Stewart. 2010.
PAGE 94: *Hellboy: The Crooked Man and Others* collection front cover. Colors by Dave Stewart. 2010.
PAGE 95: *Hellboy: House of the Living Dead* original front cover line art. 2011.
PAGE 96: *Witchfinder: Lost and Gone Forever* #1 front cover. Colors by Dave Stewart. 2011.
PAGE 97: *Witchfinder: Lost and Gone Forever* #4 front cover. Colors by Dave Stewart. 2011.
PAGE 98: *Witchfinder: Lost and Gone Forever* #3 original front cover line art. 2011.
PAGE 99: *Witchfinder: Lost and Gone Forever* #3 front cover. Colors by Dave Stewart. 2011.
PAGE 100: *Hellboy: The Fury* #1 front cover sketches.
PAGE 101: *Hellboy: The Fury* #1 front cover. Colors by Dave Stewart. 2010.
PAGE 102: *Hellboy: The Fury* #3 original front cover line art. 2011.
PAGE 103: World Horror Convention program cover. Colors by Dave Stewart. 2010.
PAGE 104: *Hellboy: The Fury* #3 variant front cover. Colors by Dave Stewart. 2011.
PAGE 105: Calgary Comic and Entertainment Expo print. Colors by Dave Stewart. 2011.
PAGE 106: *Abe Sapien: The Devil Does Not Jest* collection front cover sketches.
PAGE 107: *Abe Sapien: The Devil Does Not Jest* collection front cover. Colors by Dave Stewart. 2011.
PAGE 108: *Dark Horse Presents* #7 front cover. Colors by Dave Stewart. 2011.
PAGE 109: *Lobster Johnson: The Burning Hand* #1 Year of Monsters variant front cover. Colors by Dave Stewart. 2012.
PAGE 110: *B.P.R.D. Hell on Earth: The Pickens County Horror* #1 Year of Monsters original variant front cover line art. 2011.
PAGE 111: *B.P.R.D. Hell on Earth: The Pickens County Horror* #1 Year of Monsters variant front cover. Colors by Dave Stewart. 2011.
PAGE 112: *Lobster Johnson: The Burning Hand* #4 Year of Monsters variant front cover. Colors by Dave Stewart. 2011.
PAGE 113: *B.P.R.D. Hell on Earth: The Long Death* #1 Year of Monsters variant front cover. Colors by Dave Stewart. 2012.
PAGE 114: *B.P.R.D. Hell on Earth: The Return of the Master* #1 Year of Monsters variant front cover. Colors by Dave Stewart. 2012.
PAGE 115: *Lobster Johnson: Caput Mortuum* Year of Monsters variant front cover. Colors by Dave Stewart. 2012.
PAGE 116: *Hellboy in Hell* #1 Year of Monsters variant front cover. Colors by Dave Stewart. 2012.
PAGE 117: Trickster print. Colors by Dave Stewart. 2012.
PAGE 118: *B.P.R.D. Hell on Earth: Russia* collection front cover. Colors by Dave Stewart. 2012.
PAGE 119: *B.P.R.D. Hell on Earth: The Devil's Engine and the Long Death* collection front cover. Colors by Dave Stewart. 2012.
PAGE 120: *Sledgehammer 44* #1 front cover. Colors by Dave Stewart. 2013.
PAGE 121: *Hellboy in Hell* #1 front cover. Colors by Dave Stewart. 2012.
PAGE 122: *Hellboy in Hell* #2 front cover. Colors by Dave Stewart. 2012.
PAGE 123: *Hellboy in Hell* #3 front cover. Colors by Dave Stewart. 2012.
PAGE 124: *Hellboy in Hell* #4 front cover. Colors by Dave Stewart. 2012.
PAGE 125: *Lobster Johnson: Satan Smells a Rat* collection front cover. Colors by Dave Stewart. 2013.
PAGE 126: *Hellboy: The Midnight Circus* front cover sketches.
PAGE 127: *Hellboy: The Midnight Circus* front cover. Colors by Dave Stewart. 2013.
PAGE 128: *Abe Sapien: To the Last Man* collection front cover. Colors by Dave Stewart. 2013.
PAGE 129: *Hellboy in Hell* #5 front cover. Colors by Dave Stewart. 2013.
PAGE 130: *B.P.R.D. Hell on Earth* #115 20 Years of Hellboy variant front cover. Colors by Dave Stewart. 2013.
PAGE 131: Original art for 20 Years of Hellboy print. 2013.

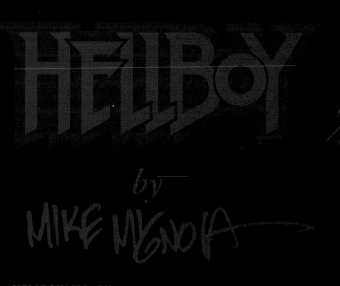

HELLBOY by MIKE MIGNOLA

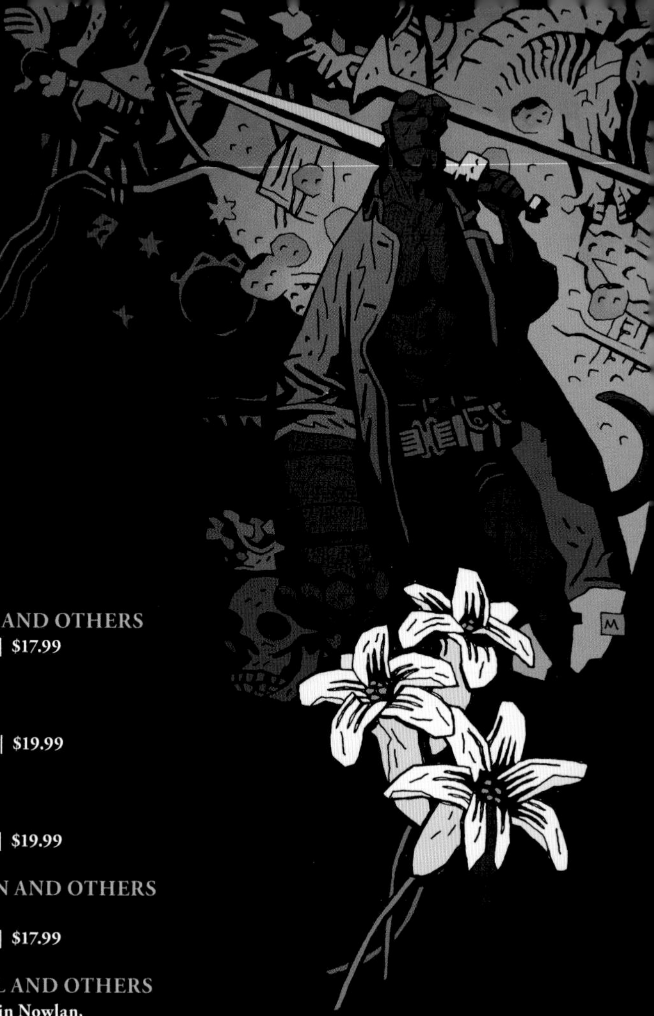

HELLBOY LIBRARY EDITION VOLUME 1:
Seed of Destruction and Wake the Devil
ISBN 978-1-59307-910-9 | $49.99

HELLBOY LIBRARY EDITION VOLUME 2:
The Chained Coffin and The Right Hand of Doom
ISBN 978-1-59307-989-5 | $49.99

HELLBOY LIBRARY EDITION VOLUME 3:
Conqueror Worm and Strange Places
ISBN 978-1-59582-352-6 | $49.99

HELLBOY LIBRARY EDITION VOLUME 4:
The Crooked Man and The Troll Witch
with Richard Corben and others
ISBN 978-1-59582-658-9 | $49.99

HELLBOY LIBRARY EDITION VOLUME 5:
Darkness Calls and the Wild Hunt
with Duncan Fegredo
ISBN 978-1-59582-886-6 | $49.99

HELLBOY LIBRARY EDITION VOLUME 6:
The Storm and the Fury and The Bride of Hell
with Duncan Fegredo, Richard Corben, Kevin Nowlan, and Scott Hampton
ISBN 978-1-61655-133-9 | $49.99

SEED OF DESTRUCTION
with John Byrne
ISBN 978-1-59307-094-6 | $17.99

WAKE THE DEVIL
ISBN 978-1-59307-095-3 | $17.99

THE CHAINED COFFIN AND OTHERS
ISBN 978-1-59307-091-5 | $17.99

THE RIGHT HAND OF DOOM
ISBN 978-1-59307-093-9 | $17.99

CONQUEROR WORM
ISBN 978-1-59307-092-2 | $17.99

STRANGE PLACES
ISBN 978-1-59307-475-3 | $17.99

THE TROLL WITCH AND OTHERS
ISBN 978-1-59307-860-7 | $17.99

DARKNESS CALLS
with Duncan Fegredo
ISBN 978-1-59307-896-6 | $19.99

THE WILD HUNT
with Duncan Fegredo
ISBN 978-1-59582-352-6 | $19.99

THE CROOKED MAN AND OTHERS
with Richard Corben
ISBN 978-1-59582-477-6 | $17.99

THE BRIDE OF HELL AND OTHERS
with Richard Corben, Kevin Nowlan, and Scott Hampton
ISBN 978-1-59582-740-1 | $19.99

HELLBOY IN HELL VOLUME 1: THE DESCENT
ISBN 978-1-61655-444-6 | $17.99

THE STORM AND THE FURY
with Duncan Fegredo
ISBN 978-1-59582-827-9 | $19.99

HOUSE OF THE LIVING DEAD
with Richard Corben
ISBN 978-1-59582-757-9 | $14.99

THE MIDNIGHT CIRCUS
with Duncan Fegredo
ISBN 978-1-61655-238-1 | $14.99

HELLBOY: THE FIRST 20 YEARS
ISBN 978-1-61655-353-1 | $19.99

THE ART OF HELLBOY
ISBN 978-1-59307-089-2 | $29.99

HELLBOY II: THE ART OF THE MOVIE
ISBN 978-1-59307-964-2 | $24.99

HELLBOY: THE COMPANION
ISBN 978-1-59307-655-9 | $14.99

HELLBOY: WEIRD TALES
Volume 1
ISBN 978-1-56971-622-9 | $17.99
Volume 2
ISBN 978-1-56971-953-4 | $17.99

HELLBOY: MASKS AND MONSTERS
with James Robinson and Scott Benefiel
ISBN 978-1-59582-567-4 | $17.99

NOVELS

HELLBOY: EMERALD HELL
By Tom Piccirilli
ISBN 978-1-59582-141-6 | $12.99

HELLBOY: THE ALL-SEEING EYE
By Mark Morris
ISBN 978-1-59582-141-6 | $12.99

HELLBOY: THE FIRE WOLVES
By Tim Lebbon
ISBN 978-1-59582-204-8 | $12.99

HELLBOY: THE ICE WOLVES
By Mark Chadbourn
ISBN 978-1-59582-205-5 | $12.99

SHORT STORIES
Illustrated by Mike Mignola

HELLBOY: ODD JOBS
By Poppy Z. Brite, Greg Rucka, and others
ISBN 978-1-56971-440-9 | $14.99

HELLBOY: ODDER JOBS
By Frank Darabont, Guillermo del Toro, and others
ISBN 978-1-59307-226-1 | $14.99

HELLBOY: ODDEST JOBS
By Joe R. Lansdale, China Miéville, and others
ISBN 978-1-59307-944-4 | $14.99

DARK HORSE BOOKS
DarkHorse.com

AVAILABLE AT YOUR LOCAL COMICS SHOP OR BOOKSTORE! • To find a comics shop in your area, call 1-888-266-4226.
For more information or to order direct visit DarkHorse.com or call 1-800-862-0052 Mon.–Fri. 9 AM to 5 PM Pacific Time.
Prices and availability subject to change without notice.

Also by Mike Mignola

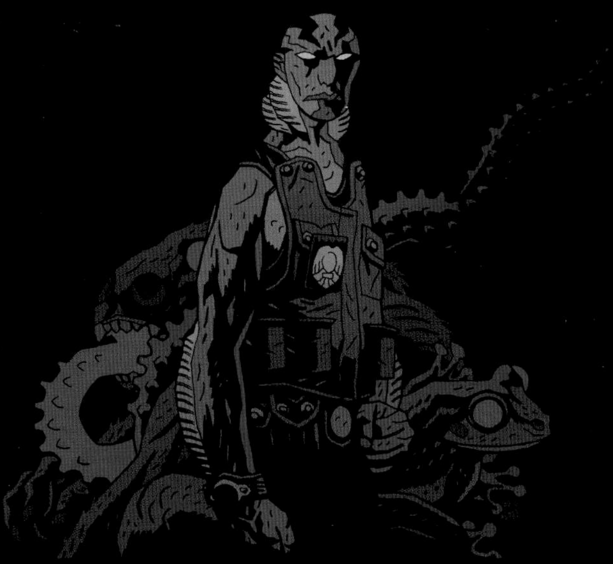

B.P.R.D.

PLAGUE OF FROGS
Volume 1
with Chris Golden, Guy Davis, and others
ISBN 978-1-59582-609-1 | $34.99
Volume 2
with John Arcudi, Davis, and others
ISBN 978-1-59582-672-5 | $34.99
Volume 3
with Arcudi, and Davis
ISBN 978-1-59582-860-6 | $34.99
Volume 4
with Arcudi and Davis
ISBN 978-1-59582-974-0 | $34.99

1946
with Joshua Dysart and Paul Azaceta
ISBN 978-1-59582-191-1 | $17.99

1947
with Dysart, Fábio Moon, and Gabriel Bá
ISBN 978-1-59582-478-3 | $17.99

1948
with Arcudi and Max Fiumara
ISBN 978-1-61655-183-4 | $17.99

BEING HUMAN
with Arcudi, Davis, and others
ISBN 978-1-59582-756-2 | $17.99

VAMPIRE
with Moon and Bá
ISBN 978-1-61655-196-4 | $19.99

B.P.R.D. HELL ON EARTH

NEW WORLD
with Arcudi and Davis
ISBN 978-1-59582-707-4 | $19.99

GODS AND MONSTERS
with Arcudi, Davis, and Crook
ISBN 978-1-59582-822-4 | $19.99

RUSSIA
with Arcudi, Crook, and Duncan Fegredo
ISBN 978-1-59582-946-7 | $19.9

THE DEVIL'S ENGINE AND THE LONG DEATH
with Arcudi, Crook, and James Harren
ISBN 978-1-59582-981-8 | $19.99

THE PICKENS COUNTY HORROR AND OTHERS
with Scott Allie, Jason Latour, Harren, Max Fiumara, and Becky Cloonan
ISBN 978-1-61655-140-7 | $19.99

THE RETURN OF THE MASTER
with Arcudi and Crook
ISBN 978-1-61655-193-3 | $19.99

A COLD DAY IN HELL
with Arcudi, Peter Snejbjerg, and Laurence Campbell
ISBN 978-1-61655-199-5 | $19.99

ABE SAPIEN

THE DROWNING
with Jason Shawn Alexander
ISBN 978-1-59582-185-0 | $17.99

THE DEVIL DOES NOT JEST AND OTHER STORIES
with Arcudi, Harren, and others
ISBN 978-1-59582-925-2 | $17.99

DARK AND TERRIBLE AND THE NEW RACE OF MAN
with Allie, Arcudi, Sebastián Fiumara, and Max Fiumara
ISBN 978-1-61655-284-8 | $19.99

LOBSTER JOHNSON

THE IRON PROMETHEUS
with Jason Armstrong
ISBN 978-1-59307-975-8 | $17.99

THE BURNING HAND
with Arcudi and Tonci Zonjic
ISBN 978-1-61655-031-8 | $17.99

SATAN SMELLS A RAT
with Arcudi, Fiumara, Joe Querio, Wilfredo Torres, and Kevin Nowlan
ISBN 978-1-61655-203-9 | $18.99

WITCHFINDER

IN THE SERVICE OF ANGELS
with Ben Stenbeck
ISBN 978-1-59582-483-7 | $17.99

LOST AND GONE FOREVER
with Arcudi and John Severin
ISBN 978-1-59582-794-4 | $17.99

THE AMAZING SCREW-ON HEAD AND OTHER CURIOUS OBJECTS

ISBN 978-1-59582-501-8 | $17.99

BALTIMORE

THE PLAGUE SHIPS
with Golden and Stenbeck
ISBN 978-1-59582-677-0 | $24.99

THE CURSE BELLS
with Golden and Stenbeck
ISBN 978-1-59582-674-9 | $24.99

A PASSING STRANGER AND OTHER STORIES
with Golden and Stenbeck
ISBN 978-1-61655-182-7 | $24.99

NOVELS

LOBSTER JOHNSON: THE SATAN FACTORY
with Thomas E. Sniegoski
ISBN 978-1-59582-203-1 | $12.95

JOE GOLEM AND THE DROWNING CITY
with Golden
ISBN 978-1-59582-971-9 | $99.99

ABOUT THE ARTIST

MIKE MIGNOLA's fascination with ghosts and monsters began at an early age; reading *Dracula* at age twelve introduced him to Victorian literature and folklore, from which he has never recovered. Starting in 1982 as a bad inker for Marvel Comics, he swiftly evolved into a not-so-bad artist. By the late 1980s, he had begun to develop his own unique graphic style, with mainstream projects like *Cosmic Odyssey* and *Batman: Gotham by Gaslight.* In 1994, he published the first *Hellboy* series through Dark Horse. As of this writing there are twelve *Hellboy* graphic novels (with more on the way), several spinoff titles (*B.P.R.D.*, *Lobster Johnson*, *Abe Sapien*, and *Sir Edward Grey: Witchfinder*), prose books, animated films, and two live-action films starring Ron Perlman. Along the way he worked on Francis Ford Coppola's film *Bram Stoker's Dracula* (1992), was a production designer for Disney's *Atlantis: The Lost Empire* (2001), and was the visual consultant to director Guillermo del Toro on *Blade II* (2002), *Hellboy* (2004), and *Hellboy II: The Golden Army* (2008). Mike's books have earned numerous awards and are published in a great many countries. Mike lives somewhere in Southern California with his wife, daughter, and cat.